© Copyright 2013

Don K. Preston D. Div.

No part of this publication may be reproduced, stored in a retrieval system, or transmitted by any means, electronic, mechanical, photocopy or otherwise, without the prior written permission of JaDon Management Inc. except for brief quotations in critical reviews or articles.

ISBN 978-1-937501-09-9 1-937501-09-4

Produced by JaDon Management Inc.

1405 4th Ave. N. W. #109

Ardmore, Ok. 73401

Original Cover Design by:

Kim Lester

P. O. Box 33741

Amarillo, Tx. 79120

kim_lester@sbcglobal.net

Contents

Introductory Comments iii

Don K. Preston's First Affirmative Presentation 1

Joel McDurmon's First Negative 26

Don K. Preston's Second Affirmative 41

Joel McDurmon's Second Negative 50

Don K. Preston's Third Affirmative 56

Joel McDurmon's Third (Final) Negative 64

Joel McDurmon's First Affirmative 70

Don K. Preston's First Negative Presentation 83

Joel McDurmon's Second Affirmative 101

Don K. Preston's Second Negative 107

Joel McDurmon's Third (Final) Affirmative 114

Don K. Preston's Third (Final) Negative 120

Question and Answer Session 127

Joel McDurmon – Afterthoughts 184

Don K. Preston – Afterthoughts 195

Introductory Comments

Thursday July 19, 2012

Mr. William Bell (MC): Good evening, ladies and gentlemen. I'm William Bell from Memphis, Tennessee. And I want to welcome each of you to this year's weekend Preterist Pilgrim weekend, and especially to tonight's event, a live public oral debate.

First, let me express thanks to God for making it possible for all of us to be here, and especially to the contenders in the debate. In a few minutes we will be introducing each of the speakers. But before that, we have a few preliminaries. And I think it's in order to express some gratitude to the following: We want to thank our participants for their dedication, for their study, for their scholarship, and their willingness to contend openly and publically for their convictions.

Secondly, we would like to thank each of you for your sacrifices of time, finances, and travel to be present in the audience tonight.

We want to thank those of you who are watching via live stream, and to those who will support the spread of this event through future recordings and media.

We thank PRI, Preterist Research Institute, for their foresight and ongoing support of our studies and growth of the Preterist community and teachings through the publishing of books, tapes, sponsoring conferences, and other media and events.

Thanks to the support staff, the Ardmore Church of Christ collectively, and to individuals who work behind the scenes to make this event possible.

We also thank our media technicians, audio and video engineers, for their support in helping us to broadcast this event. Once again, we welcome all of you.

We have just a few preliminary issues that we would like to discuss. The first is live stream. We need every one of you to look to your neighbor and say, "He's talking to me." And then I want each of your neighbors to point to you and say, "He's talking to you."

But this is what we require, please. That every one of you turn off your phones and computers -- or turn your computers to airplane mode, if that's possible, I'm not even sure. But please turn off the phones. Because what we need is to reduce the bandwidth demand and improve the live stream. This is very, very important.

Next we'd like to announce that there are three new books which are being introduced by Steve Temple, Joseph Vincent, and also Don Preston. So be sure and avail yourselves to the opportunities to get copies of these new books that are available for you.

For the debate preliminaries, there should be no demonstrations. No outbursts. Please be mindful of the fact that the person next to you is trying to listen, they're trying to take notes, they are trying to learn. There will be a lot of information dissimilated in this debate, and they will probably be moving at a rather moderate pace because they are on a time schedule. So be sure and give your neighbor that respect so that all of us can learn as much as we possibly can.

Brother Jack Gilbert from Arkansas will be the moderator of the debate. And following me, he will come up and introduce the speakers.

The format for tonight is that each man will have the following -- they will speak for 35 minutes, which will be followed by a 15-minute -- one 15-minute speech, and then that will be followed by a second 15-minute speech by each of the disputers.

Each man will have from five to ten minutes between each speech to organize his thoughts and notes.

Don Preston will be in the affirmative tonight with the following proposition: Resolved, the Bible teaches that the final end-of-the-age coming of Christ and the attended resurrection from the dead occurred at the time of the fall of Jerusalem in A.D. 70.

On Saturday, a Q and A session will be featured. There is a box for you to submit written questions for each man. Please submit those as soon as possible so that the moderator can organize them.

Don't forget the catered meal on Friday. And we do encourage and ask, very kindly, that each person attend.

We also have book tables in the back, and we have a table with the Logos Bible study program here for the first time. They will give a ten-minute presentation on Friday to tell a bit about this program.

Last for me, I would like to just make this note. The discussion tonight is one where each of these men have some very similar views. That's one of the things that make this a very momentous debate. And so please understand, they both believe that a coming of Christ occurred in 70 A.D., that a resurrection occurred in 70 A.D., and that there was an end of heaven and earth in 70 A.D.; that a judgment occurred in 70 A.D. There may be some of you in the audience who may not be quite as familiar with some of the distinctions between those two positions. That's what the discussion is about tonight.

One of the disputants believes that all of those events and related events occurred in 70 A.D., the other believes that some of those events are yet future. And that will be a matter of contention tonight.

Thank you very much. At this time, Brother Jack Gilbert.

Jack Gibbert: Thank you, William.

We have a timekeeper, Rick Jameson, sitting down here right now. And for the disputants, he will hold up his fingers at ten minutes when you have ten minutes left. He will hold up his fingers "five" when you have five left. And "two" when you have two left. And then he will call time at the conclusion of your time period.

I'm so happy to be here to listen to these two men who have studied very hard, very long, on a subject that has touched everyone in this room. Because we've all dabbled into it, some deeper than others, but we know the difficulties. We know also how exciting it is as you see these things unfold.

American Vision was one of the very first introductions that I had into preterism. I know the writers studied their works, I have spoken with some of them. Just tonight was the first time I met Joel, and I'm very excited about listening to what he has to say because I have put myself out front and let you know I've moved past that. But I'm ready to listen to everything that Joel has to say and consider very seriously the arguments that he will present.

Joel is the director of research for American Vision, which as I say I have the greatest respect for. He's written ten books. He has written over 300 articles. He is a lecturer and regular contributor to the American Vision website and to their activities. And he lives in Dallas, Georgia.

You know, I was talking as we came up this afternoon about all the places I saw in Texas where they stole names like Detroit and Pittsburgh. Those people don't have any imagination.

But he lives in Dallas, Georgia, with his wife and four sons. And we're certainly happy that he is here tonight and will be responding to Don as Don gives his speech.

Don is an old friend. Don is the one who brought me all the way over from the partial position that Joel holds over to full preterism. But as I said to Don, I'm ready to listen to what Joel has to say, because there may be things I haven't thought about, and I want to hear what he has to say.

Don's new book, *The End of the Law and Torah and Telos Volume 1*, indicates to me that Don may write another book it's volume one, so there must be more coming.

Don is the director of Preterist Research Institute. And I look forward every time to getting together with Don to hear all that he has to say. He's written so many books. The back tables are full of the books by Don. And I understand that Joel has some. I need to get back there. I'm anxious to see what he has available for us to purchase and to read.

So with nothing more to say, we're going to turn this over to Don and get this debate moving. I will call any points of order that need to be called.

Don K. Preston's First Affirmative Presentation

****

First of all, let me express my sincere appreciation to Joel McDurmon for his willingness to come and engage in these discussions. Not everyone is willing to defend what they believe in the form of public debate. And so, I very much appreciate Joel.

We were able to go out last night and eat some barbecue and we certainly share that in common. We do love barbecue. And we had a good time: no pressure, you know, no tension, just a good time, a time of good fellowship.

I obviously want to thank each of you for being here and for your support. I cannot begin to tell you how many e-mails, how many phone calls I have received over the last few days from individuals literally from all over America, and some e-mails from all over the world, expressing their appreciation for sponsoring this debate.

Many have said, being familiar with American Vision and the good work that they have done and continue to do -- and let me say with Jack, I too appreciate a great deal of the work that American Vision does. I consider Gary Demar a friend. I have spoken on lectureships with him. We've worked together, and perhaps we will be able to do so again.

I would like to appear on American Vision's lectureship one of these days. I'd like to have a formal debate down there perhaps. We have invited Joel to be here, perhaps they can reciprocate.

It is very good to have my family here from Missouri. They don't get to come down here very often. And so it's very, very good for them to be here.

Now there's an awful lot that I could say, but I will not take up any more time because I have miles and miles to go, and not a lot of time to get there. So with that said, let me begin.

Don K. Preston's First Affirmative

What this debate is about, ladies and gentlemen, and my proposition is: Resolved that the Bible teaches that the second final coming of Christ and the attended resurrection of the dead at the end of the age occurred at the fall of Jerusalem in A.D. 70. Now normally I would spend some time defining that proposition, but let me simply say that I believe it is fairly well self-explanatory. If Joel wants to challenge any of the issues that are there, he and I have discussed those through our individual conversations and e-mails, so I don't think there's any disagreement in them -- in our positions.

What This Debate Is About

This Presentation will focus on the fulfillment of God's promises to <u>Old Covenant Israel After the Flesh</u> It will be about the passing- through fulfillment- of The Law of Moses It will be about the End of the Millennium (EoM) It will be about the Promises to Abraham My premise: No matter our concept of protology, i.e. Genesis 1-3... No matter our concept of the Curse and Death of Adam... 　　　　　No matter our concept of the millennium... 　　　　　No matter our concept of the nature of the resurrection... Scripture posits the EoM resurrection to overcome the Eden Curse, at the end of the Old Covenant Age– in fulfillment of God's promises to Abraham and to Israel after the flesh.

This presentation will be about the fulfillment of God's Old Covenant promises made to Old Covenant Israel -- and listen very carefully -- Old Covenant Israel after the flesh. It will be about the passing through fulfillment of the Law of Moses. It will be about the end of the millennium. It will be about the fulfillment of the promises that God made to Abraham.

My premise very simply is this. No matter what our concept of protology -- that is, creation in Genesis, no matter what our concept of the protology may be. No matter what our concept of the curse of Adam and the death of Adam may be, no matter what our concept of the millennium may be, no matter what our concept of the body, or our concept of the resurrection may be, scripture posits the end of the millennium -- that's what EOM stands for -- the end of the millennium resurrection to overcome the Adamic curse and the Adamic death at the end of the old covenant age of

Don K. Preston's First Affirmative
Israel and fulfillment of God's promises to Abraham and Israel after the flesh.

So based upon that, I want you to consider with me the following:

Issue #1—Israel and Torah

> Fact: Paul said: <u>"There is one hope"</u> (Eph. 4:4-5).
> Paul said his resurrection doctrine was "the hope of Israel"- After the flesh– and that he preached <u>nothing</u> but what Moses and the prophets foretold
> **Acts 24:14-15**– The "about to be" resurrection
> **Acts 26:6-7**– Resurrection the hope of Israel
> **Acts 26:21f**- Nothing but what Moses said!
> The Resurrection Promise was made to Israel- "after the flesh" (Romans 8:23-9:3).
> God's resurrection promises to Israel after the flesh were irrevocable– not transferrable (Romans 11:25-29).

Point number one, Paul was emphatic. His resurrection doctrine, his doctrine of the end of the millennium resurrection doctrine was nothing but the hope of Israel. Acts 24 and verse 14, Paul said, "I believe all things are written in the law and the prophets that there is [literally DKP] about to be the resurrection of the just and unjust."

Acts 26:6-7, Paul said that it was the hope of the twelve tribes to attain unto the resurrection. And Acts 26:21 and following, Paul said, "I now stand before small and great saying *no other things* than what Moses and Prophets said should take place." [emphasis DKP]

Now I want you to listen to me very, very carefully; this is a critical point. The resurrection promise, the end of *the millennium resurrection promise* was made to Israel after the flesh, to fleshly Israel. When Paul talked about the redemption of the body, the adoption in Romans 8:23, he then proceeded to say in Romans Chapter 9:3 that the promise of the adoption belonged to Israel *after the flesh*.

So let me reiterate. God's resurrection promises to Israel after the flesh are the end of the millennium resurrection promises, and God's promises to Israel concerning those promises, according to Paul in Romans 11:28-29,

Don K. Preston's First Affirmative

were "*irrevocable.*" They would not be, they could not be, transferred to someone that was not Israel after the flesh. This is critical.

Now watch.

Matthew 5—Jesus, Israel and Torah

> Jesus: "Until heaven and earth passes, Not one jot or one tittle shall pass from the law until it is all fulfilled."
>
> **The words are unambiguous and emphatic**
>
> Not one iota of Torah, the Law of Moses– **including the Sabbaths**- would pass until everything foreshadowed in Torah was "fully accomplished" (*genetai*, Mt. 5:18).
>
> **But, Torah –Via Sabbaths- foreshadowed the EoM resurrection**
>
> **Therefore, Torah- all of it- i.e. Sabbaths-would- or will- stand binding until the full accomplishment of the EoM resurrection promise made to Israel after the flesh**

Jesus said in Matthew Chapter 5:17-18, "Do not think that I came to destroy the law and the prophets. I did not come to destroy, but to fulfill. Verily I say unto you until heaven and earth passes away, not one jot, not one tittle shall pass from the law until it is all fulfilled." The word fulfilled there is from *genetai*; it means fully accomplished.

These words are unambiguous and they are emphatic. Not one iota of Torah -- that is the Law of Moses -- which -- listen to me -- includes the festal Sabbaths would pass until everything in Torah, the Law of Moses, and the Sabbath, was foreshadowed. But the Sabbath -- listen very carefully -- the Sabbath foreshadowed the end of the millennium resurrection. Therefore, Torah, all of it, including Israel's festival ceremonial sacrificial Sabbaths would, or will, if the Sabbath -- or if the resurrection has not occurred, will stand binding until the full accomplishment of the end of the millennium resurrection made to Israel after the flesh.

Don K. Preston's First Affirmative

The Millennium—Sabbath-- Israel

> The <u>Sabbath</u> is one of the most significant but overlooked, eschatological topics (cf. Gen. 2:7)!
>
> **<u>The Sabbath was a Covenant Sign</u>** between God and Israel– Exodus 31:16-17; Deuteronomy 5:15)
>
> The Sabbath was typological of the EoM resurrection of Revelation 20! Bahnsen, Gentry, Jordan, Bull, etc. all concur!
>
> ***You must catch the power of this!***
>
> The Sabbath- <u>God's covenant with Israel</u>- is inseparably bound to the end of the millennium!

I suggest to you, ladies and gentlemen, that the Sabbath is one of the most significant, but most overlooked, of all the Eschatological topics. The Sabbath was a covenant sign between God and Israel. In Exodus Chapter 31:16-17, God said that He gave the Sabbath as a sign to Israel and for Israel of the fact that He created heaven and earth.

In Deuteronomy 5:15, God said He gave the Sabbath to Israel as a sign between Him and them of His deliverance of Israel out of bondage. The Sabbath was a typological foreshadowing of the end of the millennium resurrection.

Now I can quote to you from various Jewish sources. I could quote to you Greg Bahnsen -- great guy by the way. But it's widely acknowledged in all scholarship that the Sabbath foreshadowed the end of the millennium resurrection. *You must catch the power of this.*

Don K. Preston's First Affirmative

Sabbath-Resurrection—Matthew 5

> Jesus: Not one jot or one tittle shall pass from the law until it is all fully accomplished (*genetai*).
>
> **The Seventh Day Sabbath, part of "the law" foreshadowed the EoM resurrection- final salvation of Revelation 20.**
>
> **God's Covenant with Israel- "the law"- would remain valid until the full accomplishment of Sabbath, i.e. <u>Until the resurrection of Rev. 20!</u>**
>
> ***<u>But, Joel says the Law of Moses "died in AD 70"</u>***
>
> ***<u>Thus, of logical necessity, the EoM resurrection of Revelation 20 was fulfilled in AD 70!</u>***

The Sabbath, God's covenant with Israel, is inseparably bound to the end of the millennium. Now remember, Jesus said, "Not one jot or one tittle will pass from the law until everything in the law [-- everything foreshadowing the law –DKP] was fully accomplished." Greek word *genetai*.

Listen again. The seventh day Sabbath, part of the law, foreshadowed the end of the millennium resurrection and final salvation of Revelation Chapter 20. Now what that means is that God's covenant with Old Covenant Israel after the flesh would remain valid until the full accomplishment of Israel's ceremonial, sacrificial Sabbaths; In other words, until the resurrection of Revelation Chapter 20; In other words, of the logical necessity, if the Law of Moses has passed away, then the end of the millennium resurrection has occurred.

Now, again, Jesus said not one iota, not the single particle of the Law of Moses would pass until it was all completely fulfilled.

Now Joel, and all Dominionists that I'm aware of, insists that Israel's Sabbath days have passed away. Bahnsen says they were altered. They were purged of the ceremonial aspect and replaced with a Christian Sabbath. But, folks, that means that Israel's Old Covenant ceremonial, sacrificial, Sabbath was taken away.

Don K. Preston's First Affirmative
Listen to me very carefully.

Whatever Passed Has Come to Pass!

> Jesus: Not one iota of the Law of Moses would pass until it was all fully accomplished
>
> Joel and all Dominionists say that Israel's Sabbaths have passed away, or have been altered, replaced with the typological Christian Sabbath
>
> But, before a single iota of Torah could pass, that part of Torah had to come to pass– had to be fully accomplished!
>
> If therefore, the Sabbaths have passed, then <u>what they foreshadowed has been fully accomplished!</u>
>
> **But, the Sabbaths foreshadowed the EoM resurrection!**
>
> Therefore, if, as Joel says, Israel's "symbols and ceremonies" have been annulled, then the EoM resurrection has been fully accomplished!
>
> **Whatever Part Has Passed <u>Has Come To Pass!</u>**

Before a single iota of Torah could pass, whatever part of Torah passed away, that part had to come to pass. But again, the Sabbath foreshadowed the end of the millennium resurrection. Therefore, if, as Joel says in his book -- which is a great book by the way, available on my book table. I sell it because I love it. If as Joel says Israel's, "symbols of ceremonies have been annulled and passed away," if the Law of Moses, quote, "died in A.D. 70," unquote -- Page 47 of his book -- then that means that the end of the millennium resurrection has been accomplished.

The Sabbath could not pass away until it was accomplished. Joel says it passed away in A.D. 70. Therefore the Sabbath and what it foreshadowed was fully realized; fully accomplished in A.D. 70.

Let me reiterate. Whatever part has passed, if you say it's been altered, if you say the old has been purged, then it passed. But it couldn't pass until it was fulfilled.

Don K. Preston's First Affirmative

Joel's Self Contradiction

> Jesus: Not one iota of the Law of Moses would pass until it was all fully accomplished
>
> Joel says the Law of Moses "died in AD 70"
>
> However! -> I asked when ALL of God's OT promises to OC Israel were completely fulfilled and <u>His covenant relationship with them terminated.</u>
>
> **He says it will be at the EoM future resurrection!**
> **This is a direct, inescapable self contradiction!**
>
> If Torah passed in AD 70 then every iota was fulfilled— or, God's promises failed!
>
> If God's OT promises to OT Israel are unfulfilled, then every jot and tittle of the Law of Moses is still valid!

I want you to notice a self-contradiction by Joel in his writings. Remember now, Jesus said not one iota of the Law of Moses will pass until it was all completely fully accomplished. Joel says in his book, Page 47, that the Law of Moses, "died in A.D. 70". However, in private correspondence, I asked Joel when all, not just some, not even most, but when *all* of God's Old Covenant promises to Israel after the flesh were completely fulfilled and his covenant relationship with them consummated and terminated. And Joel said, "It will be at the end of the millennium physical resurrection."

I suggest to you, ladies and gentlemen, this is an absolutely inescapable self-contradiction.

If Torah passed away in A.D. 70, then every iota was fulfilled or God's promises fulfilled. And if God's Old Testament promises to Old Testament Israel were unfulfilled, then every jot and every tittle of the Law of Moses remains valid today. So I would ask if Joel observes the seventh day Sabbath and the ceremonial sacrifices and symbols and sacrifices and ceremonies of Torah; and, of course, he doesn't.

Don K. Preston's First Affirmative

The Resurrection: The Salvation Hope of Israel

> "**And in this mountain** The Lord of hosts will make for all people **A feast of choice pieces, A feast of wines on the lees**.... ⁷ And He will destroy **on this mountain** The surface of the covering cast over all people, And the veil that is spread over all nations. ⁸ **He will swallow up death forever**, And the Lord God will wipe away tears from all faces; ⁹ And it will be said **in that day**: "Behold, this *is* our God; We have waited for Him, and He will save us. This *is* the Lord; We have waited for Him; **We will be glad and rejoice in His salvation**." (Isa. 25:6-9)

I want to call your attention now to Isaiah Chapter 25:6 and following, in which the great prophet Isaiah said, "In this mountain" -- that's Zion of the previous two verses -- "In this mountain the Lord of host will make for all people a feast of choice pieces. A feast of wines on the lees. He will destroy on this mountain the surface of the covering cast over all the people and veil that has spread over all the nations. He will *swallow up death forever*. And the Lord will wipe away all tears from all faces. And it will be said *in that day*, behold, this is our God. We have waited for Him and He will save us. This is the Lord. We have waited for Him. We will be glad and rejoice in His salvation."

Listen very, very carefully. Paul's resurrection doctrine of 1 Corinthians 15, is the end of the millennium resurrection foretold in Revelation Chapter 20:10-12. Joel will agree with that.

Paul's One Resurrection Hope and the Millennium

Paul's resurrection doctrine in 1 Corinthians 15 is the EoM resurrection foretold in Revelation 20:10-12.

"When this corruptible has put on incorruptibility, and the mortal has put on immortality, **then shall be brought to pass the saying**, 'Death is swallowed up in victory,' and 'O, death, where is thy sting, o grave, where is your victory?"

      Paul is directly citing and drawing from:
    Isaiah 25:8 (Inclusio- 24-27)
    Hosea 6; 13:14– (Inclusio)
    Daniel 12:2- Resurrection to Eternal Life

Without Question, this "EoM" resurrection was to take place at the end of Israel's Old Covenant Age– in AD 70!

Don K. Preston's First Affirmative

Look at what Paul said. In speaking of the resurrection of 1 Corinthians 15 he says, "When this corruptible has put on incorruptibility, when the mortal has put on immortality, *then* shall be brought to pass the saying 'death is swallowed up in victory. Oh, death where is your sting. Oh, Grave where is your victory.'" Paul is directly drawing from, citing, and quoting from Isaiah 25:8, which is actually an *inclusio* of Chapters 24-27. He is quoted from Hosea Chapter 13-14, which is also an *inclusio* of Hosea Chapters 3 and following; and Daniel Chapter 12, the resurrection to eternal life.

Now without question, this end of the millennium resurrection was to take place at the end of the Old Covenant age of Old Covenant Israel after the flesh. Let me vindicate that statement.

Nothing But the Hope of Israel!

Paul said his <u>ONE HOPE</u> was "nothing but the hope of Israel (Israel after the flesh) found in Moses and the prophets" He preached the EoM resurrection! In preaching "nothing but the hope of Israel" Paul anticipated the fulfillment of Abraham's promises (Galatians 3:17-6:15)! In preaching "nothing but the hope of Israel," Paul proclaimed <u>the fulfillment of the Edenic Mandate</u> (Colossians!) Hebrews 11 Shows, Abel's Hope Was Enoch's Which Was Noah's, Which Was Abraham's Which was Israel's **ONE HOPE!!**

Remember Paul said, "I preach nothing but the hope of Israel. The hope of Israel after the flesh." Now watch this. And Ephesians Chapter 4:4, Paul said, "There is one hope." Paul did not have an eschatology based on Genesis divorced from Israel. Paul did not have an eschatology of Israel divorced from Genesis. Paul said, "There is one hope." That hope of Paul was the end of the millennium resurrection.

And listen to me. In preaching nothing but the hope of Israel, Paul anticipated the fulfillment of God's promises to Abraham, Galatians Chapter 3:17-26.

Paul said that the promise to Abraham was not nullified by the law, although it wasn't fulfilled under the law. But the law was added. Added to what? To the Abrahamic promise. What does that mean? That means that Israel's promise, Israel's hope of the resurrection, was Abraham's hope. But not only that, in preaching, quote, "nothing but the hope of Israel," Paul likewise proclaimed the fulfillment of Genesis Chapter 1.

In Colossians 1, Paul said the gospel had been preached in all the world and was bringing forth fruit in every nation and multiplying. Paul, in the book of Colossians uses Genesis Chapter 1-3 language over and over and over again, but he wasn't saying one of these days it's going to be fulfilled. He said it was *being fulfilled*.

In other words, in preaching nothing but the hope of Israel, Paul proclaimed the fulfillment of Genesis Chapter 1.

Now watch this. Hebrews Chapter 11 shows that Abel's hope, this great, great roll call of faith in speaking all the great men and women of faith that he wanted to talk about, where does he start? Abel: In other words, at creation.

Abel's hope was Enoch's hope. Enoch's hope was Noah's hope. Noah's hope was Abraham's hope. But guess what, Abraham's hope was Israel after the flesh's hope. It was the *one hope* of scripture.

Watch this. Let's look at Isaiah a little bit closer. Remember that Isaiah 24-25 is a single prophecy and is the ground of Paul's doctrine of the end of millennium resurrection.

No More Curse—Isaiah 24-25

24:1-6– "The Curse" / **"The Death"** devoured the earth" as a result of the violation of "the everlasting covenant" (The Law of Moses)
Judgment on "heaven and earth" results in YHVH's rule in "Zion" (24:19-21)
Joel On Zion
"The Curse" / "The Death" removed at the time of the judgment / Kingdom / resurrection (25:6-8)
This is the end of the millennium resurrection of 1 Corinthians 15 / Revelation 20!
Therefore, "The Curse" / "The Death" of Isaiah 24-25 removed at the EoM resurrection
Follow closely →

Don K. Preston's First Affirmative

Isaiah 24:1-6 the Lord said that the curse, that is *the* death, had devoured the earth as a result of the violation of the everlasting covenant, and that's the Law of Moses. Joel agrees with that, by the way, in his book.

Judgment has passed upon heaven and earth. Heaven and earth is clean dissolved. The earth is dissolved. The earth falls. It totters and falls and will never rise again. But why? Well, judgment on heaven and earth results in Yahweh's rule after the destruction of heaven and earth. Guess what, Yahweh rules gloriously in Zion after putting in bondage, after putting in chains, *for the millennium,* the powers on high. And he rules gloriously in Zion.

And then, catch this," *in that day"* -- what day? In the day in which the Lord rules gloriously in Zion, *in that day*, the curse and the death is removed at that time of judgment, the time of the kingdom God ruling gloriously, and the time of the resurrection of 25:8.

Again, this is the end of the millennium resurrection. Paul said his doctrine of the end of the millennium resurrection would be when Isaiah was fulfilled. Therefore, the curse and the death of Isaiah 24-25 would be removed at the end of the millennium resurrection. Well, there's no controversy really about that, but let's look a little closer.

"The Death"

The NT writer's anticipated the end of **"the death"** designated by the definite article– i.e. the death of Adam (Rom. 5:12)-- in fulfillment of God's OT Promises to Israel after the flesh
The end of "the death", "the curse" is the focus of Romans 8, 1 Cor 15, 2 Cor. 5, Revelation 20-22!
It is not the end of "the deaths" or "death" but *"the death!", "the curse." There are not two ends, two "the deaths", two "the curses"!*
*They had **ONE HOPE**, the end of "the death", "the curse"– Of Genesis– At the End of Torah!*

The New Testament writers anticipated the end of "the death." And they designated it by, just like I have here, the definite article. This is the death of Adam that was introduced by Adam, Romans Chapter 5:12, "Wherefore as by one man sin entered into the world, and death by sin; therefore death is passed upon all men because all men have sinned." But the New Testament writers anticipated the end of that death -- listen to me -- in fulfillment of God's Old Testament promises made to Old Covenant Israel after the flesh.

The end of *the death* and the end of *the curse* is the focus of Romans 8, 1 Corinthians 15, 2 Corinthians 5, 1 Thessalonians 4, and Revelations 20-22. It is not the end of the deaths, plural. It is not the end of death, an anatharously; that is, without the article. It is the end of the death. It is the end of "the curse."

There are not in scripture two ends of two "the deaths" or the curses. Remember, the New Testament writers as well as the old, all the way back to Abel had one hope. And that was the end of the death, the curse of Genesis, and it would come at the end of Torah.

This is what Paul and the rest of the New Testament teaches.

1 Corinthians 15- Revelation 20 / 21- The Death

I Cor. 15:54- At the time of "the end", "*the death*" is swallowed up in victory, when "the law" "the strength of sin" (Torah!) would be overcome
Rev. 20:14 – "*The death*" Cast into the Lake!
Rev. 21:1-4 – In the New Creation, at the end of the Old-- there is no more "*the death*", "no more curse no more" (22:3) -- Inside the city– not outside!)
Joel says the New Creation, where there is no more "*the* death" / "no more curse no more" arrived in AD 70-> Rev. 22:6 →"These Things Must shortly come to pass!"
Joel, give us your Hermeneutic of Distinction between "the death" to be overcome in 1 Cor. 15 / Rev. 20– and "the death" of Revelation 21-which arrived in AD 70!

Notice in 1 Corinthians Chapter 15:54 at the time of "the end" -- 1 Corinthians 15:24, the death is swallowed up in victory. Most translations do not render the definite article in 1 Corinthians 15:54 unfortunately, but it's there in the Greek. And that -- the overcoming of "the death" would be

Don K. Preston's First Affirmative

when "the law," which was the strength of sin, and only one law was the strength of sin, and that was Torah, would be overcome.

Revelation Chapter 20:14, "the death" was cast into the lake of fire. Revelation 21:1-4, in the new creation -- listen to this -- at the end of the old creation, there is no more *the death*. And verse 3 says that in that New Creation, in the new heaven and new earth, there is *no more curse no more*. That's the literal rendering of the Greek.

Now notice this is inside the city. It's not true outside the city. Now watch this. Joel says that this New Creation of Revelation 21 and 22 where there is no more the death and no more curse no more arrived in A.D. 70. And even if he didn't agree with that, Revelation 22:6 says, "These things must shortly come to pass."

We cannot escape the imminence of the text. So what I'm going to ask Joel to do is to give us his Hermeneutic of Distinction between the death to be overcome in 1 Corinthians 15 and Revelation 20, and the death of Revelation Chapter 21, which was destroyed, according to Joel, in A.D. 70.

Notice now, here's my argument. Very simply stated, this is the syllogistic argument.

The Argument

"The Curse" / "The Death" that entered through Adam would be overcome at the resurrection of 1 Cor. 15 / Rev. 20– in fulfillment of Isaiah 25:6-8.

In the <u>New Zion</u> of Revelation 21-22, there is no more "the curse" no more "the death."

But, the New Creation of Revelation 21-22 arrived in AD 70 – (Joel)→ "Must shortly come to pass!"

Therefore, "The Curse" / "The Death" that entered through Adam was overcome in AD 70.

This is inescapably true!
If not, what is the <u>Hermeneutic of Distinction</u>?

Don K. Preston's First Affirmative

The curse and the death had entered through Adam would be overcome at the resurrection of 1 Corinthians 15 or Revelation 20 in fulfillment of Isaiah 25:6-8.

In the new Zion of Revelation 21 and 22 there is no more "the curse." There is no more "the death."

But the New Creation of Revelation 21 and 22 arrived in A.D. 70, Joel McDurmon. And remember, even if he wanted to argue with it, the text does say, "These things must shortly come to pass." *Therefore*, the curse and the death that entered through Adam was overcome in A.D. 70.

I suggest to you that this is inescapably true. If not, once again, we ask for the Hermeneutic of Distinction.

Now I want to shift gears just a little bit, but I want to look a little bit closer to Isaiah 25.

Resurrection and Zion

The EoM resurrection of 1 Cor. 15 would be *in fulfillment of Isaiah 25:8*.

The EoM resurrection of Isaiah 25 would be on Zion– "On this mountain... He shall destroy death..." **Joel On Zion**

Zion is the locus of the EoM Resurrection– **The One Hope** of Abel-Noah-Abraham-Moses→ **Zion**! (Heb.11:11-35)!

This is not **Jewish eschatology** Divorced From Genesis!

Abel's One Hope Was Abraham's One Hope Which Was Israel's One Hope– Located in Zion!

Hebrews 12:21– "You have come to Mt. Zion!"

Joel: "Zion has been spiritualized and fulfilled" →

The end of the millennium resurrection, 1 Corinthians 15, would be in fulfillment of Isaiah 25, "Then shall be brought to pass the saying."

Don K. Preston's First Affirmative

There's no question that Paul's doctrine, the end of the millennium resurrection, is Isaiah 25, but watch this. That means that the end of the millennium resurrection of Isaiah 25 would be on *Zion*; "On this mountain He shall destroy death." Folks, that's old Zion.

Zion in Old Testament scripture is the locus of the end of the millennium resurrection. It is the focus of all of Old Covenant Israel's eschatological and soteriological hopes. It was the one hope of scripture.

By the way, it was the hope of Abel. It was the hope of Noah. It was the hope of Abraham. And it was the hope of Moses- Hebrews 11:11-35.

I want to suggest to you something that -- this is very important. This is not Jewish eschatology divorced from Genesis. This is Genesis eschatology, pure and simple.

Abel's one hope was *Enoch's* one hope, which was *Noah's* one hope, which was *Abraham's* one hope, which was *Moses'* one hope, which was *Paul's* one hope. And guess what, that hope was focused on the heavenly city, the heavenly country. The better resurrection -- Hebrews 11:11-16, and Hebrews 11:35, they anticipated the better resurrection.

That focus was on *Zion*. What does the writer of Hebrews say? "You have come to Mount Zion." Now if Zion is the location of the end of the millennium resurrection and the writer of Hebrews says, "You have come to Mount Zion," folks, I suggest to you the time of the end of millennium resurrection had arrived.

Now by the way, Joel says the Zion promises have been spiritualized and fulfilled. I want to read to you a great quote for Joel. I love this quote. I love it not only because of who he was writing against, but I love it because it's true. He's arguing against the Dispensationalists -- this article can be found on American Vision's website.

Don K. Preston's First Affirmative

Joel On Zion

> When the argument of faith and pilgrimage in Hebrews 11 finally does turn to "us" it notes a complete change of status. While all of those Old Testament pilgrims died and "did not receive what was promised," New Testament believers are different: "God had provided something better for us" (Heb. 11:40). <u>So, we are categorically not like them. We are in a better position than they. The promised Kingdom has indeed come, it is given to us.</u> We are not exiles waiting to receive the promise. Indeed, the author tells the first-century believing Jews in the very next chapter, ... "you have come to Mount Zion" (Heb. 12:22). They had arrived! This arrival verse is very important. ... Hebrews makes it absolutely clear that New Testament believers "have come to Zion." This is in the past tense> *(My emph., DKP)...* (AV Article)
>
> **Amen and Amen!**
> But, <u>Zion is the locus of the EoM Resurrection</u>-Fulfilling Genesis!
> **Joel has affirmed the EoM Resurrection!**

Quote, "When the argument of faith and pilgrimage in Hebrews Chapter 11 finally does turn to, quote, us," unquote, it notes a complete change of status. While all of those Old Testament pilgrims died and, quote, did not receive what was promised, unquote, New Testament Christians or believers are different."

God had provided something better for us, Hebrews 11:40, so we are categorically not like them. We are in a better position than they. Listen carefully. *The promised kingdom has indeed come*. It is *given* to us. We are not exiles to -- waiting to receive the promise. Indeed the author tells the first century believing Jews in the very next chapter, Chapter 12, "You have come to Mount Zion." They had arrived. This arrival of course is very important. Hebrews makes it abundantly clear that the New Testament believers, quote, 'have come to Zion,' unquote. 'This is in the past tense,'" unquote.

All I can do is say Amen. And Amen. But let me say this again. Zion is the focus and the locus of the end of the millennium resurrection: the one eschatological hope of Abel, Noah, Abraham, Moses, and Paul. There is no Jewish Zion eschatology divorced from Genesis. It is one eschatology.

Don K. Preston's First Affirmative

Now I suggest to you, ladies and gentlemen, Joel has affirmed the end of the millennium resurrection.

Now let's go back to Isaiah Chapter 25 and look just a little bit closer.

Isaiah 25- The Banquet and the Resurrection

Isaiah 25:6 = Messianic Banquet
Isaiah 25:8 = EoM Millennium (Edenic) Resurrection
Banquet and EoM Resurrection are Inseparable
Follow Closely….
Matthew 8 = Messianic Banquet (Abraham's Hope)
Thus, Matthew 8 = <u>EoM Resurrection!</u>
But, Matthew 8 was fulfilled in AD 70 when the Sons of the Kingdom were cast out (Joel)→ Gal. 4
Therefore, the EoM resurrection was AD 70
This is irrefutable!

In Isaiah 25:6 it says, "In that day" -- what day? In which the Lord would judge heaven and earth -- destroy heaven and earth. He would cast the wicked into bondage. He would rule gloriously on Zion. "In that day the Lord shall make a great feast. A feast of wine on the lees. A feast of fat things." This is the Messianic Banquet. And by the way, Joel won't disagree with that.

So Isaiah 25:6 is the Messianic Banquet. But wait, Isaiah 25:8 is the end of the millennium resurrection. Now notice the connective terms. "*In that day* the Lord will make a feast." *In that day*. What day? "In the day he makes the feast." *In that day* he will destroy death. The Messianic Banquet and the end of the millennium resurrection are absolutely inseparable.

Now follow closely. In Matthew Chapter 8 we have the prediction and the statement concerning the Messianic Banquet. Jesus commended the faith of the Centurion who had tremendous faith and Jesus said, "many shall come from the east and the west and shall sit down with Abraham, Isaac, and Jacob in the kingdom, and the sons of the kingdom will be cast out."

Now follow this. Isaiah 25:6 is the messianic banquet. Isaiah 25:8 is the end of the millennium resurrection. But Matthew Chapter 8 is the Messianic

Don K. Preston's First Affirmative

Banquet, therefore, Matthew Chapter 8 is the end of the millennium resurrection.

But guess what? My friend Joel says that Abraham sat down at the messianic banquet when the sons of kingdom were cast out in A.D. 70. I concur one hundred percent. But that means the end of the millennium resurrection was in A.D. 70. I consider that irrefutable.

Daniel 12	**1 Corinthians 15**
Hope of Israel	Hope of Israel (54-55)
Time of the End	Time of the end
Resurrection	Resurrection
Everlasting Life	Immortality
Righteous shine in the kingdom	Entrance into the kingdom
AD 70	AD 70
When the power of the holy people is completely shattered	When "The Law" Terminated (54f)

Notice now the complete parallel between Daniel 12 and 1 Corinthians 15. Both are speaking in the hope of Israel.

Both speak of the time of the end. Both speak of the resurrection at the end of the age.

Both speak of the resurrection to everlasting life -- everlasting life and immortality.

Both speak of the time in which the righteous will shine forth in the kingdom.

By the way, Daniel Chapter 12 says that resurrection out of the dust of the earth to everlasting life would be when the power of the holy people is completely shattered. By the way, Joel agrees with that. That was A.D. 70: - unless he's changed his mind.

Well, what did Paul say as he talked about the resurrection to eternal life at the end of the age of 1 Corinthians 15? Writing to the Corinthians -- first century generation Christians, he said, "Brethren, we're not all going to sleep." And he said that that resurrection would take place when the law

Don K. Preston's First Affirmative

that was the strength of sin, i.e., the Law of Moses, was done away with: Perfect correlation between Daniel 12 and Revelation as well.

Notice Daniel 12 and Revelation Chapter 20.

Daniel 12	Revelation 20
Great Tribulation	Satan loosed at the end of the millennium **Tribulation**
Those in the books rewarded	Those in the books rewarded
Resurrection the (One) Hope of Israel	Resurrection- The Hope of Israel
Time of the end	Time of the end
Righteous shine in the kingdom	Righteous in the New Creation
When the power of the holy people (Torah) is shattered– AD 70! **(Daniel is not typological!)**	Behold, I come quickly! Joel, give us your Hermeneutic of Distinction!!

Both speak of the great tribulation. When did Revelation 20 put the great tribulation? *At the end of the millennium.*

Now watch: Both Daniel 12 and Revelation 20 talk about the rewarding of those written in the books.

Both are speaking of the resurrection and remember Israel only had one resurrection hope, not two. Paul didn't have two resurrection doctrines nor did John.

Both speak at the time of the end when the righteous would shine in the kingdom. Daniel 12 was when the power of the holy people have been completely shattered. Joel agrees that was A.D. 70.

What does Revelation say? "Behold, I come quickly." So, again, we ask for Joel's Hermeneutic of Distinction. If he says that Revelation 20 is not Daniel Chapter 12, tell us the difference between eternal life in Daniel and eternal life in 1 Corinthians 15 and Revelation Chapter 20 and on.

Here's my argument in syllogistic form.

Don K. Preston's First Affirmative

Resurrection and the End of Torah

> Daniel 12 / 1 Cor. 15/ Rev. 20
> The resurrection of Daniel 12 is the resurrection of 1 Cor. 15 / Revelation 20– If Not, Why Not?
>
> The resurrection of Daniel 12 was to be (was) "when the power of the holy people is completely shattered" (Daniel 12:7)– AD 70
>
> Therefore, the EoM resurrection of 1 Cor. 15 / Revelation 20 was when the power of the holy people was completely shattered– AD 70.
>
> Joel agrees that the Law of Moses "died in AD 70"
>
> This demands that the EoM was in AD 70!

The resurrection of Daniel 12 is the resurrection of 1 Corinthians 15 and Revelation Chapter 20. *If not, then why not?*

The resurrection of Daniel 12 was to be, and was, when the power of the holy people's completely shattered, i.e., A.D. 70. Therefore, the end of the millennium resurrection of 1 Corinthians 15 and Revelation Chapter 20 was when the power of the holy people is completely shattered.

Joel agrees. Remember the law died in A.D. 70. This demands that the end of the millennium resurrection was in A.D. 70.

I'm going to talk in my remaining time about the hope of Israel.

> Abraham's Hope? -- Abraham longed for ONE Zion-Banquet- Resurrection (Mat. 8 / Heb. 11-12) - Fulfilled AD 70 Says Joel! (Rev. 21-22)
> Abraham's Hope? - NT proclaimed ONE Resurrection / Zion / Banquet- Mat. 8 / Gal. 4/ Heb. 12 / Rev. 22 - End of time? Unfulfilled? (Rev. 20) - What is the Difference, Joel?
> Abraham Had One Hope– <u>Zion, Banquet-Resurrection-</u> and Hebrews 12 Said: "You have Come To Mt. Zion!
> The EoM Resurrection Was Near– 1 Peter 4:5-17!!

Don K. Preston's First Affirmative

I want you to notice that in Isaiah 25 and in Hebrews Chapter 11, Matthew Chapter 8, Abraham longed for one heavenly Zion. According to Matthew Chapter 8, he longed for one Messianic Banquet. He longed for the better resurrection. Abraham did not have two resurrection hopes.

Joel says -- do you remember the quote? Joel says that Abraham and all of those worthy have received the kingdom. Notice he didn't use the term "resurrection"? He used the word "kingdom."

They were promised the resurrection, and that was their hope. That was their kingdom hope. Resurrection and kingdom go hand in hand. But wait a minute. The New Testament proclaimed one resurrection, one Zion, one banquet, and Joel comes to Revelation Chapter 20 and creates a new eschatology and says in Revelation Chapter 20 is a different eschatology from what Abraham received in A.D. 70. No, Abraham had one hope.

Abraham and the One Resurrection Hope

Hebrews 11– 12
From Creation (Abel)→ To Noah → To Abraham→ To Moses→ ***To Zion!***   ***There was One Hope***!
Those OT worthies anticipated Zion (11:13-16) - the "better resurrection" (11:35)- Zion and the EoM Resurrection are Inseparable– Isaiah 25:6-8!
You cannot divorce Genesis–Noah- Abrahamic eschatological hope from Israel- from the EoM!
Abel's One Hope Was Abraham's One Hope Which Was Israel's One Hope!
"You have come To Mt. Zion!" (Heb. 12:21)   The **One Hope** Was About To Be Realized!

So Abraham had one hope, Zion, banquet, and the resurrection. Remember Hebrews Chapter 12 says, "You have come to Mount Zion." So here we go again.

In Hebrews Chapter 11 and 12 from creation, that is from Abel to Noah to Abraham to Moses to Zion, there was *one hope*. Those Old Testament worthies anticipated Zion, the better resurrection, Hebrews 11:35, and the end of the millennium resurrection and Zion are absolutely inseparable. You can't divorce them, ladies and gentlemen.

You cannot divorce Genesis from Noah from Abraham. And their eschatological hope from Israel or the end of millennium. Abel's one hope was Abraham's hope which was Israel's one hope. And remember, Paul said, "You have come to Mount Zion." Their one hope was about to be realized.

Remember, Paul said there is *one hope*, not two. He didn't say Israel has a hope about to be fulfilled and Genesis will be fulfilled a couple of millennia later.

One Hope—Not Two!

> Paul: There is One Hope (Eph. 4:4)
> That One Ultimate Hope was the reuniting of "heaven and earth"- *purposed before time* (Eph. 1:9-10)
> That One Hope was to be fulfilled "in the stewardship of the Fullness of Time" (1:10)
> But, the fullness of time was the last days of the Old Covenant World of Israel (Gal. 4:4).
> Therefore, the fulfillment of the ONE HOPE was to be fully accomplished in the last days of Old Covenant Israel– which Joel admits was finalized in AD 70!

Now I want you to watch Ephesians 1:9-10, Paul said it was God's eternal purpose, purpose before time began, that He would reunite heaven and earth. This is Genesis 1-3. That one hope was to be fulfilled, quote, "in the stewardship of the fullness of time," Ephesians 1:10.

But wait, the fullness of time was present in the first century and the fullness of time was Israel's last days. "In the fullness of time, God sent forth His son, born of a woman, made under the law, to redeem them that are under the law" (Galatians 4:4)

Do you catch this? God's one ultimate hope was the uniting of reuniting of heaven and earth; He purposed that reuniting that restoration before time. That one hope, that restoration, was to be fulfilled in the stewardship of

Don K. Preston's First Affirmative

the fullness of time. But the fullness of time was present in the first century and the fullness of time was Israel's last days, not our days.

Therefore the fulfillment of that one single eschatological hope from Genesis onward was to be fully accomplished in the last days of Old Covenant Israel, which Joel admits was finalized in A.D. 70.

All the Prophets Spoke of "These Days"

Paul said it was God's eternal purpose to re-unite heaven and earth– Paul's One Hope (Eph. 1:9-10; 4:4)

Peter likewise anticipated the "restoration of all things" at the parousia of Christ– This is Genesis eschatology (Acts 3:19-24).

Peter said all the OT prophets who spoke of the restoration of all things "spoke of these days" - that is his generation!

Paul's "the fullness of time," and Peter's "these days" is the fulfillment of Genesis in the first century!

Both Paul and Peter affirm that the time for fulfillment of God's Ultimate Plan, the One Hope, Was Present!

Notice in Peter and Acts Chapter 3 as he spoke of the restoration of all things; this is the reconciling of heaven and earth to be sure, Ephesians Chapter 1; this is the fulfillment of Genesis 1-3. But notice that Peter anticipating the restoration of all things, that the parousia of Christ said all of the old testament prophets who foretold that restoration, quote, "spoke of these days," unquote.

Those were Peter's days; they're not these days of 2012. Notice that Paul's fullness of time and Peter's "these days" are the fulfillment of Genesis eschatology in the first century. So both Paul and Peter affirmed the time for the fulfillment of God's ultimate plan, *the one hope,* was present.

Let me summarize and conclude.

Don K. Preston's First Affirmative

> We have proven beyond disputation that:
> The end of the EoM resurrection was the one eschatological hope of the OT and NT saints– From Abel-Noah-Abraham-Moses→ Zion!
> That one hope became known as "the hope of Israel"
> Paul's one eschatological hope was based on Isaiah 24-27, Hosea and Daniel 12– This is indisputable.
> The end of the millennium resurrection foretold in these prophecies was to be fulfilled at the end of the Old Covenant age of Israel in AD 70- The End of Torah
> It does not matter what our concept of Genesis 1, resurrection, the body, the millennium, the curse of Adam, might be– Scripture undeniably posits fulfillment of the end of the millennium resurrection in AD 70

I have proven beyond any disputation I believe that the end of millennium resurrection was the one eschatological hope of the Old Testament and New Testament saints from Abel to Noah to Abraham to Moses to Zion. That one hope of Abel became the hope of Israel.

Paul's one eschatological hope is based upon Isaiah 24-27, Hosea, Daniel 12; this is indisputable. And the end of the millennium resurrection foretold in these prophecies was without a doubt to be fulfilled at the end of the Old Covenant age of Israel in A.D. 70 at the end of the Law of Moses.

Let me reiterate. It does not matter what our concept of Genesis 1 may be. It does not matter what our concept of the resurrection or the body to be raised might be. Doesn't matter what our concept of the millennium might be, or the curse of Adam or the death of Adam might be. Scripture, as we have shown, posits the fulfillment of that one eschatological hope at the end of the millennium resurrection and fulfillment of God's Old Covenant promises to Old Covenant Israel in A.D. 70. Thank you very much.

Joel McDurmon's First Negative
****

First of all, let me say a word of thanks for being invited to this event. It is an honor to be asked to come debate anyone on such a detailed intellectual topic in front of this many people that are interested in it. So, I thank Don for that invitation, and I also thank all of you for coming out to listen to what I consider to be an extremely important issue, one that has been important to the church at least enough in the early days to enshrine a particular view in their creeds. I'm not going to approach it from that angle tonight, but I do want you to each keep that in the back of your minds.

Before I start, let me say to Don, thanks for drawing attention to my books. And I wanted to especially unveil tonight a brand-new book written by a man who, as most of you probably know, Samuel Frost, one-time intellectual leader in this movement, and who has returned to the partial preterist world, if you want to use that term. And he has written a small booklet, which American Vision has published just this week. This is hot off the press entitled, *Why I Left Full Preterism*, a 70-page booklet. Wonderful read. I enjoyed reading it and editing it.

And I also wanted to say that a donor has made it possible for that entire box of books back there for you to take one each home free. So help yourself. Please don't take two. Unless there are some left over after Q and A on Saturday, and then we'll talk about that.

The refutation of Don's position that the final, end-of-the-age coming of Christ and attendant final resurrection of the dead occurred in A.D. 70 occurs under three headings. They are Biblical Theology, Systematic Theology, and Practical Theology.

Let's begin with the Biblical. My argument for the defense of the bodily resurrection of the dead is nothing less than Jesus' argument for the bodily resurrection of the dead. And that appears in Luke Chapter 20 in exchange with the Sadducees. Most of you know this passage. I'll elucidate on my argument tomorrow night.

Tonight I bring it up just to introduce my critique of Don's position as has been expressed in his statement.

Joel McDurmon's First Negative

Jesus began his refutation of them by saying "you guys are wrong." For two reasons: You don't understand the scriptures and you don't understand the power of God. Now it wasn't that the Sadducees didn't understand -- didn't know the scriptures. They knew the scriptures inside and out.

And as I level this same charge at Don Preston's position and to full Preterism in general, I am obviously not saying he doesn't know the scriptures. I would be a lunatic to say that after that magnificent presentation and journey through the scriptures. But this is talking about a more intimate type of knowing. Knowing Biblical Theology.

Let's talk about the nature of Biblical Theology. My major criticism of the way his arguments progress is that God's word is not put together like an erector set. Do you remember those things when you were a kid? Little metal pieces with holes in them and you bolt them together, and you build little buildings and robots and things.

God's word is not built out of two-by-fours and steel-frame structure. There's not a piece here and piece here, and these two pieces come this far and another piece spans in between. And it's all rigid and you put the structure together and you can count all the pieces, and if one piece is missing, you know it's not fulfilled yet. And if a piece is there, you know it's been used up and that piece can never be used again. God's word is not like that at all. It has elements of that in it in some places; they're actually more few than you might imagine.

Instead God's word in Biblical prophecy is more like fine art. In particular, I have in mind a symphony. Yes, there are many pieces, but they're all working together at the same time in harmony, adding different timbers and different colors and different sounds to make one whole that covers one theme over one long period of time.

That period of time has different movements within it in which there are stops and starts, and the theme is replayed in different ways. And there are variations upon a theme, and each variation is a little different than the theme, but the theme is recognizable in it. Its image is recognizable in its children, so to speak.

Joel McDurmon's First Negative

Biblical prophecy is much more like that than it is the rigid structure that Mr. Preston has put before you tonight. Why is this the case? How is this the case?

A favorite verse is Luke 21 used by full preterists to prove that all things must come to pass in A.D. 70. You know the verse. "But when you see Jerusalem surrounded by armies, then know that its desolation has come near, then let those who are in Judea flee to the mountains. Let those who are inside the city depart, and let not those who are out in the country enter it for these are the days of vengeance to fulfill *all* that is written."

Now, why is there any debate at all after that passage? Well, it's because if you take a very rigid view of that verse and the words in it and the concepts and the prophecies in it that it's talking about, you run into serious problems.

Let's start with the word "all." Now don't sit there and say, "Oh dear, is this guy really going to tell us that the word all doesn't mean all? Does the word all really mean some? Is this guy Bill Clinton sitting up there telling us about the meaning -- what the word 'is' is?"

Well, I think Don himself would acknowledge that at least in some circumstances you have to qualify the meaning of the word "all." It doesn't always mean "all, every single one." It's not always meant to be taken that way. From just a couple of examples you can see that this is not the case with prophecy.

Nineveh was judged under the prophet Nahum. That prophecy was final, fulfilled, over with in 612 B.C., Nahum is quoted nowhere in the New Testament.

Better yet, the virgin birth of Christ, prophesied in Isaiah 7. Takes place in Matthew 1:23 at Jesus' birth. Now obviously that doesn't need to wait until the siege of Jerusalem in A.D. 70 to be fulfilled. And so all prophecy is not fulfilled in A.D. 70. Minor qualification.

What you learn from this is when the word all is used in that way, it has qualifications that actually do make it mean some. Maybe a little bit,

Joel McDurmon's First Negative

maybe to a larger degree, but it at least opens the door to the discussion that needs to be had.

What we learned really is that the days of vengeance are not a necessary and sufficient condition for all of the prophecies of the Old Testament to come to pass; it's merely a necessary condition. Which is to say, yes, this has to happen that all prophecy must be fulfilled, but that doesn't mean that all prophecy is fulfilled because of that one piece. Either before it or after it or anything else.

This phrase, by the way, is peculiar to Luke that all that has been written. It only appears in Luke and Acts. And its other uses show this word needs to be qualified more. Luke 18:31-33, talking to the 12, he said to them, "See, we're going up to Jerusalem and everything that is written about the son of man but the prophets will be accomplished. For he will be delivered over to the Gentiles, mocked and shamefully treated and spit upon. And after flogging him, they will kill him. And the third day he will rise."

Jesus is here saying that all that is written in the prophets about him is fulfilled in the crucifixion, death, burial, and the resurrection.

Same thing in Acts 13. "For those who live in Jerusalem and their rulers because they did not recognize him nor understood the utterances of the prophets, which are read every Sabbath, fulfilled them by condemning him. And though they found him not guilty, worthy of death, they asked Pilate to have him executed. And when they had carried out all that was written of him, they took him down from the cross -- from the tree, and laid him in the tomb."

Here it says that all that was written about him was fulfilled on the cross before they even took him off. So do we really expect that this is meant to be taken literally? Does it mean "all, every single one, at this very time, and not before it or after it?" No, it doesn't.

Biblical words are not meant to be used that way. I am reminded as I go through this discussion of the meaning of words of an old pastor one time who pulled me over -- and this is highly relevant to this discussion, by the way, because it talks about 1 Corinthians 15. And he pulled me over and he said, "Son, you do realize what perfect scripture verse there is to go on the

Joel McDurmon's First Negative

door to the nursery of the church?" I said, "Nursery? Oh, the babies? The cry room?" I said, "Yeah." He says "It's 1 Corinthians 15. 'We shall not all sleep, but we shall all be changed.'"

Now obviously it wasn't meant to be understood in that way, but it can be understood in that way. So we have to be very precise based on positional context, book chapter verse context, whole context of the Bible, whole context of redemptive of history before we start pinning definitions on words and then carrying them through the rest of scripture.

Secondly, let's talk about the nature of the word of "fulfill." Don used this in his presentation. He indicated, at least to me, that that meant final, over with, done. Maybe he would qualify that in some cases.

Too many people think that fulfill means finish, done, over with, gone. But I think that's wrong, and I'll show you why. Just as Francis Shaffer used to talk about a category of" true truth." I think we need to have a Biblical hermeneutical category of "fully fulfilled" and then we can start this discussion in reality.

In Joshua 21:43-45, a verse you all know I'm sure. "Thus the Lord gave to Israel all the land that he swore to give to their fathers and they took possession of it and they settled there. And the Lord gave them rest on every side just as he had sworn to their forefathers. Not one of all their enemies had withstood them for the Lord had given them all into their hands. Not one word of all the good promises of the Lord had made to the house of Israel had failed. All came to pass."

Let that sink in. Obviously not everything was fulfilled at that time because there was more, thousands of years of history to come yet. Second Samuel 7 is said to be fulfilled. This is God's promise to David that he would have a son on his throne forever.

In 1 Kings 8 this is said to be fulfilled: "Now the Lord has fulfilled this promise that He made," Solomon says, "For I have risen, in the place of David, my father, sit on the throne of Israel as the Lord promised and I have built the house in the name of the Lord, the God of Israel. You have kept with your servant, David, my father, what you declared to him. You've spoken with your mouth and with your hand you have fulfilled it."

Joel McDurmon's First Negative

The Hebrew word is *Male*. The Greek LXX renders that with *pleroo* or *pleroma*, which is the same word used mostly in the New Testament to indicate fulfillment of prophecy.

Lamentations Chapter 4, Ezekiel 7. Lamentations 4 says "Our end drew near. Our days were fulfilled" -- *pleroo*, same word. "For our end had come." People, this is the end of Israel.

Ezekiel 7:2-3 calls it "the end" with the definite article. Don's big on definite articles tonight; throw that in there.

With the definite article says it had come now, literally in his day. "An end has come." And "The end has come." Jeremiah admitted that exact same end, which was the carrying off into Babylon of Israel, called it "our end," and he said that the time for it has been fulfilled, *pleroo*.

Now we know that the prophecy was not fully fulfilled because it's fulfilled later again in the death and burial of Christ in, A.D. 70, and who knows?

My point here is to show you that the word fulfillment is used in this way in many places in scripture. Does the word of God contain contradictions? Does it say something is fulfilled here and then say it's fulfilled here again? Does it say it will be fulfilled twice? Don likes to use that question.

Or do we fallible humans have an indefinite understanding of what fulfillment really means?

But suppose, Mr. or Mrs. full preterist, that you have lived at any one of those times. You had lived after Joshua crossing the land and made this bold proclamation that not one of the promises of Israel had failed to come to pass, all was fulfilled.

You lived in that time and you embraced Preston's Hermeneutic. Just imagine the arguments that took place. Leveraging the very word of God through David and Joshua and Moses and Solomon, Jeremiah, Ezekiel. "There is nothing more to come, people. What are you talking about pie in the sky for? What are you talking about more? There is nothing more. This is the end. It's over with, done, fulfilled, gone."

Joel McDurmon's First Negative

But someone might respond, What about -- what about the curse? What about this ground? I'm still plowing my garden and it's still got thorns and thistles. And you know what, I'm still sweating an awful lot when I plow it. What about the pain? And the tears? And what about -- what about death?

"Ah, you knothead. All that's spiritual. All that's spiritual. Spiritual reality. You're still going to suffer here, but when you die you get to go be with the Lord up in heaven." The reversal of the curse, so-called.

You could have maintained at any one of those times in history -- when those promises were said to be fulfilled, you could have maintained a very powerful full Preterist argument, sustained it, and been very difficult to refute. And you would have been wrong.

I'm not saying that necessitates that you're wrong this time, but I'm saying think real hard about it.

Secondly, you can't do what Don Preston does continuously, and that is quote a passage from the Old Testament that is cited in the New Testament as fulfilled, and then drag the entire context of that Old Testament prophecy along with it as proof that all that must take place at the same time.

This is very important. Because most of his arguments and most of his syllogisms are built on equating scripture to scripture in this way. I'm a big fan of *analogia scriptura*, but it has its limitations when it's not used properly. It must be used properly.

Luke 4:18-21, Jesus says, "The spirit of the Lord is upon me because he's anointed me to proclaim the good news to the poor. He sent me to proclaim liberty to the captives, recovering of sight to the blind and set at liberty to those who are oppressed, to proclaim the year of the Lord's favor. And he began to say to them today this scripture has been fulfilled in your hearing." That's Isaiah 61:1.

The very next sentence of Isaiah 61:1 includes in that long list of things that he had come to give and that is the Days of Vengeance. This is at the very beginning of Jesus' public ministry. He doesn't really publicly announce the

Joel McDurmon's First Negative

Days of Vengeance really not until much, much later. You could say all of that, but it's questionable whether there was a whole crowd of people there. And really if you get into the New Testament and the Apostles, it's not proclaimed until much later.

So if you are able to drag the entire context of a prophecy forward, you would have to drag that forward to Luke 4:18 as well. But ironically, Jesus stops and he doesn't quote that very next sentence.

Matthew 1:23, Isaiah 7:14, we already mentioned the virgin birth. This is quoted in Matthew 1:23. But Isaiah 7-9, if you read it, is a single, seamless prophecy.

Matthew again quotes it from Isaiah 9 in Matthew 4:15-16 that Jesus travels through the land of Zebulon and Naphtali and preaches the gospel. And these people laying in darkness have seen a great light. So Matthew is jumping from Isaiah 7 to Isaiah 9. What's the problem with that? Isaiah 8 is all about judgment. And the judgment that is to come on Jerusalem.

If Don Preston's hermeneutic is correct, then you have to -- you have to, must, obligatory, irrefutably drag that also into the early phase of Jesus' ministry, his birth, and his public announcements.

Matthew 2:15, you're all probably familiar with, the quotation of Hosea 11:1. It is used to describe the fulfillment when Jesus and his family flee into Egypt from Pharaoh. "Thus it was done that it would be fulfilled out of Egypt have I called my son." It's baffled commentators for years. It's very simple.

What's the problem with that? Hosea 11-13 is a seamless prophecy. Hosea 13 is about the resurrection. Don mentioned it a while ago, very graphic passage on resurrection. Why is not the resurrection fulfilled here in Matthew 2:15? Why not? Because you can't treat Bible prophecy that way. It's much more piecemeal; it's much more fluid. It's used with much more authority by the Apostles who were inspired.

Zechariah 13 "Strike the Shepherd and the sheep of the flock will be scattered." But the very next verses talk about judgment on Israel. "I'll turn my hand against the little ones, and the whole land, declares the Lord,

Joel McDurmon's First Negative

two-thirds shall be cut off and perish, one-third shall be left alive." According to Zechariah, as you read through the seamless prophecy of Zechariah 13 and 14, he says twice this will happen "in that day." Let me yell it like Don does. "In that day."

So why did not the crucifixion of Jesus and the resurrection and the destruction of Jerusalem -- judgment on Jerusalem all happen in literally the same day at the same time? Why is there a 40-year space between Jesus and the coming -- *that coming*? (Had to throw that in there or I'd get quoted and put on the screen tomorrow.)

It's because you can't treat Bible prophecy that way. Isaiah 53 is quoted by John 12 in the middle of Jesus' ministry. It's quoted in Mark 15 at the crucifixion. Matthew says this was fulfilled at the beginning of Jesus' public ministry when he healed people. Peter applies it later in 1 Peter 2:24 and puts in the past tense, "You have been healed."

If Isaiah is one seamless prophecy, why was it not all fulfilled at the same time? And why can't we drag the entire context into every one of these spaces in scripture? Because Bible prophecy is not meant to be treated that way.

The fulfillments and applications are sometimes cited in a much more piecemeal way, and I'm not sure that anyone has ever developed a clear hermeneutical rule for it. But it is irrefutable that it does happen that way.

My view is that all of it was fulfilled in the death, burial, resurrection, and ascension of Jesus Christ. Anything that happens before that or after that is completely dependent upon what happened to him. Because he is the focus of all the Bible, of all Biblical prophecy, of all redemptive history. Jesus -- the man, Jesus, who is the mediator of this New Covenant. And so even destruction and everything else of Jerusalem happened at the cross, and was only later worked out in history by God's will. When the goodness and loving-kindness of God our savior appeared, he saved us, past tense. Not because of works done in righteousness, but because of his own mercy.

2 Timothy 1:9-10 says this: "God who saved us" -- past tense -- "and called us to a holy calling not because of our works, but because of his own

Joel McDurmon's First Negative

purpose and grace. Which he gave us in Christ Jesus before the ages began, which has now been manifested through the appearing of our savior Jesus Christ who abolished death."

Let that sink in, folks. You don't have to wait until 1 Corinthians for death to be swallowed up in victory. It was fulfilled on the cross.

What happens as a, "resurrection" in A.D. 70, and anytime thereafter is a recapitulation of what happened to the person of Jesus Christ.

But it's undeniable that that was abolished in Christ. You don't have to say, oh, well, where does it say this will be done twice? It doesn't have to say it will be done twice. The nature of Biblical prophecy is variations upon the theme until you reach that vast final conclusion. Of course that's the argument going on here tonight. So you'll say to me: Well, how do you know you've reached the end of that whole symphony? And I will go to something that Don virtually dismissed in his opening statement and I will reply to that more fully in my actual response times. And that is the curse.

What is the curse exactly? Let's read the curse. Before we go talking about how it's mentioned in Revelation or anywhere else, what does it say?

To the woman he said, "I will greatly multiply your pain in childbearing. In pain you shall bring forth children. Your desire shall be for your husband, and he shall rule over you."

And to Adam he said, "Because you have listened to the voice of your wife and eaten of the tree which I commanded you, you shall not eat of it, cursed is the ground for your sake."

Get in mind what he's saying there. The word for ground in Hebrew is *adamah* from which he was taken, Adam. Cursed is the *adamah* because of *Adam*. There is a final organic connection between those two. "In pain you shall eat of it all the days of your life. Thorns and thistles it shall bring forth to you and you shall eat the plants of the field. By the sweat of your face you shall eat bread until you return to the ground. For out of it you were taken, for you are dust and to dust you shall return."

Joel McDurmon's First Negative

Don may say it doesn't matter what this means. I say it matters -- definitely matters what this means. The curse involves the ground; it involves intensified labor. Sweat. Have you ever done a Biblical study of the word sweat? It appears three times. It will change your life.

Thorns, scarcity, and by implication poverty. Power struggles in marital relationships, and by implication other authoritative relationships. Great pain in childbirth, and of course, the death of returning to that cursed ground.

My wife, I can promise you, will never in her life -- in this life, become a full Preterist. She has given birth to four baby boys, three of them by natural childbirth. The average weight of all four being almost ten-and-a-half pounds. She knows something about the curse.

If there is no removal of this curse in the earth, then full preterism runs you into Neo-Manichaeism. I don't agree with everything Gary North said in critique of that -- of full Preterist position, but I do agree with this: Theologically it becomes a dualism. You have an irredeemable earth. You have an irredeemable body. It is the body itself which causes you to sin, some full preterists say. I don't know if Don holds that position or not. But you're led to an eternal dualism in which the curse is never removed from this earth.

We're also told that physical death is part of the curse. I mentioned the language there. "Cursed is the ground -- *adamah* -- because of you, Adam. By the sweat of your face you shall eat bread until you return to the ground" -- *adamah* -- "For out of it you were taken, for you are dust and dust you shall return."

Later in scripture death is referred to as corruption. If this curse is natural in Genesis, then corruption must be good. And yet it's spoken of all through the Psalms as an enemy, as something to be feared, as something to run from.

In Isaiah 11 and 65 it's spoken of in terms of something that is horrible, something that you want to avoid and overcome and see the end of. And yet if Preston's position is correct and the curse is never removed or the curse never involved death to begin with, more particularly -- if the curse

Joel McDurmon's First Negative

never involved physical death to begin with, then that corruption, which the Psalms and Isaiah berate must have been something that God originally created, and which he therefore pronounced good at the end of the day and very good at the end of the seven days.

Is corruption something very good? According to later scripture, no. So aside from the language and the very clear flow of the passage, we have a Biblical argument that shows you physical death was part of the curse. If that curse is going to be removed, ala, Revelation 22. Whether it's in the city temporarily or out of it later, then it has to be overcome.

Systematic theology: Now I'm not going to be able to get to all of this, unfortunately.

I will take a little bit more time of my next talk to cover some more of the topics I don't get to. But I have promised Don Preston face to face that I will address his toughest arguments from the pulpit. So I promise you I'm not avoiding the arguments he's made; I just need to get through this material.

Systematic theology. If Preston's position of the eternal dualism is in place and "flesh and blood shall not inherit" means that our bodies will never be resurrected, nor enter the kingdom of heaven, then that means Jesus' body is not in heaven. He must have shed his flesh and blood as he went or before and thus there is no continuing incarnation. At least not in a form in which he is like us. And if there is no continuing incarnation of Christ in heaven, which the church has affirmed for the entirety of its existence, and of course, scriptures teach in Colossians 2 and 1 John 4:2, then our high priest in heaven is no longer like us in flesh, and therefore he cannot represent us adequately. If there is no more of that, there's no more progressive sanctification. We're not trying to save this body after all. We're not trying to overcome the sin that resides in our members as Paul put it.

So why -- why would the Holy Spirit work with us on those regards? Our ultimate job is to escape this body, just as Plato taught and go to heaven. So there's no progressive sanctification.

Why was -- why is the church called a priestly nation? A priest of what? If everything is done and finalized and our only goal is to get to heaven in the

Joel McDurmon's First Negative

end, then why are we priests? Priests of what? We're priests for the same reason Israel was a priestly nation, and that was we would shine forth that light in this earth and bring everyone else into it. And that is transferred to the church in the New Testament of 1 Peter 2 as you all know.

More importantly, how can Don's full preterist position ever talk about the fulfillment of the ruling on the earth of the saints and of Christ? Matthew 5:5 clearly says, "Blessed are the meek for they shall inherit the earth." Not that they'll inherit heaven. They will inherit the earth. Now, if Preston's position is correct that we all go to heaven and that's our ultimate reward, then Matthew 5:5 was wrong. Someone should have told Jesus.

By the way, as a side note on time texts, Matthew 5:5 is quoting from Psalm 37:9 in which it says: "The wicked shall not prosper essentially and the meek shall inherit the earth." The very next verse says: "Yet a little while and the wicked will be cut off." If every time text must be taken exactly literally in its place, then this doesn't work. Jesus can't quote this passage later because it would have been fulfilled in a little while in David's day.

In Revelation 5:9-10, the 24 elders say to Jesus: "By your blood you ransom people for God from every tribe and language and people and nation. You have made them a kingdom and priests to our God, and they shall reign on the earth." When did the saints ever reign on the earth? Never. If that scripture is ever to be fulfilled, bodies must be resurrected.

And, in fact, some of the manuscripts of that actually say that they do reign on the earth. Revelation 1:5: "Jesus is the ruler of the kings of the earth." Matthew 28:18: Jesus, "All authority in heaven and on earth has been given unto me." By the way, that's Daniel 7 language; he has received a dominion at that point, didn't have to wait until A.D. 70 to get it. Didn't have to wait until any other time; he had it after the resurrection and before the ascension into heaven. All authority in heaven and on earth. Daniel 7 must have been fulfilled in some way at that point.

The Lord's prayer, which hopefully you all pray, "Your kingdom come, your will be done, on earth as it is in heaven."

Joel McDurmon's First Negative

Now I want to hear Don in his position tell us how -- or any full Preterist's position explain any earthly rule of the saints, not just a specific one, any earthly rule of the saints. It can't, because it rejects the earthly nature of the kingdom. The kingdom is in heaven. The ultimate phase of our salvation and presence with the Lord is after we die and shed the flesh and blood. There is no earthly kingdom. No earthly rule. And there certainly is no growth or advance of the kingdom progressively on earth.

I want to know how the full preterist's position can ever see this fulfilled. Only in a highly qualified spiritualized way could it say that. With dualism. With the stark separation of heaven and earth. Of rewards coming ultimately only after the body is shed. There's only one way those scriptures can be fulfilled, and that is if Don Preston's claim to finality in A.D. 70 is false.

I want to talk about real quickly the defeat of God's enemies, 1 Corinthians 15:24-26, "Then comes to the end when he delivers the kingdom to God, the Father, after destroying every rule and every authority and power[hooray]. For he must reign until he has put all enemies under his feet. The last enemy to be destroyed is death."

If A.D. 70 was the final resurrection, then death has forever been defeated and destroyed. But if death has forever been defeated and destroyed, so has every other single enemy of God, period. For death was the last one. Ergo, there are no more enemies of God.

How can sin exist anywhere in creation, anywhere in the corner of God's universes (if He has more than one), if all of His enemies are defeated?. It can't happen. But if that verse is true and you cling fast to that verse, then I say this position leads irrevocably to the position of Tim King and others who have gone into universalism. Why? If death is definitive and finally defeated, then there is no more death, period. And if death means by definition separation from God, then there is no more separation from God, period.

Not just those -- for those who believe now, but for everyone after that time, period. And not surprising, universalism is exactly where several of Max King's' disciples have gone.

Joel McDurmon's First Negative

Real quick, as I have a couple moments left. Mentioned a couple of things in Practical Theology. If this position is true, then there is no more Lord's Supper. I know Don doesn't hold that position, but I see it as logical. No more great commission. There are no more offices in the church. If Ephesians 4 is fulfilled and that means not only Apostles, prophets, and evangelists, but also pastors and teachers. There are no more teachers. Hebrews 8 clearly affirms that they will not teach one another the law because they will all know the Lord being taught of him.

Don, if your position is true, I want you to quit teaching it because there are no more teachers or pastors.

There's no more Lord's Supper as I said, and finally there's no more marriage. Luke 20 says this very clearly so that those sons of this age marry and are given in marriage, but those who are considered worthy to obtain that age and to the resurrection of the dead neither marry nor are given in marriage. Or they cannot die anymore; they are equal to the angels, being sons of the resurrection.

If this is the age of the resurrection, then every one of you living in a married relationship is wrong. You need to disband it right now. And so my direction is for every one of you full preterists who maintain this position, and Don, is to quit teaching it and disband your marriages. Thank you.

Don K. Preston's Second Affirmative

****

Well, I found an awful lot of what Joel had to say interesting. Obviously, I disagreed with it. And he said he would answer my questions; he did not answer my questions. He did not answer the majority, the huge majority of my salient arguments. And he tried to divert attention away from them. So I'm going to present another affirmative argument. And in doing so, I'm going to address some of the things that he said. I want you to notice that's what we're going to talk about in this lesson the promises of Abraham. According to Hebrews Chapter 11, that I gave an awful lot of attention to in my very first lesson, again, that Joel ignored.

RESURRECTION: THE HOPE OF ABRAHAM

> Hebrews 11:4ff– Abel, Enoch, Noah, Abraham, etc all had **ONE Hope!** **That One Hope** was a heavenly country, **a city**, the better resurrection (15-16, 35).
>
> They all died in faith, not having received the promise. **Take note:** Abel's Hope Was Enoch's Which Was Noah's, Which Was Abraham's **Which was Moses / Israel's!**
>
> **There was but ONE HOPE, From Genesis to Israel!**
> There is no dichotomy between the hope of Genesis, Abraham, Israel.
>
> **There are not two resurrections!**
>
> - **ONE RESURRECTION HOPE!**

We are told that there was one hope. Now according to Joel we can see many hopes, because, you know the story of the Bible is multi-variegated. And it's this, and it's that.

But according to Joel, because we have all of these recapitulations down through history, we are actually supposed to see -- in Abel, Enoch, Abraham and everything: we're actually supposed to see many hopes. But that's not the story of Hebrews, is it? There is *one hope*.

Don K. Preston's Second Affirmative

Ladies and gentlemen, throughout the entirety of this debate, do not lose sight of that.

It's interesting that Joel said, "My argument is that God's word is not like an erector set. It's not a piece here and not a piece there"; well, as a matter of fact, Isaiah 8 said it was, -- not Isaiah 8, but Isaiah. But he said "it's like a symphony, and it's working together to make one whole." Well, amen. That's what Paul said. "*One hope*."

Now, you didn't notice it, but what Joel was very subtly saying is, well, Israel does have hope. But there's a story of Genesis -- and I know it's not fulfilled, because my wife has had four kids and suffered through every one of them. Now that's what you call an *ad hominem* argument, ladies and gentlemen. It's not a scriptural argument. My wife would never become a full preterist because she experienced pain in child birth. That's not a scriptural argument.

By the way, his appeal to saying, If Don Preston is right, then look at what follows from it. I've got in my bag down there a book on Biblical logic by Joel McDurmon. In it he talks about what's known as a logical fallacy called "the Red Herring." And a Red Herring is -- do you know what a Red Herring argument is? It's saying, "Well, if Preston's right, look what this means."

What did Joel McDurmon say? And you know what he says? "If we come to realize that the results of a doctrine do not determine truth, we will avoid the Red Herring error."

Now that's from Joel McDurmon's own book. But what does he do? He gets up here and he makes a Red Herring argument. "If Don Preston is true, everybody here is not married; they ought go home and disband your marriage." Folks, that's a Red Herring argument.

Okay. Let's go on. That one hope of Abraham was a heavenly hope, Zion. Did Joel say a word about Zion? If he did, I missed it. It was the better resurrection. Did Joel say anything about Hebrews 11:35 about the better resurrection? If he did, I missed it.

Now watch, they all -- and Joel says, see, we've got to qualify all. Well, does that even -- does the word "all" here include Abel, Enoch, *et cetera*, or does

Don K. Preston's Second Affirmative

it exclude some of them? Does it include Abel, but exclude Moses? No. All in the context is defined by the context from Genesis all the way to Moses.

Now take note, just as I said, he ignored it, Abel's hope was Enoch's hope, which was Noah's hope, which was Abraham's hope, which was Moses' hope, which was the hope of Israel; *one hope.*

One hope. Let me reiterate. Joel created in his speech -- very subtly, but he created a dichotomy between Genesis and Israel; between Abraham and Israel. He created a dichotomy between resurrection -- oh, yeah, Abraham might have experienced a resurrection in A.D. 70. You notice he didn't deny all the quotes I gave where he said that Abraham and those experienced what was promised to them. Instead, he says there's this multi-variegated, many-layered promise and we can't see it fulfilled here. We can't see it fulfilled there.

The Promise to Abraham And Torah
Abraham was given the promise of the Heavenly Zion / Resurrection **430 years before Torah** (Gal. 3.17)
Torah did not annul the promise, or create another resurrection promise: **Abraham's resurrection hope became Israel's resurrection hope!**
However, The promise was not **through Torah** (v. 18).
The inheritance would be at *the end of Torah- Under Guardians until the time of the inheritance* (3:24f; 4:1f).
Thus, **the promise of Zion** / Resurrection- **Inheritance!- would be at the end of The Law of Moses**
Joel says the Law of Moses "died in AD 70"!
Therefore, the City / Resurrection was not the hope of Israel Isolated from Genesis/ Noah / etc.– It was One Hope! Fulfilled at the end of the Law of Moses!

Don K. Preston's Second Affirmative

Isn't it interesting though that he said, "Well, it was fulfilled here, and it's got a fulfillment here, and it's got a fulfillment there. But, yes, it will have an ultimate fulfillment."

How would we know if the Biblical writers were intending to point to the consummative end? Wouldn't they say something like the end of all things has drawn near? 1 Peter 4. Okay. Now watch, the promises of Zion -- the promise of the end of the millennium resurrection, the time of the inheritance would be at the end of the Law of the Moses.

Now remember, Joel says the Law of Moses died in A.D. 70. Therefore, the city -- the resurrection was not the hope of Israel isolated from Genesis, Noah, et cetera; it was the one hope of all of those men. Joel divorces A.D. 70 from Genesis eschatology. He says Genesis is to be fulfilled at some point in our future, i.e., at the end of the Christian age. However, again, Hebrews 11-12 inseparably joins the one hope of Abel, Noah, Abraham, and Moses.

Now that's not one hope, Joel. If that's many hopes, you need to show us from the text, not some *ad hominem* argument, but you need to show us from the text that Abraham's resurrection hope -- hope of the better resurrection was different from that of Noah. Show us where Abraham's resurrection hope was different from Paul's end of the millennium resurrection of 1 Corinthians 15. Show us from text, not philosophizing. Not talking about Systematic Eschatology -- theology. Not talking about Practical Eschatology. Let's have some exegesis of text and that will help us along our way.

The Abrahamic resurrection promise was given 430 years before Moses. But according to Paul, in Galatians Chapter 3, Abraham's hope was joined to -- or it's more accurate to say, Israel's hope was joined to Abraham's hope, thus it became, guess what, *one hope*. It was not a hope of Israel distinctive from Abel from Noah to Abraham; there is one eschatological hope.

Again, Abel, Noah, Abraham, and Israel longed for one, *One*. Joel, tell us how one can be many? They longed for *one* better resurrection.

Don K. Preston's Second Affirmative

Now watch. Since Paul tells us in Galatians Chapter 3 that Israel's hope was joined to Abraham, and Abraham's hope was that of Noah, and Enoch, and all the way back to Abel, I want to know how they're different. The law was added to that. It wasn't different. It continued it.

Abraham and the One Resurrection

Abel-Noah-Abraham-Israel longed for **ONE** "better resurrection" (Heb. 11:35)!!
 Isaiah – Hosea – Daniel thus predicted the fulfillment of the hope of Abel / Abraham's eschatology!
 You cannot divorce Abel -Abraham's Resurrection Hope from Israel and Isaiah 25 / Hosea / Daniel 12 etc.
   The Question is: Has That Been Fulfilled?
   The Unequivocal Answer is: Yes!

You cannot divorce Abel or Abraham's resurrection hope from Israel. What this means is, since Torah was added to Abraham, which was added to Noah, which was added to Genesis, that means when the prophets of Israel made the promise of the resurrection, i.e., Isaiah Chapter 25, they are giving the hope of Genesis. Not a different promise. The question is, has that been fulfilled? Well, let's look again.

Abraham, The Resurrection of Isaiah 25
The EoM resurrection of 1 Cor. 15 / Rev. 20 would fulfill Isaiah 25:6-9 (1 Cor. 15:54f)   **That resurrection promise was the One Resurrection Hope of Abel-Abraham-Israel**   **Isaiah 25:6-9: Two Constituent Elements:**   **#1- Messianic Feast On Zion: On This Mountain He Shall Prepare a Great Feast**   **#2- Resurrection on Zion: On this mountain He Shall Destroy Death.**

The end of the millennium resurrection, 1 Corinthians 15 and Revelation 20, would be fulfilled or would fulfill, Isaiah 25:6-8 or 6-9.

Don K. Preston's Second Affirmative

By the way, Joel had a lot to say about the definition of the word "fulfill." What was interesting to me is that he ignored the word that was used in Matthew 5:18. He used the word -- Greek word *pleroo*. Well, *pleroo* is the first word used in Matthew 5:17, but *genetai* is the last word, and according to Greg Bahnsen -- one of his instructors by the way, Greg Bahnsen says it means "fully accomplished." And when you join it with "not one jot, not one tittle shall pass from the law until it's all" -- all what? Every jot, every tittle, was fully accomplished: not recapitulated, not reiterated, not typological; when it was all fully accomplished.

Now I presented several charts on the Sabbath. The Sabbath predicted, foreshadowed the end of the millennium resurrection. Jesus said not one jot or one tittle will pass from Torah, the Law of Moses, until everything foreshadowed there. Everything foreshadowed there, typified there, everything found there was fully accomplished, ladies and gentlemen. Not *pleroo, genetai*. And if that's wrong, he needs to show us. Now once again -- and it was really interesting that Joel says you can't go to an Old Testament prophecy and bring over the entire context. Really interesting.

He is right. This is a tremendous question of hermeneutics. But you know what? The Jews believe that is exactly precisely what you did do. N. T. Wright, Scott McKnight, R. T. France, some of the greatest Jesus scholars in the world today are acknowledging -- and I don't have time to draw up the quotes, but I've got tons of quotes from them -- to demonstrate that, in fact, the Jewish hermeneutic was precisely that. When one part of the verse of the Old Testament prophecy was cited, they were bringing the entire context over there.

Now Joel made the mistake of saying, "Well, okay, look, in Luke Chapter 4 when Jesus said, "This day this prophecy is fulfilled in your sight," that must mean the day of vengeance would have been fulfilled." No, it doesn't. It means it will be fulfilled in that generation though. Why? Because Jesus said so, that's why.

And so it is simply a hermeneutical error, I believe, on Joel's part, to say you don't go back there. Now here's the question. When was the Messianic Feast fully accomplished? Joel McDurmon says in A.D. 70 when the sons of the kingdom were cast out. But notice Isaiah. Notice the organic unity, ladies and gentlemen. Notice the organic unity of Isaiah "in that day."

Don K. Preston's Second Affirmative

Now do I think that that's a single 24-hour day? I didn't say that. But it's certainly in the same time frame that Peter said all of the prophets, all *whoever wrote*, spoke of the restoration of all things that encompasses the Genesis restoration, and they spoke of "these days."

So Joel needs to tell us since he is taking a tack that's really interesting, that I'm seeing among some partial preterists, in fact Sam Frost in his new book undoubtedly does this because he's doing it in a lot of his writings now. Whereas they have honored the temporal statements of scripture that "at hand" must mean "at hand," all of a sudden now they're going, well, maybe it doesn't mean at hand after all.

It may not be too long before some of these folks become dispensationalists because I can guarantee you right now dispensationalists are loving -- are loving-- what some partial preterists are doing with the time statements right now. And they've never, ever, ever denied the time statements before. But now when full preterists start pressing them on the time statements, it's like, "Well, okay, you know, maybe at hand shortly, quickly; maybe it doesn't really mean that at all!"

Well, we go on. So once again Abel, Abraham, Isaac, Jacob, Israel longed for the heavenly city, the better resurrection. Now again, here's the question to Joel. Is the better resurrection of Abraham, is it the end of the millennium resurrection or not? It goes all the way back to Genesis. So tell me why it's not.

Matthew Chapter 8 again, that end of the millennium resurrection is inextricably tied, ladies and gentlemen, with the Messianic Banquet. Now catch the power of this.

Don K. Preston's Second Affirmative

Isaiah 25- The <u>Banquet</u> and the Resurrection
Isaiah 25:6 = Messianic Banquet
Isaiah 25:8 = EoM Millennium (Edenic) Resurrection
Banquet and EoM Resurrection are Inseparable
Follow Closely….
Matthew 8 = Messianic Banquet (Abraham's Hope)
Thus, Matthew 8 = <u>EoM Resurrection!</u>
But, Matthew 8 was fulfilled in AD 70 when the Sons of the Kingdom were cast out (Joel)→ Gal. 4
Therefore the EoM resurrection was AD 70
This is irrefutable!

Joel says the sons of the kingdom were cast out and Abraham, Isaac, and Jacob and all of the worthies sat down at the Banquet in A.D. 70. Thus Abel's hope, which is Abraham's hope; Noah's hope, which was Abraham's hope; and Israel's hope, which was Abraham's hope which was filled in A.D. 70. If it wasn't, he needs to tell us how it wasn't.

Abraham—Resurrection: Zion
Abel- Abraham-Israel longed for the "better resurrection"- of Isaiah 25!- -- This is the EoM Resurrection of 1 Cor. 15/ Rev. 20
The EoM Resurrection of Isaiah 24-25– would be on Zion: "<u>On this Mountain…</u> He shall destroy death…"
Therefore, <u>if the Zion Promises Are Fulfilled</u>, The EoM resurrection of 1 Cor. 15 / Rev. 20 have been fulfilled– <u>No Matter Our Concept of Genesis.</u>
You Cannot Affirm the Fulfillment of Hebrews 11-12 – The Zion Promises-- Without Affirming the End of the Millennium Resurrection!
What Does Joel Believe About the Zion Promises?

You cannot affirm the fulfillment of Abraham's hope. Now here's a good question since Joel said we got to have all this recapitulation over, over, and over. We've got many, many fulfillments. Is Abraham expecting a yet future fulfillment of the Messianic Banquet, or did he partially enter the kingdom? Did he just sort of kind of enter the kingdom and he's waiting for a fuller entrance of the kingdom? How much of the Banquet does he get to enjoy?

You cannot affirm the fulfillment of Abraham's hope without affirming a fulfillment of the end of the millennium; that is, Genesis resurrection.

Don K. Preston's Second Affirmative

Once again, Abel through Abraham and Israel longed for the better resurrection of Isaiah 25. That is the end of the millennium resurrection. The end of the millennium resurrection of Isaiah 25 -- look, any way you want to put it, "in that day" he would destroy death. "On this mountain He will destroy death." On what mountain? *Zion.* You catch this? "*On this mountain* He will destroy death." What mountain is that? Zion.

Well, Joel says -- Joel says the Zion promises have been spiritualized and fulfilled in Christ. Remember the chart I gave you with the beautiful quote that he had to say? Those promises are past tense, "We have received."

Once again, you cannot affirm the fulfillment of Hebrews 11 and 12, the Zion promises as Joel McDurmon does, without affirming the end of the millennium resurrection. So what does Joel believe the Zion promises? It doesn't matter what you want to associate with Zion, the Old Testament associates resurrection, salvation, redemption, the kingdom, et cetera, et cetera. Well, here's the quote again:

"When the argument of faith and pilgrimage in Hebrews 11 finally does turn to "us" it notes a complete change of status. While all of those Old Testament pilgrims died and "did not receive what was promised," **New Testament believers are different:** "God had provided something better for *us*" (Heb. 11:40). <u>**So, we are categorically not like them. We are in a better position than they. The promised Kingdom has indeed come, it is given to us.**</u> We are not exiles waiting to receive the promise. Indeed, the author tells the first-century believing Jews in the very next chapter, … "you have come to Mount Zion" (Heb. 12:22). They had arrived! **This arrival verse is very important. … Hebrews makes it absolutely clear that New Testament believers "have come to Zion." This is in the past tense>** *(My emph., DKP)… (AV Article)*
Amen and Amen!
But<u>, Zion is the locus of the EoM Resurrection</u>-Fulfilling Genesis!
Joel has affirmed the EoM Resurrection!

I'm not going to take the time to read the entire quote. But you can see it for yourself that Joel McDurmon is emphatic. He's clear; he is unambiguous, that they, the Old Testament saints and we have now entered Zion. Folks, Zion is the end of the millennium resurrection. Thank you.

Joel McDurmon's Second Negative

****

First of all, let me say in response that I'm disappointed with some of the things that I heard from Don. I said even in my speech -- my first intro-- that I would get to Don's toughest arguments. And I said but first I want to cover a few things. He pretends that I ignored everything he said on purpose and am not going to get to it.

Interestingly enough here is from an e-mail I sent to Don on Monday July 9th, just ten days ago. And I said, Don, I've noticed -- essentially I want to summarize the first paragraph - I said, I've noticed there's this phenomenon where people who debate you don't answer your questions and this back-and-forth ensues. Well, he didn't answer my questions. Well, he didn't answer my questions. Well, I'm not going to answer his unless he answers. And it devolves into this kind of childish thing. And I said, Don, I want to avoid this at all costs. But then I went on to say after that –"in our debate, I hope to avoid this phenomenon entirely. I'm sure you will reciprocate. That said, I did want to point out that our debate format is a bit different in my understanding than your Simmons debate" -- that was with Kurt Simmons. "I specifically wanted each side to have the opening statements for our positions *before we go into our responses*. Thus, this is the wording of the contract"-- and I can produce that for anyone who would like to see it. "Thus while I plan to respond, and will respond directly to your arguments as best I can, my opening allows me to introduce my own negative material before I'm obligated to do so."

And I just wanted to share that with you. And I thought that I had said something similar to that in my opening statement. And maybe Don missed it. But I thought it was unfortunate that he thought that was important to attack me in that regard.

Don said in his opening -- his first opening-- that this thing about the hope of Israel being completed in the resurrection of A.D. 70 -- he said this is going to hold true and it's going to be final, no matter what concept of creation you have, no matter what concept of the body or of death, and then there were a bunch of other alternatives in there that I didn't get to write down. But then a little bit later he went into this discussion about

Joel McDurmon's Second Negative

Paul did not have an eschatology divorced from Genesis. And then of course in this last statement you saw him accuse me of divorcing the two, which I'll address that a little bit later.

Well, I agree. Paul didn't have an eschatology separate from Genesis. But if that's the case, then I think it's *highly* important how you define creation and how you define body and death and all of those things. If death means physical death and Paul's eschatology is Genesis eschatology and in Paul's eschatology death is defeated, what does that tell you? I think that's highly relevant. So don't give me this business of no matter of what concept you have, this doesn't matter. It does matter. It matters highly. And I can see why Don would want to avoid that topic. Because if death is physical death, then you have to deal with that at the final resurrection. And if the A.D. 70 resurrection didn't involve physical death, then it wasn't final.

We hear a lot about this one hope and I was -- this was thrown at me that I apparently -- because of all these variegated, multiple fulfillments that I have, that there must be many hopes. And then he actually answered that very argument for me in saying that Joel sees all of those many variations within a theme under the umbrella of one overarching theme. Well, there's the answer to your question, Don. You did it for me; I didn't have to do it. There is one overarching hope. The question is, is it all right to take the word hope here in scripture and the word hope over here in scripture, and the word hope somewhere else in scripture, and say these must all be the exact identical thing all the time, and therefore they all have to take place at the same time? No, these are the very type of errors I was trying to warn you against.

Now if it does say they happen at the same time, we have to deal with that. But the one thing I haven't seen yet is any of those with the word final on it or any of them with a concept final on it.

Don says, well, don't you think that if they wanted to say that it was going to be the final fulfillment, they would have used a word something like, this is the end?

Well, maybe they will. Maybe they do. But I provided you three examples from the Old Testament -- not a single one of which Don responded to by the way -- in which the word –"fulfilled" was used -- specifically used in the

Joel McDurmon's Second Negative

same way that the New Testament uses it to answer fulfillments of prophecy in the Old Testament. And yet they weren't final and yet if you were living in those days you could have proved they were final simply by pointing to the word and saying it's final. And no one could have controverted your evidence. And yet we know from thousands of years of redemptive history afterward they weren't final.

Ezekiel and Jeremiah and Lamentations both used the word "the end" when they go into exile. "This is the end now." And yet it wasn't *the* end, was it? No.

So, no, you can't pull something out like that. You can't "absolutetize" words like that and then force them to mean something they mean all across the board.

Don likes to quote from other scholars and reference other scholars as authorities on occasion, although I would recognize that he sees ultimately Scripture's the ultimate authority.

But I would refer him to a book he's probably already read *D. A. Carson's Exegetical Fallacies*. He goes over these types of word fallacies that are very common among commentators; let alone people who are considered radical and trying to advance a radical position and who are much more prone to those types of errors.

Don says the covenant was a sign with Israel -- or the Sabbath was a covenant sign of Israel. I think that's very important too. And I think the ceremonial Sabbath was done away with in A.D. 70.

He says it was a sign in Exodus of creation in six days. I say I totally agree. That forces us to hold a six-day creation viewpoint. It also forces us to take creation seriously -- Genesis 1-3 seriously as literal physical things when it comes to resurrection and finality. Just because the Sabbath was done away in the interim, which Don admits, was added by the Mosaic Law, maybe you would make a distinction there and I would obviously grant that if you do.

Joel McDurmon's Second Negative

But as far as it was added by the Mosaic Law and it was done away in A.D. 70, then that doesn't answer the aspect of this is pointing to Genesis -- literal Genesis.

This aspect about how I have affirmed that the Mosaic Law died in A.D. 70 is nonsense. You might have noticed when Don quoted me on that verse, that he only quoted three words with the quotation marks around it. This is something we -- and of course later he wanted to quote me, he went to this big long quotation that brought in a lot more context. And I would say it's always important to bring in the context. I see Don reaching for his copy of my book right now.

I was going to read it to you, but I already closed my laptop so I won't waste the time. Basically what I said in that whole paragraph, I'm talking about the Old Covenant *administration* of the law, not the law itself necessarily. Now we can have a debate over whether all the law itself was gone at that point, but in that paragraph I specifically say the Old Covenant administration is replaced by the New Covenant administration and that -- the topic of the chapter is actually when the end of the old age begins and the new age starts.

And I say -- quoting Hebrews 8:13 and say, yes, that old administration is passing away. And what happened to it? Then I say, quote, "it died in A.D. 70." I didn't say the law itself died in A.D. 70. I said the Old Covenant *administration* of the law died.

Now you say that's a fine distinction, you're splitting hairs, and I say it's a discussion we need to have, a little bit longer discussion than I have time right now to take. But it is a distinction. And if Don Preston was as intellectually rigorous and honest as he presents himself to be, he would have put up the whole context and dealt with it in those terms instead of trying to pin me in a corner with a quotation taken out of context.

The idea of Isaiah 25 being pulled up again, Hosea 13, Daniel 12, this was the whole reason I went through the exercise of giving you multiple examples of how scriptures are quoted in the New Testament as fulfilled and yet it is impossible that the whole context of that scripture be imported at that place.

Joel McDurmon's Second Negative

I gave five examples at least of this happening; Don mentioned one of them. And the one that he did mention he got -- in my opinion got wrong.

He does say this is a single prophecy, Yaweh rules Zion after judgment. But I have shown you multiple examples of where you can't pull that in. I would like for Don to deal with each one of those examples and show us a hermeneutical principle by which you have to do this, have to pull in the context. He says, well, this is how Jews interpreted the context. Well, praise the Lord, hallelujah. The Jews also believed in a physical literal resurrection. So why don't you come on over with me on that one, Don?

The Jews of first century don't determine how we interpret Scripture. We're specifically told that they did not understand Scripture and the New Testament and that's why they crucified the Lord of Glory.

Now if you want to be on that same path, maybe you should continue embracing Don Preston's hermeneutic. But I'm telling you that I have given you five examples of why you cannot bring the full context of the Old Testament into every citation of the New Testament.

So, yeah, it's a single prophecy, but the New Testament doesn't always treat it that way.

Don said to provide my hermeneutic of distinction of why I can take one word one way and place one word another place. Well, I would say this to that. Number one, that doesn't get to the nature of this debate tonight. I don't have to prove that tonight. Don has to prove his affirmative tonight, and I have pulled the rug out from under it by showing all doesn't always mean all, that fulfilled does not always mean final. Don hasn't shown us a single passage in which any resurrection or any prophecy he has talked about *has to* -- has to, mean final. If he can't do that, people, his affirmative is un-established.

You say, well, maybe you haven't refuted it all the way. That's not my job tonight. My job tonight is to show you that in everything he said, and all the shots that he's taken at me, that he has not yet established that. And I'm telling you that he can't establish that, because scripture nowhere attaches the word final to any of these things. He gets on to me because I quoted *pleroma* as the Greek word that means fulfilled and I dealt with

Joel McDurmon's Second Negative

that. And he says he totally ignored the other word in Matthew 5 and that's *genetai*, which is not pronounced correctly; it's *genetai*.

And all you got to do is open up your BibleWorks, open up just about any lexicon, open up Gingrich's abridged Lexicon of the Greek language, and the very first sentence after *genetai*, which is from -- *ginomai* -- is actually the root, the very first sentence says, "capable of many translations." Don forgot to tell you that part. It doesn't always mean fully accomplished. In fact I would say it rarely means fully accomplished. It certainly never has the absolute meaning of finally accomplished. It doesn't mean that. I don't know anywhere in scripture it means that, and Don can't show you anywhere in scripture it means that. And if he can't, then that argument is absolutely bogus.

And building an argument for the finality of death and resurrection upon it is absolutely bogus.

Now this business about talking about my wife as an *ad hominem* argument. I'm as capable at *ad hominem* as everybody else. I'm as capable of red herrings as everybody else. One of the reasons I wrote the book was to say, look, Christians do this as much as, if not more, than everybody else, even scholars. But I did not make that argument that my wife has this many children and, oh, well, full preterism must be false. I did not use that as an argument; I used it as what I thought was a humorous illustration of the fact that child -- pain in childbirth still exists in this day. Some people in our race understand that better than others do.

But if it does still exist, this is -- not, this is not saying that if full preterism is true, look what must come about. This is saying this is true, and if it's true, then the curse is not gone. And if the curse is not gone then full preterism -- then the final resurrection has not happened yet. That was my argument. And I just used my wife to illustrate that. I hope you enjoyed it as much as I did. She thought it was funny. I always pass it by her before I ever mention her in public. I certainly didn't mean to make her the object of ridicule, and of course she wasn't, at least not on my part.

That's probably enough for now. I'll get to a couple of these arguments in the next section. Thank you.

Don K. Preston's Third Affirmative

****

First of all, let me offer an apology to Joel in regard to, you know, whether or not he was going to respond to my material in his first -- first negative. I did misunderstand. I apologize for that, Joel. I never want to misrepresent anyone. Joel says that I did misrepresent him in regards to some things.

He said I misrepresented him in regard to Hebrews Chapter 8 in the passing of law. I'm going to go ahead and read this for you. I'm going to read the entire context:

Joel and Torah
Joel (J v J, 47, Heb. 8:13) – "The Old was becoming obsolete and was ready to vanish away. It has not yet been completely wiped out, but it was certainly in its dying moments. It died in AD 70, when the symbols and ceremonies of that Old System– the Temple and sacrifices– were completely destroyed by the Roman armies. This was the definitive moment when "this age" of Jesus and Paul ended completely and gave way to "the age to come." **DeMar on the Types**   If Torah, Temple and Sacrifices Ended in AD 70 that is when they were fully accomplished– in the end of the millennium resurrection!!

Hebrews 8:13- (Preston—reading from Joel's book): "From the teaching of Jesus, Paul, and the author of Hebrews; We get a very clear picture of two primary agents, one that endured up until the time of Christ, another that began around that same period. I believe these two periods may have hinged upon the coming and work of Christ and pertain obviously to the Old and New Covenant administrations."

He did use the word, but listen very carefully: "Indeed this is what the author of Hebrews himself relates. He says the New Covenant -- New *Covenant* makes the Old – [*Old Covenant*, DKP] -- obsolete."

The word "covenant" there is elliptical. He says the New Covenant makes the Old obsolete. And what is becoming obsolete and growing old is ready to vanish away.

Don K. Preston's Third Affirmative

Ladies and gentlemen, it wasn't simply an administration that was growing old. It was Torah that was growing old, the law. Notice the new had in fact made the old obsolete definitively. But as he wrote in his time the old was becoming obsolete and was ready to vanish away. It had not been completely wiped out. But it was certainly in its dying moments. It died in A.D. 70.

Listen to this: "When the symbols of ceremonies of that old system, the temple and sacrifices, were completely destroyed by the Roman armies, this was the definitive moment when" -- catch this -- when the *"this age,"* unquote, "of Jesus and Paul ended and completely gave way to their," *"age to come,"*.

Now, ladies and gentlemen, there was no administration without Torah. Torah provided the administration. Did you notice that Joel admitted that the Sabbath has been done away? Now what did Jesus say about the passing of the law?

I want to share something with you here, and I may not be able to get to too much affirmative, but I've just got to share something with you, because he keeps arguing that all doesn't mean all, and all this kind of stuff. I want you to notice what Greg Bahnsen in the book *Theonomy* page 83 had to say about the use of all of Matthew Chapter 5:17-18.

What Does "All" Mean?
"A verse like Matthew 5:18, with its unparticularized panta is prey for such treatment… Nothing in the context or vocabulary of Matthew 5:18 warrants the induction of speculative meaning; a phrase as colorless and abstract as panta should not be particularized, personalized, and steered into this theological preconception. …. Page 83— "In Matthew 5:18 the commencement of the law's passing away is made dependent upon <u>panta genetai. Panta, when used without an article or preposition indicates "all things, everything."</u> It is to be taken in this absolutely general sense unless the context dictates some antecedent whole of which <u>panta</u> constitutes the complete parts." (Bahnsen, *Theonomy*, 83, my emp).

Don K. Preston's Third Affirmative

Quote, "A verse like Matthew 5:18 which its un-particularized panta -- panta is the Greek word translated as all -- is prey for such treatment. What kind of treatment? For making it mean some, part, partial, not all. Nothing in the context of -- or vocabulary of Matthew 5:18 warrants the induction of speculative meaning. A phrase as colorless and as abstract as *panta* should not be particularized, personalized, and steered into theological presuppositions." I can only say amen.

On Page 83 it continues. "In Matthew 5:18 the commencement of the law's passing away is dependent upon *panta genetai*. That's fine. *genetai* -- you'll notice he pronounced it *genetai* too, but that's okay. Any Greek teacher will tell you it's hard to know exactly how to pronounce Greek words.

"*Panta*, when used without an article or preposition, indicates all things, everything. It is to be taken in this absolutely general sense unless the context dictates some antecedent whole of which *panta* constitutes in complete parts."

Now Joel gave us Luke Chapter 18:30-31, Jesus fulfilled -- fulfilled all things. That's right. But the context determines *panta*. The context is everything concerning his suffering. It's not concerning all things written. Okay?

So I think we need to understand exactly what's going on. Now, notice then what Jesus has to say in Matthew 5 in regard to *panta*. "Not one jot or one tittle." Now Joel needs to tell us if that's a comprehensive term or if it really just means some, part, a little bit, or most.

"Not one jot, not one tittle shall pass from the law until it is all *genetai*." And then Joel makes a rather bold claim saying that *genetai* has, you know, so many -- all these different applications, and it doesn't mean fully accomplish.

What does every jot -- or not one jot or one tittle mean? Okay. And let's see if he'll stick with his definition of *genetai* not meaning fully accomplished.

1 Corinthians 15:54, "When the mortal has put on immortality, and the corruptible has put on incorruptibility, then shall be brought to pass, *genetai,* the saying 'death is followed up in victory.'"

Don K. Preston's Third Affirmative

Now according to Joel's definition of *genetai*, it doesn't have to mean full or final at all.

Oh, by the way, he says, I don't see the word final anywhere. There is no word final in any of Don's arguments. Well, Paul's doctrine of the end of the millennium resurrection is taken from Isaiah 25:8. That's *final* resurrection.

The end of the millennium resurrection would be on Zion (Isaiah 25:8). Joel says all of the promises concerning Zion have been "spiritualized," which means by the way, "the death" has been spiritualized, and fully accomplished.

Unless Joel wants to tell us that maybe 1 Corinthians 15 is not the full accomplishment of the overcoming of the death of Adam after all, maybe it's -- maybe it's just one of many more to be, sometime in the future.

Oh, by the way, the word "final" does not appear in Revelation Chapter 20:11-12 either, when he talks about the resurrection and those being brought out of the sea. But it's the end of "the death." And in my first affirmative, I demonstrated how that term is used definitively and consistently throughout scripture.

It's really troublesome to me when people seem to be -- seem to be-- establishing a disunity in the story of the Bible. What did Paul say? "There is one hope."

Now Joel said he agrees with that. He says there's one overarching hope. Well, okay. Again that hope went from Abel to Enoch to Noah to Abraham to Israel.

Joel says Israel's eschatology, one of many under the overarching, was fulfilled in AD 70, but it wasn't final, because the word final is not used. But the word final is not in Revelation 20. And the word final is not in 1 Corinthians 15, either.

But what does Joel believe when it says "then comes the end"? Does Joel believe that's the final end? Yes, he does.

Don K. Preston's Third Affirmative

But you see, the resurrection of 1 Corinthians 15, the final resurrection, is the resurrection on Zion, which Joel McDurmon has told us was fulfilled. The resurrection of 1 Corinthians 15 is Paul's doctrine of the one hope which was nothing but the hope of Israel after the flesh. When did Joel say God was basically through with Old Covenant Israel? Well, he tells us the Sabbath was removed, taken away, annulled at A.D. 70.

Folks, you've just simply got to catch the power of this. What did Jesus say? "Not one jot, not one tittle will pass until it's *genetai*." What did the Sabbath symbolize?

What did the Sabbath symbolize? I didn't hear Joel say anything denying that Sabbath represented, symbolized, and of course Edersheim, Kurtz, Bahnsen, Gentry on and on I could go with citations and quotations. And that's -- you know, that's an appeal to authority if you please. *(Argumentum ad veracundiam)*. I won't make that argument, but the point of fact is, guess what? Sabbath represented the final rest, (Revelation 14:13) of the coming of the Lord, "Blessed are the dead who die in the Lord from now on for yea says the spirit they shall rest from their labors." Greek word *anapausis* which is the Greek word that is used in the Septuagint of the Old Testament to speak of the Sabbath rest, over and over and over.

When would that rest come? When would the Sabbath rest come in other words? When will the Sabbath be fulfilled? Every jot, every tittle of it? At the coming of the Lord.

So, just because the word final is not in a given text, doesn't mean it's not final. Because Joel appeals to Revelation 20, 1 Corinthians 15 and says that's the final resurrection when final is not there. Why doesn't he accept 1 Peter Chapter 4:7, that says, "The end of all things has drawn near"?

Now I want to know Joel's justification for dichotomizing that from the final. As a matter of fact, 1 Peter 4:5, Peter said, "Christ was ready" -- Greek word **hetoimos**-- "to judge the living and the dead.

Now I want to make a point here. It's very important.

Don K. Preston's Third Affirmative

1 Peter 4:5-17- The Anaphoric Article
• Peter said Christ was, "ready to judge the living and the dead" (1 Peter 4:5), and, "the appointed (*kairos- the divinely appointed time*) has come for <u>THE</u> judgment" (*to krino*, 4:17). • Peter said THE TIME HAD COME for "THE judgment" (*to krino*). Peter uses *the anaphoric article.* • The anaphoric article is <u>the preponderant use</u> of the definite article: "The anaphoric article has, by nature, a pointing back force to it, reminding the reader of whom or what was mentioned previously." (D. Wallace, *Greek Grammar Beyond the Basics: An Exegetical Syntax of the NT*; pg. 218-19). • In 1 Peter 4:5 Peter said Jesus was ready to "judge the living and the dead." • *The anaphoric article in v. 17 points back to v. 5.* • Peter was saying "the (divinely appointed) time has come for *the* judgment- THE JUDGMENT OF THE LIVING AND THE DEAD." • *<u>The imminence of the resurrection is undeniable.</u>*

In 1 Peter Chapter 4:5 Peter said that Christ was ready, *hetoimos*, which is a word that means not only morally prepared, but temporally ready to do that.

But notice in 1 Peter Chapter 4:7, he then said the end of all things has drawn near, the perfect tense of *engus* is *eggiken*. Then in verse 17, he says "the time." Definite article, the time is *kairos*, the appointed time, for judgment, but it's not judgment; it's *the* judgment.

Now wait a minute. An interesting thing takes place here. Peter -- in 1 Peter Chapter 4:17 is using what's known as the anaphoric article.

The anaphoric article is the preponderant usage of the article in the Greek. According to Daniel Wallace in his-- *Greek Grammar Beyond the Basics: Exegetical Syntax of the New Testament* Page 218 and following.

Joel knows this. This is not even an argument. What is an anaphoric article? Well an anaphoric article is used by a writer or even a speaker sometimes. He's mentioned a topic, he's mentioned a subject, but he hasn't used the definite article. But then a little bit later he mentions it again and in order to reference what he's already mentioned -- in order to reference the

Don K. Preston's Third Affirmative

previously talked about subject, he uses the definite article. Well, what does that mean?

That means that 1 Peter Chapter 4:17 when Peter said, "The time has come for the judgment," he's referring back to the judgment of verse 5. Well, what's the judgment of verse 5? The judgment of the living and the dead. Just like Paul said in 2 Timothy Chapter 4:1, "I charge thee therefore before the God and the Lord Jesus Christ who is about to judge the living and the dead and is appearing at the judgment."

Now I want to know the distinction between those. Here's Christ, his coming, the appearing, the judgment of the living and the dead.

Why is that not the end of 1 Corinthians Chapter 15? Well, the word final is not used. Well, the end of all things is used. And 1 Peter Chapter 4, and it's the judgment of the living and the dead, and the judgment of the living and the dead is the resurrection of the dead, Revelation Chapter 11: "The time has come." What time? The time of the judgment of the city where the Lord was slain. The time has come for the judgment of the dead that they should be judged and the prophets rewarded.

By the way, Joel applies Revelation Chapter 11 to A.D. 70 according to my understanding of where he has been at least. Now I want to know why it's not the same. I've got to get to Luke Chapter 20..

Joel says – insists-- that a physical death -- if there is a physical death -- if death in the Garden was physical, that demands a physical resurrection. Well, let's see if he'll stand up to that.

The question, ladies and gentlemen, is not what happened here in Genesis *in one sense*. The question is how does the New Testament -- how do the New Testament writers interpret that?

Don K. Preston's Third Affirmative

Does Physical Demand Physical?

Joel insists that since / if Genesis 1 speaks of the literal creation, that this demands the end– or regeneration-- of the literal cosmos.
        This overlooks how the NT Interprets OT realities!
Israel had a literal temple and literal sacrifices
Israel dwelt in a literal land
Israel practiced literal circumcision
It overlooks that <u>Eden Was Incorporated into Israel!</u>
Millennialists insist these physical realities demand a physical fulfillment!
        How did the NT writers interpret the OT realities?
        Joel knows the NT interprets those things spiritually!

And by the way, notice Israel had a physical literal temple, didn't they? Israel dwelt in a literal physical land. Israel practiced literal physical circumcision.

Now my millennial friends absolutely insist that those physical realities demand a physical fulfillment, a physical restoration of Israel. Joel denies that, as I do. How did the New Testament writers interpret the physical realities, the physical things of Israel?

Joel knows they interpreted them spiritually. Just like Zion has been spiritualized and fulfilled in Christ. Just like Paul in Colossians Chapter 1 quote, cites, and alludes to Genesis Chapter 1, and the old creation and says Christ is the first born of the new creation. He's the second Adam, and he talks about the new man and the old man being regenerated and being made in the image of Christ. Not one word about a physical restoration in order to reset or re-correct and to restore what was lost in Adam. It was all spiritual in Colossians Chapter 1. If Paul, the inspired Apostle, interprets Genesis 1 curse, Genesis 1 image, Genesis 1 eschatology, *spiritually* I suggest you and I need to interpret it spiritually as well. Thank you.

Joel McDurmon's Third (Final) Negative

****

Let's make a beginning. Let's have a beginning for our end. That is what this is all about afterwards, Genesis to Revelation, beginning and the end, the Alpha and the Omega.

All right. A few concluding responses. I'm accused of believing in many hopes, and that based on what I'm saying, I have to show that there are many hopes and that somehow Abel's hope was different from Abraham's hope was different than Paul's hope and -- no, I don't think that's the case. Although they probably are if you sat down and studied - different hopes and scripture based on different times and things of that nature. Although ultimately they are hoping in one hope. Preston says that that hope was the A.D. 70 resurrection destruction of Jerusalem and he points to the fact that Paul uses the word hope in Acts 24 to prove that that's the end of the millennium. Folks, "end of millennium" doesn't show up there. There's no phrase "end of millennium" there. There's no phrase "end of the millennium" in Isaiah 25:8. There's no end of the millennium mentioned anywhere. There's only one millennium mentioned in one verse -- or two verses in Scripture in Chapter 20 of Revelation. And the only way you could arrive at saying the resurrection and the hope that Paul talked about over here and the hope that's mentioned in Hebrews 11 has to mean that same end of the millennium hope, the only way you arrive at that is by assuming that all those words mean the exact same thing and point to the exact same thing, when they don't necessarily do that. Don has done nothing but reassert that as a fact. He has not given you any further arguments or rebuttals to prove that that's the fact. And I say that his position on that fact remains un-established.

Don wants to know about the better resurrection. Hebrews 11:35, the saints were told that they were looking for a better resurrection. Well, if you actually read the verse, it is talking about many things that the saints endured and did through the power of God -- through the power of their faith in God, and yet never received the promise. And Hebrews 11:35 says among them -- you remember this passage where it talks about they -- you know, they braved lions and they were sawn asunder and all of this stuff, they subdued kingdoms. And at one point, it says, "And women received

Joel McDurmon's Third Negative

their dead raised back again." This is, of course, talking about Elijah (or Elisha - I maybe forgetting the name exactly). In the Old Testament, there was a resuscitation of a corpse; she had her dead raised back again. And then he says, "But they were waiting for a better resurrection."

Okay. I agree they were waiting for a better resurrection. Does that therefore prove it was A.D. 70 that they were waiting for? Does that therefore prove it was anything specifically that they were waiting for? No. It says they were waiting for a better resurrection.

There is no data on that whatsoever until you get to Chapter 12. And we're told that since the saints that this letter is written to in Chapter 12 are told that you have arrived at Mount Zion, therefore this must be the end of the millennium resurrection. That's not there. And besides, if that was there, think about it. That verb is in the perfect tense, that is past tense; that has been done and has continuing results into the future. In other words, the point is, it was already done when the author of Hebrews wrote it. So if that verse is talking about the fulfillment of Israel's hope and the end of millennium resurrection of A.D. 70, then why is it saying it was already fulfilled? Why is he telling these saints you've already arrived it?

Folks, what they had already arrived at was the kingdom of God accomplished through faith in Jesus Christ and the kingdom that he secured on the day that he said all power has been given to me in heaven and on earth. Again, all of the multiple fulfillments, whatever they may be, whenever they may be, point back ultimately to the fulfillment made by Christ. He is the focus of all prophecy and all of the New Testament -- of all the Bible, Old Testament as well.

I am accused of putting a dichotomy between Genesis and Israel and the resurrection. Nothing could be further from the truth. But Don told you in his own talks that the Mosaic Covenant was added to the Abraham Covenant in the Old Testament administration. Well, I agree with that. It did come later. Paul says very clearly it did. Do you not see therefore that it is -- if I could use the phrase -- a covenant within a covenant. So that when the one covenant comes to an end, it doesn't necessarily have to mean the end of the overarching covenant that it is within.

Joel McDurmon's Third Negative

Yeah, they may have been looking at the same overarching hope that's down the line somewhere. But just because that Mosaic Covenant comes to an end and its Sabbath rests come to an end and its feast days come to an end and its laws come to an end doesn't mean that God's redemptive history is done in total.

So, yes, you can speak of a death, burial, and resurrection of Mosaic Covenant in A.D. 70. That doesn't mean it's final by any means. It means it was one movement in God's symphony, which is still yet to play out.

There was confusion over the word *genetai*, the letters an *eta* not an *epsilon*. I don't know any Greek scholar who would say that that's pronounced as an *epsilon*. But these are ticky-tack things. And we can settle it by arm wrestling afterwards if you'd like.

We're told that if I continue down this road of saying things like "all doesn't mean all," and "fulfilled doesn't necessarily mean fulfilled," then we're -- all of a sudden us partial preterists, as we're called, are going to become dispensationalists. Well, you want to talk about an *ad hominem* argument if I've ever heard one, that's about as ridiculous as it gets. Dispensationalists also believe in the Trinity; so do I. Does that make me a dispensationalist? No. And I can assure you that if it came down to it and I had to debate these issues with a dispensationalist, I would be able to refute them on it. That's a whole different story. But it's also a distraction of Don Preston proving the finality of his argument without simply restating it. It's a distraction. Whatever I believe at this night is totally irrelevant to his position. Totally irrelevant. Because he's not established his position, and he knows it. He'd not addressed a single one of those five passages I drew on to show you that you can't bring the full context of the Old Testament into a new context -- he addressed one and I'll cover it in just a second.

But he hasn't touched the others. He hasn't touched the places in the Old Testament where I said the word fulfilled was used. With the Joshua Chapter 24. Clearly fulfilled all the promises God had ever given to Israel. Fulfilled that day, done, they were in rest. Notice the language: all their enemies had ceased around them. God gave them all into their hand. Folks, that is final rest if I had ever heard it.

Joel McDurmon's Third Negative

Didn't address Lamentations where it says, "Our end has come upon us." "The end has come upon us." Didn't address Ezekiel who said the same thing. The end, definite article, not addressed. Why? Because it falsifies his position. It shows that his physician -- his position – (I don't know about his physician; I have never met him) -- his position has not been established.

I didn't hear anything about the reign of the saints on the earth. Notice that all of my questions for the most part were ignored totally. Now here we're at the end of the debate. He's had all of his time for response. He spent it attacking me and my arguments, but he didn't address a single one of the arguments I presented against his position except for a couple, I will admit.

Psalm 37:9 says "The meek shall inherit the earth." Jesus appropriates that in Matthew 5:5. If you can drag the context in, as I said you can't, then you also have to drag in Psalm 37:10 that says it would be a little while. But that means that scripture was sitting there saying it would be a little while since David wrote it. Some little while. Now does that make me in danger of becoming a dispensationalist because I point that out? No. All I'm showing you is there's a problem with Don's hermeneutic. I'm not affirming necessarily anything because of it.

We have come to Mount Zion, I agree. That has been spiritualized, I agree. I don't agree with his treatment of my paragraph again. I think he's adding some things to it that aren't necessarily there. But when I say that those promises were spiritualized, yeah, we're all resurrected already in Christ. We were before A.D. 70 ever thought about happening. And Paul affirms this in Ephesians 2. He says, "We are seated in the heavenly places with him." We were not only resurrected, folks. We were ascended into heaven at the right hand of God reigning with Christ in Ephesians 2 before A.D. 70 ever happened.

So, yeah, we came to Mount Zion, and, yeah, that was spiritualized. Does that mean it was final? Not a word. Not a word on it. Not a word on it. It's no more final than it was final in Joshua. It's no more final than it was in 1 Kings. It's no more final than it was in the captivity of Babylon. Why not? Simply for the one verse -- one of the things he really hasn't addressed at all -- well, I shouldn't say at all -- mostly, is that the curse is still in place.

Again, you would not have convinced my wife tonight.

Joel McDurmon's Third Negative

New Covenant makes the old obsolete. And this -- I use in my paragraph -- he says this is an elliptical statement on a New Covenant. I didn't mean it like that at all. The whole reason I added before it the phrase New Covenant -- Old Covenant and New Covenant administrations -- and if you look in my book, it's capitalized -- is simply for the fact that I didn't want anyone to construe this as an argument against Theonomy, which believes that there are applications of Old Testament law for saints today and society. And I didn't want anyone coming back to me specifically saying, "Oh, well, if you're a Theonomist, then this argument knocks you down." No, I was talking about the *administration* of the law, particularly in the Old Testament ceremonies.

Now I have my reasons why those things were ended, and yet some aspects of the law continue. I don't have to give them tonight; it's not my purpose. But I can say that I have my reasons for that. Don's insisting that I have to justify that is him distracting you from the fact that he doesn't have an answer to my arguments that he hasn't addressed the scriptures I brought forth all the while saying I have given philosophizing and scriptural or *ad hominem* arguments. "Well, how about some solid exegesis?" I gave you tons of exegesis. You didn't talk about any of it. That's loathable.

I specifically mentioned in that paragraph that this is when the symbols and ceremonies of the Old Covenant were done away with. Yes, there is a definitive moment here when this age gives way to the age to come. But, again, that doesn't say anything about the finality of the resurrection, does it?

Don says, "Well there is no administration without Torah and that's what passed away. And therefore there's no more administration." What in the world do you think Jesus did? Jesus Christ I the administration of the New Covenant; that's why the Bible calls him the mediator of the New Covenant.

In his body, he fulfilled all the Old Testament ceremonies and rights. Again, don't think that fulfillment means done, gone, over with, out of here. Those ceremonies and rights live on to this day in the body of Jesus Christ who fulfilled them in his body. Therefore that writing of handwriting -- that handwriting ordinance was blotted out. We don't have to worry about

Joel McDurmon's Third Negative

them -- we don't have to worry about circumcision. Thank the Lord. And yet the New Testament is filled with citations of Old Testament including the Old Testament case laws for things like paying pastors or paying ministers. Very obscure things like this. Love your neighbor as yourself, the second most quoted Old Testament passage in the New Testament.

Jesus says this is the summary of the law. Well, if every jot and tittle is gone in the way that Don says, then you've got to throw out love your neighbor as yourself too, because that was part of Leviticus. And you've got to throw out love the Lord as your God with all your heart and soul and mind and strength because that's Deuteronomy 4 -- or Deuteronomy 6.

Folks, you've got to be careful about, as I said in the beginning of my opening statement, absolutizing words and then trying to build these doctrines on them and then trying to equate them all across scripture. Scripture is not put together like that. It's put together in a much more artistic way. And by that, I'm not saying, "Oh, there's all these variegations floating around out there." No, that's not the point. It is -- remember what I said -- harmony, symphony, order. There is order in time and it will end. And there is one overarching theme through all of it, and it is the coming of the Messiah that theme begins in Genesis 3:15 when the promised servant -- it is said -- is going to come crush the head of the serpent and have his heel bruised.

Now you could have never gotten the fullness of that just from that one verse, but that theme is played out from creation to Revelation. And it involves the removal of the curse and that curse is not removed.

There may have been some things that Don has emphasized that I missed. If that's the case, please do not get the idea that I am, as he says, totally ignoring them. I took notes at a feverish pace because he talks at a feverish pace, which is admirable in some cases.

And if there is something that I missed that's outstanding and really important to address and you think it's going to put me on the floor, or not that, but if it's just as important, bring it up in Q and A and let's hear it. Thank you all very much.

Joel McDurmon's First Affirmative

****

As I said last night, my argument for a future bodily resurrection of the dead is Jesus' argument for the future bodily resurrection of the dead, which comes in his confrontation with the Sadducees in Luke 20. I will read the entire passage.

There came to him some Sadducees, those who denied that there is a resurrection, and they asked him a question saying, "Teacher, Moses wrote for us that if a man's brother dies having a wife but no children, the man must take the widow and raise up offspring for his brother. Now there were seven brothers, the first took a wife and died without children. The second and third took her, and likewise all seven left no children and died. And after -- afterward the woman also died. In the resurrection therefore whose wife will the woman be? For the seven had her as a wife." And Jesus said to them, "'The sons of this age marry and are given in marriage. But those who are considered worthy to attain to that age and to the resurrection from the dead neither marry nor are given in marriage." And I still think that's a valid argument.

"For, they cannot die anymore because they are equal to the angels and are sons of God being sons of the resurrection. But that the dead are raised even Moses showed in the passage about the bush where he calls the Lord the God of Abraham and the God of Isaac and the God of Jacob. Now, He is not the God of the dead, but of the living, for all live to Him."

Well, there you go. Case closed. The Lord is the God of Abraham and of Isaac and of Jacob. He says, "I am the God of Abraham, Isaac, Jacob," and therefore He is not the God of the dead, but of the living. And therefore there shall be a future bodily resurrection of the dead. Couldn't be any more clear than that to me.

You say, wait a minute, something is wrong here. Well, a full Preterist looks at this verse and generally responds to it by saying Jesus completely baffled the Sadducees by refuting their assumption that the resurrection is going to be a fleshly bodily resurrection, and instead shows that since Abraham is still alive with God in heaven, Jesus was spiritualizing the definition of

Joel McDurmon's First Affirmative

resurrection. So he completely overthrows their assumptions and presuppositions.

And I just have a hard time accepting that because if that were the case, I just have a feeling that the Sadducees would have laughed him off the face of the earth. Is this passage really teaching, do you really get that from there, that God is not the God of the dead but of the living? It doesn't say that in the scripture. Jesus added that part; that was his explanation. So are we really supposed to assume simply because you quoted this verse that Abraham, Isaac, and Jacob are still alive in heaven?

And I have a feeling that they wouldn't have been convinced. In fact, I have a feeling they would have laughed at him if that's what he meant.

Many people have thought that in this passage Jesus -- full preterists have taken this passage and said Jesus is refuting and baffling the Sadducees simply by redefining the definition of resurrection. They had come to him with the assumption that their resurrection is a physical bodily resurrection, which is of course the view of their rival sect, the Pharisees.

And Jesus was baffling them by saying, no, this is a heavenly reality; it is a spiritual resurrection, for Abraham, Isaac, and Jacob are alive with God in heaven now, and therefore the resurrection happens. And I have a hard time accepting the fact that that's what he was saying simply because the scripture is not clear on that. Jesus adds the next part that God is not the God of the dead but of the living. That is not in the Old Testament's text that he's quoting from. That was his explanation of that text or at least an explanation of that text, an addendum, a codicil.

So simply quoting that passage that "I am the God of Abraham, Isaac, and Jacob" was not a redefinition of the resurrection, and I think if that's what he meant it to be, the Sadducees probably would have laughed at him. And I don't think it would have been convincing to anyone, especially in the very next following verses one of the scribes is standing by overhearing this. And a scribe is by definition a Pharisee. And he says, "Master, you have answered well." So here's a guy who presupposes belief in a physical resurrection, and he thinks Jesus has completely put these people to silence with that argument. So obviously he's not redefining the resurrection or the Pharisee might have thought otherwise.

Joel McDurmon's First Affirmative

And the very next verse says, "And after that no one asked him any more questions." You know what, Jesus? That was a pretty good answer. I'll see you later.

So what is going on here? Well, go back to the passage that he's quoting. It's from Exodus Chapter 3. It is the burning bush passage of Moses in the wilderness.

In Exodus Chapter 3 verses 5 and verses 8 are very relevant. The bush begins to burn. Moses says I want to turn aside and see what's going on here. And he walks up to it and he hears the voice speaking to him out of the bush: "Do not come near. Take your sandals off your feet, for the place on which you're standing is holy ground." (*Adamah*, by the way.) And he said, "I am the God of your father." "I am the God of your father. The God of Abraham, the God of Isaac, and the God of Jacob. And Moses hid his face for he was afraid to look at God."

And if you skip down to verse 8 after God explains to Moses that He has chosen this time to deliver His people out of the bondage of Egypt for He has heard their cries, and the time has come for Him to remember his covenant people, He says, "I have come down to deliver them out of the hand of the Egyptians and to bring them up out of that land and unto a good land and to a large" ... "unto a land flowing with milk and honey."

In other words, God's revelation of this name is directly tied to his promise to Abraham. His covenant promises, plural, to Abraham that he and his seed after him would inherit the land.

Argument still not over with. There's still one more aspect of that. So we know Jesus is invoking the name of the covenant God. The God of the covenant with Abraham. The God who made a covenant that you will inherit this land. The problem with that is that promise was *never* fulfilled.

Now you might say, wait a minute, Mr. Joel. You said last night -- you quoted right there from Joshua Chapter 24 where it said all these promises were fulfilled. They possessed all the land that God said they would possess, and not one of the promises to any of the fathers was not fulfilled. Not any of the promises made to the fathers was not fulfilled. So how can

Joel McDurmon's First Affirmative

you say now that that promise was never fulfilled to Abraham? Because it wasn't. Abraham went into the land. He sojourned into the land, but for him that promise was never fulfilled.

Now this is very important. You may think at this point that I'm just splitting hairs. But I'm not. In the Book of Acts Chapter 7 as Stephen is giving a rundown of the entire redemptive history of Israel, what does he say? Verses 5 -- 4 and verse 5. God is calling Abraham out of earth. "And then he came out of that land of the Chaldeans and dwelt in Charran: and from thence, when his father was dead, he removed him into this land wherein you now dwell." He's speaking to the Jews of course.

And now listen. "And He gave him none inheritance in it. No, not so much as to set his foot on. And yet He promised that He would give it to him for possession."

If you go back and read the original promises in Genesis 13, Genesis 15 -- Genesis 12, 13, and 15. In one place, he says, "I'll give you a seed and your seed shall inherit this earth." In two other places, he says, "I'm giving this land to *you and your seed*." And that's exactly what Stephen is referencing, that God promised to give him -- *him and his seed* to inherit the land. And that promise was never fulfilled, per Stephen's words.

Now, "I am the God of Abraham, Isaac, and Jacob" invoking the covenant God's name, and the covenant He made with Abraham, which includes that land promise. There's only one way for that promise to be fulfilled, and that's if there is a future bodily resurrection of Abraham.

Now, when you go to a lynchpin like that and then back up to all the other promises made about resurrection, all through scripture, all of the other coming out of the tombs imagery that is talked about in Isaiah 25, 26 and Daniel 12, I don't care where it shows up. Wherever it shows up, Ezekiel 37, all of that, why is God continually invoking this image as an image of salvation? I just happen to be fool enough to believe that He's going to do it someday.

And when I look at the promise made to Abraham and the fact that it was never fulfilled and that there's only one way for it to be fulfilled, I'm convinced it will happen. So however we typologically apply those

Joel McDurmon's First Affirmative

resurrection passages in the interim, keeping in mind of course all the hermeneutical difficulties I explained last night, there is still yet one grand fulfillment of that. It is the dominant image all through Biblical theology with the exception perhaps of the crushing of the head of the serpent, which was, of course, the proto promise in Genesis 3:15.

So there you have it. Now Don will probably try to respond to this by going to Hebrews Chapter 11. And yet in Hebrews Chapter beginning with verse 8, it says, "By faith, Abraham, when he was called to go out into a place which he should hereafter receive for inheritance obeyed. And he went out not knowing where he went. By faith he so journeyed in the land of promise as in a strange country dwelling in tabernacles with Isaac and Jacob, the heirs with him of the same promise. And he looked for a city which has foundations whose builder and maker is God. Through faith also Sarah herself sought to receive strength to receive seed and was delivered of a child when she was past age because she judged him faithful who had promised. Therefore sprang there even of one, and him as good as dead, so many as the stars of the sky in multitude-- as the sand which is by the seashore innumerable. These all died in faith not having received the promises, but having seen them afar off and were persuaded of him. And embraced them and confessed that they were strangers and pilgrims of earth. For they that say such things declare plainly that they seek a country." The Greek word is *patrida* -- *patrida*, I believe, which means a father land. "Country" is a very anachronistic translation.

"And truly if they had been mindful of that country from which they came out," that is the land of Ur, "they might have had opportunity to return, but they didn't. But now they desire a better -- that is a heavenly. Wherefore God is not ashamed to be called their God, for He has prepared for them a city. He has prepared for them a city. By faith Abraham when he was tried, offered up Isaac," et cetera, et cetera.

So I believe Don would probably try to go to this passage and say, look, he was not looking for the land, he was looking in verse 9, for verse 10 for a city which has foundations which builder and maker is God. And again in Verse 16, "For they desire to better by implications a better country," but I don't believe that's what it means, "that is a heavenly country, and wherefore God is not ashamed to be called their God for he has prepared them a city." Therefore, I believe a full preterist view would be that, well,

Joel McDurmon's First Affirmative

God didn't give him the land because He had something better in mind, a heavenly country. But you'll notice that even in this very passage in which the writer of Hebrews is talking says, "By faith Abraham, when he was called to go out into a place, which he should receive for an inheritance, obeyed."

In other words, it's calling the very same place that he went into, the land of Canaan, the place of inheritance that he should afterwards receive for inheritance. By the way, the word should after there is *mello*. And -- which means he was "about to inherit," but we know he didn't inherit, so there's another time/text difficulty for you to work with.

And in the next verse, "By faith and sojourned in the land of promise." So obviously the writer of Hebrews is -- when he talks about God preparing a heavenly city is not talking about the location of the city, because he calls the very place Abraham was in, "The land of promise." This is it, folks. But when we talk about a city whose builder and maker is God that has foundations, he's talking about the source of that building and that is God. That is heaven. And of course what do we find in Revelation? We find the new city of Jerusalem coming down out of heaven, *"Eck tou ouranou"*, out of heaven. Well, if it's coming out of heaven, where is it going?

Heaven is coming to earth, folks. And it's not just the land of Canaan. When God makes the original promise to Abraham, He restates it then in verse -- in Chapter 13 verse 4 of Genesis. And He says, "Abraham, I want you to stand here and look in all directions as far as you can. And as far as you see, that's going to be yours. That's your inheritance." I believe He was saying that there are no boundaries to this inheritance ultimately.

Now in the very next chapter, He does -- when he makes the covenant with Abraham and rips the animals in half and passes through, He does set some boundaries; they're fairly vague. Those boundaries get elucidated a little more, I believe, in later chapters in Exodus and Leviticus and Deuteronomy. And they get very explicit in Ezekiel 47, I believe.

But the original promise to Abraham was as far as you could see, which to me is a parallelism to your seed shall be as innumerable as the sands on the seashore. And sure enough -- sure enough when Paul picks up his theme in Romans Chapter 4:13: "For the promise that he should be heir of the

Joel McDurmon's First Affirmative

land" -- nope -- "heir of the *world*, was not to Abraham or to his seed through the law." It's not tied to Torah, folks. The death of Torah has nothing to do with the fulfillment of this promise. "To his seed, not through the law, but through the righteousness of faith."

Heir not of the land -- not the land of Israel, but of the world. And the Greek word is *kosmos*. It's in the genitive it's *kosmou*, but it's the same word.

Now, you have something to deal with here. Paul explains the promise to Abraham as inheriting the entire world. You have a choice to make whether you believe that that means the entire earth, which, of course, dovetails very nicely with Jesus' teaching that the meek shall inherit the earth. But Daniel's teaching is that the stone that is cut out without hands strikes the image on the feet and grows to fulfill the whole earth.

And the other passages I mentioned last night about the reign of the saints on the earth. Or you can go the route of the beyond creation science guys and say *kosmos* only refers to the institution of Israel. But then, of course, that forces you to redefine everything going backwards, and that would challenge your doctrine of creation too, I believe.

So I think this is a pretty firm, solid argument that there must be some bodily resurrection in the future -- at least of Abraham. But then if it's of Abraham, you have to wonder what this event is going to be, and I assume -- strange assumption I'm sure -- that this is the general resurrection of all the dead.

Along with this I want you to consider some statements made in some classic passages that I know you guys have dealt with, but we'll bring them in for discussion anyway.

John Chapter 5 and 6. John chapter 5:24 and following says, "Truly, truly I say to you, whoever hears my word and believes him who sent me has eternal life. He does not come into judgment but has passed from death to life. Truly I say unto you, an hour is coming and is now here when the dead will hear the voice of the Son of God and those who hear will live. For as the Father" -- of course, all of this is A.D. 70. "For as the Father has life in

Himself, so he has granted the son also to have life in himself. And he has given him authority to execute judgment because he is the Son of God."

What, Jesus? The dead are going to pass to life? It says, oh, don't marvel at this. Follow on. "For an hour is coming", not, "and now is," "an hour is coming when all who are in the tombs will hear the voice and come out. Those who have done good to the resurrection of life and those who have done evil to the resurrection of judgment." Now this can be applied to A.D. 70. I believe he's speaking of something yet different because of the change in the time text.

If we're going to honor time texts, perhaps we should also honor when they're not there. Compare this to the discourse that follows in the very next chapter, which brings in yet another systematic doctrine that I hope by going systematic, I won't get accused again of philosophizing.

"This is the will of him who sent me," John 6:39, "that I should lose nothing of all that he has given me, but raise it up on the last day." *The last day.* The last day, a phrase peculiar to the Gospel of John, used nowhere else in scripture. We also like definite articles very much. Let's honor this one: "For this is the will of the Father, that everyone who looks on the Son and believes in him should have eternal life. And I will raise him up on the last day." Everyone who looks on the son. What about the people who look on him after A.D. 70? When is their last day? Was their last day 2,000 years ago?

Five verses later, verse 44, "No one can come to me unless the Father who sent me draws him. And I will raise him up on the last day." These are the doctrines of grace, folks. This is the doctrine of election, and the doctrine of irresistible grace. No one can come to Jesus unless God draws him to Jesus. And that person who is among the elect will be raised on the last day.

This is the will of the Father. Every one of those who looks on me will have eternal life. There is a definite number of the elect. "Of all that he has given me I should lose nothing, but will raise it up on the last day." Jesus is talking about an inclusive number of people. This means there must be a definite number of people. This means history cannot go on to infinity as the full Preterist doctrine says.

Joel McDurmon's First Affirmative

Jesus again -- John 12:48, "The one who rejects me and does not receive my words has a judge: the word that I have spoken will judge him on the last day."

John 11, Martha said to Jesus, "Lord, if you had been with me, my brother would not have died, but even now whatever you ask of God, God will give you." And Jesus said, "Your brother will rise again." And Martha said to him, "I know that he will rise in the resurrection on the last day." And Jesus said to her, "I am the resurrection and the life. Whoever believes in me, though he died, yet he shall live. And everyone who lives and believes in me shall never die. Do you believe this?" The last day. The resurrection. So I just happen to be fool enough to believe that when Jesus says there will be a last day, there will be a last day. Sure enough there is supportive material for this in scripture. For all of these doctrines.

2 Timothy 2:19, "The Lord knows them that are his". They are the elect. They are finite in number. You can compare this, if you will, to the 2 Peter 3:9. And, of course, we know 2 Peter passage. We all, for the most part, apply that to A.D. 70 in some way or another. But think about what's being implied here. The scoffers say, "Why is this taking so long? Where is the promise of this coming, of his parousia?" And Peter says, "Be patient. The day with the Lord is like a thousand years, a thousand years is like a day." But why is it taking so long? What's he waiting on? All the conditions are right to be fulfilled for the destruction. What are we waiting on? Peter says, "He's not willing that any should perish, but that all should come to repentance."

And he begins that verse by saying the Lord is patient toward us. Not willing that any should perish, but all come to repentance. Who is us? Go back to the beginning of the book. The introduction to the book. Peter, the apostle of Jesus Christ: "To those who have obtained like precious faith." He's writing a letter to the elect, folks. And when he says that he was not willing that any should perish, but all come to repentance, obviously within that historical window, he's saying there's a definite number out there and the Lord is waiting until that comes to fruition in history.

Now, you have a choice to make here. Either the number of elect ends in A.D. 70 at the resurrection, and that's the finite number, or it extends beyond that. Or it extends beyond that, there's some point in the future at

Joel McDurmon's First Affirmative

which that number is reached and history is going to end and God is going to come back and judge and resurrect the dead.

You have to deal with the doctrine of election. And you have to deal with finitude of the doctrine of election.

There will be a last day in history. God speaks of this allusion in several places. Ecclesiastics 3:11 says that God has put eternity in man's heart. But no man may find out what God has done from the beginning to the end. That tells me God has an end in mind. A final end. An end, if you will, in which everything is fully fulfilled.

And as I argued last night, that will come when the curse is fully reversed in heaven and on earth. Isaiah 41:4, "Calling the generations," God says, "I am the one calling the generations from the beginning. I, the Lord, the first and with the last, I am He." It's a very strange Hebrew construction to read it. What it says literally is "and with the end," or "and with end, I am He." God envisions there being an end to all of this.

Isaiah 46:10, God declaring the end from the beginning and from ancient times things not yet done. My Counsel shall stand and I will accomplish all my purpose." Sounds to me like there is a very definitive set of criteria God has in mind from the beginning to the end. There is a "the end", and it will be a time in which God has all of his counsel accomplished, period.

Finally I'd like to look at a passage, which as soon as I mention it many of you full preterists are going to say, "Easy." Job 19: I do realize that there are some difficulties with this text applying into a final resurrection. I don't think they're insurmountable, and I think this passage has not gotten the due it's required.

Virtually right smack-dab in the middle of the book of Job he has this one discourse in which he says the following (19:25. "For I know that my redeemer lives and at the last he will stand upon the earth. And after my skin has been thus destroyed, yet in my flesh I shall see God, whom I shall see for myself and my eyes shall behold and not another."

And the first strike against this always is, well, the notoriously difficult Hebrew to translate here. And if you look at some of the attempts some

Joel McDurmon's First Affirmative

people have made, especially in the paraphrased translations, they don't even mention resurrection at all. They don't have any allusion to what's going on here. And absolutely it's just nonsense. If you stick with the more literal translations and the ones that have really made an effort to get in what's going on here, especially in the context of Job -- the Book of Job, and then if you can read the Hebrew yourself, you realize that this is not nearly as difficult as some people say. Especially in regard when full preterists throw that at me then go try to build doctrines on Daniel 9 and the book of Revelation as if those were just simple easy things to translate and interpret. This is a cake walk in comparison.

Some translators and some interpreters have said that there's no physical resurrection envisioned here at all. This is simply talking about when Job finally recovers from his condition, he believes that by the power of his Redeemer he will be restored to his former state, that he will overcome this temporary medical setback.

And, in fact, most of the Jewish writers, if you care to read them, held this view. And, in fact, many modern theologians. If you go to N.T. Wright's book on the resurrection, which is a big fat 7- or 8- or 900-page book, kind of the definitive work on it at this stage, he doesn't even spend more than two pages on this verse and says, I don't really think it's really talking about the resurrection. Didn't spend a lot of time explaining why, really repeating things I've just already told you. I thought that was fairly unfortunate.

But the problem is that all through the book of Job, and up and to this point, you have references from him where he had no clue -- no idea of recovering from what he was in. Recovering his health or his finances. He had lost hope. He was in despair. And it seems strange that all of a sudden, out of the blue, he would turn around and say, "Oh, you know, I want to recover some day and get everything I lost back."

When he spent several times in Chapter 6 verse 11, Chapter 7 verses 7-8, Chapter 10 verse 20, Chapter 16 verse 22, Chapter 17 verse 1, and verses 14-16, virtually saying there is no more hope here in this life. I'm going to die.

And the doctrine Sheol is dealt with several times in the book, even up to this point where Job is fearing the grave. And that is his finality. He says

Joel McDurmon's First Affirmative

there's no hope of recovery, because I'm going to the grave and you don't come back from that. And a lot of people are pointing to that and say, see, there it proves that Job didn't believe in the resurrection. No, that's not what the point is. If you read the context, he's simply saying, I'm about to die, and when you die, it's over with. There's a finality. But he's not talking necessarily a full finality because you get to this verse. And it can't be talking about the recovery of his health, or his wealth.

It's interesting to back up to the previous chapter. Chapter 18 verses 12-14. This is Bildad speaking. And Bildad back up in verse 5 says that the light of the wicked shall be put out, and the spark of his fire shall not shine. Now it doesn't take a whole lot of imagination to know what he's talking about when he says that. The wicked man is going to be put out. And down in verse 12, "His strength shall be hunger bitten and destruction shall be ready at his side. It shall devour the strength of his skin, even the firstborn of death shall devour his strength. His confidence shall be rooted out of his tabernacle." That is his skin. "And it shall bring him to the king of terrors, death."

Immediately in response to that, Job gives this passage in which he references his *skin*. So it seems to me that Job is referring directly to the physical death of man that Bildad had just brought up. And, in fact, the text says, and then Job answered. "Job responded." And he responds by saying, "I know that my Redeemer lives, and at last He will stand upon the earth. And after my skin has been thus destroyed, yet in my flesh shall I see God."

And I can say, well, that means there must be a resurrection in the future yet. And the full preterist says, no, flip over to verse -- to Chapter 42 and look right there. It says very clearly, God reveals Himself in a whirlwind in Job. They have this exchange. Job is almost weeping in repentance before God, and he says, you know what, I have heard about you, God, but now I have seen you with my own eyes. So there you go. Proof positive in the flesh. Job saw God. This was fulfilled and it has no reference to death, except it's a direct response to what Bildad was saying. And except the context in which he's saying is vindication, not repentance, before God for his condition.

So what's going on here in Job? I know that my Redeemer lives and at the last He shall stand upon the earth. The Hebrew word is *aphar*, ashes. The

Joel McDurmon's First Affirmative

Hebrew land for -- word for land is *eretz*; it's not here. The Hebrew word for ground is *adamah*; it's not here. It's ashes.

What was Job doing? We kind of forget. We lose this context as we get in. We forget that way back in the early chapters, Job finally lost it, and he begins to curse the day in which he was born. And he puts on a sack cloth and he pours ashes on himself in a big heap on the ground and he sits down in the pile of ashes. Symbolic of what? From dust you came and to dust you shall return. *Aphar.* And he says, you know what, the Redeemer is going to stand right here on these very ashes to which I have returned.

What happened to Job's body? Boils all over it. His skin is literally pussing and peeling off with boils and he takes a shard and pottery and scrapes off his corrupted dead skin. Yeah, I know this skin's going to corrupt. But you know what, after this skin is dead and gone, I'm still going to see the Savior, the Redeemer in the flesh, in the last.

There are some things said by the imagery of Job that are not said by the words directly. So I think this passage has not gotten its due.

And thank you very much.

Don K. Preston's First Negative Presentation

****

I appreciate Joel's presentation. He began with Luke Chapter 20. Let me begin with what I call some housekeeping issues from last night.

Joel said that I didn't respond to a lot; I said he didn't respond to a lot. I think we both realized that time constraints are extremely, extremely tight. Sometimes it's just time constraints; sometimes it's the fact we just don't get to things. Sometimes it's inadvertence; sometimes it's purposeful.

But let me address several things, housekeeping, that I'm going to get directly into responding point by point to what he brought up. And I'll cover as much material as possible.

But the very first thing I want to cover is Luke 20, because he brought it up last night and he brought it up again tonight as his leading one.

The Age To Come Has Come!

Jesus' "This Age" Was the Mosaic Age- Joel
"The Age To Come" Would Follow Jesus' "this age" And Be The Age *Introduced By The Resurrection*
We are living in the "age to come" that followed Jesus' "this age" (Joel)
Therefore, The Resurrection Luke 20 Has Been Fulfilled!
This is the Edenic-Abrahamic- Comprehensive Hope!
If not, why not?

I want you to notice that Jesus spoke of two ages. The sons of *this age* marry and are given in marriage. But the children -- the sons of that age neither marry nor are given in marriage. They never die.

And here's what you need to understand. Joel has properly acknowledged that we need to examine the time or temporal statements of given texts. He called our attention to some tonight. I hope to be able to address what he had to say.

Well, notice these temporal statements that we have. They're very definitive. Jesus was living in what he called *this age*. And he said the sons of *this age* marry and are given in marriage. Now here's something absolutely critical to note. The "this age" in which Jesus was living, was the age in which -- well, a man was married. He died: not having children. His brother married her [the wife of the deceased]. Bore no children. His other brother married her. Bore no children.

Folks, this is directly from Deuteronomy Chapter 25 called Levirate marriage. What age therefore was Jesus referencing? Number one, when he said the sons of *this age* marry and are given in marriage. And he talks about the sons of *this age* being that age in which the Levirate marriage was practiced. Well, it's not the Christian age.

And here's what's interesting about this.

Joel McDurmon says on Page 45 and following of his book, *Jesus -V- Jerusalem*. Jesus' this age was the Mosaic age." In fact, he says Jesus and Paul's "this age" was the Mosaic age. And he says, "the age to come," which they were anticipating is the age in which you and I are now living." You catch the power of that?

So let me reiterate because, folks, this is extremely important. Joel McDurmon himself has identified Jesus' this age, the age in which he was living at the time he spoke in Luke Chapter 20 as the Mosaic age. He has identified the age to come in which there would be no marrying and giving in marriage as the Christian age: the age in which you and I are living.

Now Joel may get back up here and say, yeah, but it can't be that way because we all are married today. Well, it's interesting because Paul says, "In Christ there is neither male or female." How does that work out?

But the point of it is, we are living in the age to come that followed Jesus' "this age" by Joel McDurmon's own theology. Therefore, since the age to come is the age of the resurrection, since the age to come would arrive at the end of Jesus' "this age," and since Jesus' "this age" was the Mosaic age, that means that the resurrection of Luke Chapter 20 is the resurrection of Job.

Now I can go into an awful lot and -- you know, he brought up Job and he said there are difficulties. Well, folks, he didn't give you half of the insight of the translational issues there are with Job 19. And if I have time, I'll get there.

But here's the point again; The resurrection of Luke Chapter 20 has been fulfilled because Joel himself identifies the age to come, the age in which Jesus said there'll be no marrying and giving of marriage, as the age to follow the Mosaic age.

Now, this is Edenic restoration. This is Genesis. Oh, but wait a minute. We've got a really severe problem here. I want you to notice: Per Joel, Luke 20 is the "final," consummative resurrection, even though the word "final" doesn't appear in Luke Chapter 20 anywhere by the way. But Luke 20 is the final resurrection. It is the restoration of Eden prior to the fall. Everybody, follow really, really closely here.

Joel-Genesis- Luke 20

Per Joel, Luke 20 is the "final" resurrection- the restoration of Eden- prior to the fall

Adam and Eve were married- with the mandate to be fruitful and multiply- Prior to the Fall!

But wait!

Jesus said that in the age to come- when Eden was restored– there is no marriage!

Per Joel's position: Marriage (being fruitful and multiplying) ends at the very time that Joel says it is restored!

This is a hopeless contradiction!
Luke 20 is a Contrast of Covenant Worlds!

But prior to the fall, Adam and Eve were married and were given the mandate be fruitful and multiply. Do you catch the power of that? Do you see the train coming?

Jesus said that in the age to come when Eden is restored, there is no marriage. Well, per Joel's position therefore, marriage, being fruitful and multiplying, ends at the very moment -- i.e., the arrival of the age to come -- in which Joel says it's supposed to be restored. You see, he says Eden --

Don K. Preston's First Negative

Adam and Eve marry. Adam and Eve bearing children, restored in the age to come. But in the age to come, there is no marrying and giving of married.

Folks, this is an irreconcilable contradiction. You cannot have it both ways. You can't have the restoration of Eden, marrying and giving in marrying in Eden, multiplying and being fruitful in Eden prior to the fall, that being the object of the restoration of all things, and then turn right around and appeal to Luke Chapter 20 and say, oh, but wait, in that age -- in the restoration of all things when Eden is restored, there's no marrying and giving in marriage after all. There is no bearing of children. Only if we keep Luke 20 within the framework which Joel McDurmon has acknowledged.

This age -- Jesus' this age-- was the Mosaic age. In the age to come, the age to follow the Mosaic age, there is no marrying or giving in marriage.

Now it's very important because he contrasts the Pharisees and the Sadducees and Joel said -- I think that -- yeah, it must have been last night. He said the Pharisees believed in physical resurrection. Well, does that prove that they were right? It really is an important question, isn't it?

Well, I want you to notice that resurrection and kingdom go hand in hand as to nature. Paul said in 2 Timothy Chapter 4 verse 1, "I charge thee therefore before God and before Jesus Christ who is about the judge of the living and the dead at His appearing and his kingdom," resurrection and kingdom go hand in hand.

Now what kind of concept do the Pharisees have about the kingdom of God? Physical. Was their concept of the kingdom right? No.

In John Chapter 6 verse 15 when Jesus perceived that they, the crowd led by the Pharisees evidently. Jesus perceived that they were about to come and to make him king; he withdraw himself. Why? Because Jesus did not come to establish a physical kingdom.

Well, guess what? The kingdom doesn't come with observation. But the kingdom of the resurrection comes at the same time. Therefore the resurrection doesn't come with observation. That means the resurrection is of the same nature as the kingdom. The kingdom is the spiritual nature.

Don K. Preston's First Negative

Now again, I suggest to you that Joel's own statement on Luke Chapter 20 in regards to the age to come or this age and the age to come presents him an insurmountable problem.

Secondly, his position that the resurrection that introduces the age to come would demand no marrying and giving in marriage contradicts his own position that Adam and Eve married, bearing children, is to be restored at the age to come.

You see, folks, what we have is a question not only concerning resurrection, but *the nature of the kingdom of God.* Sadducees are very clearly leading and postulating and arguing against the Pharisees that the kingdom was going to exist -- keep on existing under *Torah*. Deuteronomy Chapter 25.

Well, then he went to Exodus Chapter 3:5-8 and had some very interesting things to say there. And I must -- I must say that I was somewhat taken back.

Joel may have to correct me on this, but for the world, and for the life of me, it sounded exactly like Joel expects Abraham to be resurrected in a physical body and live on a physical earth. That's sure what it sounded like because he said Abraham never got the physical land. And he's got to have the physical land, because that promise was made to him.

ABRAHAM'S RESURRECTION HOPE

The EofM Resurrection of 1 Cor. 15- in fulfillment of Isaiah 24-25- **was the resurrection hope of Abraham and all the faithful worthies**– all the way to Creation (Heb. 11:13-35).

The EoM Resurrection of 1 Cor. 15- in fulfillment of Is. 24-25– **would be on Zion: "On this Mountain...** He shall destroy death..."

But, Abraham and the worthies have now received the fulfillment of All Zion Promises!– McDurmon (JvJ, 178), Gentry, DeMar, Mathison, et. Al! **Therefore, the EoM resurrection of 1 Corinthians 15 has been fulfilled.**

You Cannot Affirm the Fulfillment of Hebrews 11-12 Without Affirming the End of the Millennium Resurrection!

Don K. Preston's First Negative

You know, it's interesting that he went to Acts Chapter 7 verses 4-5. Now -- well, you need to know this. In Genesis Chapter 15:15 and following, when God gave the land promises to Israel; Joel says they're kind of vague and nebulous. Not really. Not to geographers who know those boundaries. They were so clear that in 1 Kings Chapter 4:20-21 the Chronicler said that under Solomon Israel possessed all of that land, and he gave the very borders -- actually he gave more than the borders, which shows the grace of God in His abundant gift. And Israel ruled over all of that territory. But anyway, he appealed to Acts 7:4-5 and says that Abraham did not get the land, but he overlooked this.

Back to Genesis Chapter 15 -- 15 and 16. It said that in the fourth generation, after going down into Egypt, Israel would come out and possess the land. That was the Abrahamic promise of the land. Now watch this. Acts 7:17. "When the time of the promise drew near which God had sworn to *Abraham*, the people grew and multiplied in Egypt until another king arose who did not know Joseph."

Now God set a time limitation for the fulfillment of the land promise *to Abraham and his seed*. Now if Abraham's seed got it, Abraham got it through them.

But I want you to notice, when the time drew near -- what was the time frame? The fourth generation, Acts 7:17, "When the time for the promise," what promise? Land promise. "When the time for the promise drew near" -- now I want to know from Joel if God fulfilled that land promise or not. It was supposed to be in the fourth generation. God said, I'm going to give it to you and your descendants in the fourth generation. Acts 7:17 when the time drew near. Did God keep his word?

Well, in regard to the physical land promise, I would call your attention to Nehemiah Chapter 9: 6 and 7. In Nehemiah 9, which is a post exilic passage, they returned out of Babylonian captivity. Nehemiah recounts that the Abrahamic land promise, how God promised to give the land to Abraham and his descendants, to give them the land of the Amorite – Cadmonites, the Canaanites, the Hittites, the Gittites, and all those "ites."

Don K. Preston's First Negative

What did Nehemiah say? What did Nehemiah think about God's promises *to Abraham* of the land promise? He said He made the promise to *Abram* and his descendants. And he says to Yahweh "and he has *kept His promise* for You are faithful."

Now he gives the very boundaries listed in Deuteronomy Chapter 11. The reiteration of the land promise of Genesis Chapter 15. And let's not forget, Joshua 21 does say they possessed the land.

Now here we are in Acts Chapter 7. Did Abraham himself set foot on the land? Well, Acts Chapter 7 indicates that he didn't. But it was to him and his seed. If his seed got it, Nehemiah says *Abraham got it* because God was faithful.

Now let's go on just a little bit more. Again, he's arguing for Abraham to receive the physical earth. Now I want to tell you what, ladies and gentlemen. I mean no disrespect to Joel whatsoever. I know that he rejects the Dispensational Premillennial view, but if this doesn't smack of Dispensational millennial earthly kingdom, I don't know what does.

It's Abraham in the physical body living on a physical earth reigning over a physical earth.

I said last night -- and, again, I mean no disrespect whatsoever, but I said last night the direction of some of my close Postmillennial Dominionist friends are going -- if that doesn't sound like Premillennialism, I don't know what does, and I've been debating Premillennialist and Dispensationalists for many, many years. I don't see a whole lot of difference -- now I know Joel is going to say no, no, no, I think this is spiritual, because he said, well, it comes down from God out of heaven. Well, guess what? My Dispensationalist friends say, oh, that's right the New Jerusalem comes down from God out of heaven. And it's Abraham and Isaac and Jacob ruling on a restored earth for a literal thousand years.

Now Joel certainly disagrees with them about the time of the millennium; there's no question about that. But in form and nature, they're saying essentially the same thing.

Don K. Preston's First Negative

Now he said I'll go to Hebrews Chapter 11; I certainly will. Let's go to Hebrews Chapter 11. Keep in mind that Nehemiah was absolutely adamant, in a post-exilic world. Now look what you have. You have Joshua at the time of conquest saying that God gave them all the land. You have the time of the United Kingdom, 1 Kings Chapter 4:20-21 saying they possessed all of the land. You have a post-exilic time saying they possessed all of the land, that God kept all of his promises. And you go to Acts Chapter 7 and actually they're corroborating everything saying the time had come --the fourth generation had come. I don't know how much more evidence we need to accept to know that Abraham and his descendants received that land.

Well, let me go on because I've got so much to cover. But Hebrews Chapter 11, and he said, well, yeah, this is a heavenly country, it's a heavenly city. Folks, remember my arguments on Zion and the Abrahamic hope? Joel hasn't breathed on this argument. He hasn't touched it top, side, or bottom.

ABRAHAM'S (ONE) RESURRECTION HOPE

From Creation (Abel)→ To Noah → To Abraham→ To Moses→ *To Zion!*

There was One Hope!

Those OT worthies anticipated Zion (11:13-16) - the "better resurrection" (11:35)- Zion and the EoM Resurrection are Inseparable– Isaiah 25:6-8!

You cannot divorce Genesis–Noah- Abrahamic eschatological hope from Israel- from the EoM!

Abel's One Hope Was Abraham's One Hope Which Was Israel's One Hope!

"You have come To Mt. Zion!" (Heb. 12:21)

The **One Hope** Was About To Be Realized!

Hebrews Chapter 11 and 12 – now, follow me very carefully. Abraham's hope was the hope of Noah. Noah's hope was the hope of Enoch. Enoch's hope was the hope of Abel. Remember what Paul said that I have emphasized over and over and over again? Where Paul said there is one hope. There is *one* resurrection hope in Hebrews Chapter 11. *One resurrection hope.*

It's interesting to me -- and let me interject a little bit of a discussion of Job right here. All right. Somewhere -- because we're not really certain about exactly when Job was written, but somewhere between Abel and Moses, insert Job. All right? Somewhere in there. I don't care where you put him.

Now, Joel said Job's hope had nothing to do with Torah. He says it is not tied to Torah. Well, what does Hebrews say once again? Abel's hope was Enoch's hope, which was Noah's hope, which was Abraham's hope, which was *Israel's hope.*

Now I want Joel to answer a question. Is the resurrection hope of Job -- and I am not at all convinced that Job was predicting the end time judgment. I hope to get to that material here in a moment.

But if he -- if Job was predicting resurrection, is the prediction of Joel -- excuse me -- Job 19, the resurrection of 1 Corinthians 15:54 or 1 Corinthians 15? I want Joel -- Joel -- Joel and Job are just too close together here. Is -- or are these the same resurrection hope? Is it the *one* resurrection hope?

Remember now somewhere between Abel and Moses you got to put Job. Is Job's resurrection hope the same as 1 Corinthians 15? If it is, what did Paul say? "I preach nothing but the hope of Israel." Israel after the flesh. Now what did Jesus say about Israel's hope found in Torah? "Not one jot nor one tittle shall pass from the law until it is all fulfilled."

Now let me go back to my housekeeping a little bit because this is really important.

> **Joel's Misguided Hermeneutic**
>
> Joel offered three texts where "all" or "the end" are particularized and defined and proclaimed that he had negated my entire argument on Matthew 5
>
> **Joshua 21:43f** – The "all" is defined as the land promises– Where is Matthew 5 particularized?
>
> **Ezekiel 7**- "The end" is specified– Where is "the end" or "all things" limited or specifically identified in 1 Pet. 4?
>
> **Lamentations**-- 6th Century DoJ– context specifies!
>
> Joel is guilty of illegitimate transfer of context.
>
> Joel is arguing that because he finds a text where "all" is not "all" that it negates Matthew 5!
>
> If Joshua/Ezekiel/Lamentations negates "all" in Matthew, it negates ALL in every other context!
>
> What kind of Hermeneutic is This?
>
> Those texts are not discussing what Matthew 5 Is Discussing!

I want you to notice Joel gave three passages last night in which the word all or a definite article is used, and I didn't get around to answering the passages. So in two different speeches Joel pronounced that I didn't address it because I couldn't because they definitively defeat my entire argument. He said I avoided them tremendously. Well, I didn't avoid them; I just didn't have time. Let me address them.

He gave us Joshua Chapter 21 verse 43 and he says the all, there, "See Don, all, all, all." Let me make an observation.

The "all" is defined in the context. Remember what Greg Bahnsen said on Matthew Chapter 5. It is "un-particularized." In other words, it's not defined. It's not limited in the context of Matthew Chapter 5. The all of Joshua is defined by the context.

He pointed out Ezekiel Chapter 7, *the end*. The end is near. Seven times in Ezekiel Chapter 7, as a matter of fact. Well, Joel says, "Don, that was the fall of Jerusalem in A.D. 70, (circa—586 BC) therefore the end is a qualified or limited end." That's right.

Don K. Preston's First Negative

He gave us a Lamentations, likewise. Lamentations is about one event. The fall of Jerusalem in 586 B.C. Now I want to suggest to you, ladies and gentlemen, that Joel is guilty of what is known as illegitimate transfer of context.

Here's what I mean. Listen. Neither Joshua or Ezekiel or Lamentations are talking about passing of the law. Not one of those texts is talking about the passing of the law. Not one of those texts is talking about fulfilling every jot and every tittle of the entirety of Torah. Talking about fulfilling the land promises and all of those land promises were fulfilled.

I want you to notice that this is a really strange and I would suggest a very dangerous hermeneutic. If Joshua and Ezekiel and Lamentation negate the all in Matthew 5, why do not those limited alls also negate the comprehensive all in *any and other context?*

You see what Joel is doing? He's saying, "I have found a couple of exceptions to the comprehensive definition of all, therefore that means that *Matthew 5* can't be comprehensive." Why not? They're talking about totally different alls.

What kind of hermeneutic is this, ladies and gentlemen, in which you go to passages that have nothing whatsoever to do with Matthew Chapter 5, and which are clearly delimited in their own context and you impose that limitation on a text that has no limitations? No limitations.

Again, I would suggest to you that this is a totally untenable hermeneutic. But that's not all. You notice that Joel said repeatedly about my arguments and he said, "Don, I don't see the word final in any of the texts that you give." Now Joel is guilty just like Kenneth Gentry, Gary DeMar, and other Dominionists and post-millennialists of another very, very questionable hermeneutic. He distinguishes between text and events because of the use of different words in given texts from one text to another, or the omission of words. For instance, "Don, the word final is not there."

> ### Joel's "Final" Hermeneutic
>
> Joel Distinguishes Between Texts Because of the Use of Different Words, or the Omission of Words, i.e. "Final Is Not There!"
>
> Consider the Following, However...
> Acts 1 Does Not Mention the "Final" Time of the End, The Trumpet, the resurrection, or use the word "parousia" – Like 1 Cor. 15 does
>
> 1 Corinthians 15 does not mention the 1000 yrs, "final end", coming with the angels, opening of the books, the Book of Life of Rev. 20
>
> 1 Thessalonians 4 says not one word about the millennium, the passing of earth and heaven of Revelation 20- the "final end!"
>
> Revelation 20:10-12 Does Not Mention the parousia with the angels, the trumpet, the shout, the "final" end of time!
>
> Yet, Joel says these texts are the same
>
> **Different Elements– Or Omission of Elements / Words– Does Not Demand "Different times or Topics in Apocalyptic literature!**

I want you to consider something with me. Acts 1 does not mention the word final. Not there. Doesn't mention the time of the end. Certainly doesn't mention the end of time. Doesn't mention the sounding of the trumpet, the resurrection, and does not even use the word *parousia*. But Joel believes it's the same *parousia* of 1 Corinthians 15, I believe. If he doesn't, he can correct me on that.

First Corinthians 15 simply does not mention the one thousand years, the millennial reign of Christ. It's not there. Doesn't mention the final end at all. Doesn't mention the coming of the Lord with the angels and the opening of the books. It does not mention the book of life, but Joel believes that the resurrection of 1 Corinthians 15 is the same resurrection of Revelation Chapter 20.

Don K. Preston's First Negative

1 Thessalonians 4 says not one word about the millennium or a thousand years, the passing of heaven and earth, like Revelation 20, but Joel believes they speak of the same event.

Revelation Chapter 20:10-12 does not mention the word *parousia*. Doesn't mention the Lord's *coming*. Doesn't mention the coming with the angels, the trumpet, the shout, or the *final end*. And yet Joel says all of these texts are the same.

Ladies and gentlemen, we have to understand; different elements, omission of elements, the use of different words in apocalyptic literature does not demand different times or different events in apocalyptic literature.

I can demonstrate this over and over and over again by Old Testament texts that described the kingdom when it would come for instance. There would be no? lions there. And in other texts describing the identical event, the identical time which says there would be lions there. Well, is that a contradiction? No.

It is that apocalyptic language cannot be screwed down so tight like that as to say, "Well, Don, the word final is not in any of those words, or passages that you gave, therefore it cannot refer."

Okay. I've got to hurry. We talked about the passing of the law, and Joel says Hebrews Chapter 8 was not the passing of the law itself; it is the *administration of law that died*. Folks, that's just simply false.

PASSING OF THE <u>LAW</u>- OR ADMINISTRATION?

Joel says it was not the law that died in AD 70, but "the administration of the law."

This is false!

Hebrews 8 does not mention "administration" It mentions **"the covenant"**- **"I will make a new covenant. He has made the first (covenant) old…"**

Hebrews 7:10-12- "The priesthood being (present tense) changed, **there is made of necessity a change of the law.**

Don K. Preston's First Negative

Hebrews does not mention administration. Here's a classic example. Joel says that if the word's not there, then that's not it. Well, the word administration is not in Hebrews Chapter 8. So I use his words or his hermeneutic and see what he thinks. It does, however, mention *covenant*. I will make a new covenant. He has made the first (elliptical statement), meaning the first *covenant*, old, that which is old, which is the covenant, is ready to pass away.

Now notice Hebrews Chapter 7, verses 10 and 12. The writer speaks of a priesthood of Christ, and says is the priesthood *being* present (active -- indicative in the Greek) -- being changed there is made of necessity a change of the *law*. That's not administration; that's the law itself.

Now, I must indeed go on. He says once again that the Abrahamic promise is not tied to Torah. Go with me to Galatians Chapter 3 very, very quickly. I've called attention to this. Joel basically ignored it. Galatians Chapter 3:17 and following. "This I say that the law," which was 430 years later -- that's later than Abraham- "cannot annul the covenant that was confirmed before by God in Christ that it should make a promise of no effect. For if the inheritance is of the law, it is no longer promise but God gave it to Abraham by promise. What purpose then does the law serve? It was *added* because of the transgressions until the seed should come."

Now watch this, folks. He doesn't say that the promise made to Abraham was modified, deleted, or annulled or different from Torah.

He says the law was added to the Abrahamic promise. By the way, I've got to take note of this. Remember what Hebrews 12 says about the Abrahamic hope? Do you remember what Joel says? Let's look at it again.

Don K. Preston's First Negative

THE HOPE OF ABRAHAM

ABRAHAM'S HOPE? (Heb. 11-12; Abraham longed for Zion, Banquet, Resurrection
Fulfilled in AD 70- Joel (Mat. 8 / Rev. 21-22)
ABRAHAM'S HOPE? Isaiah 25→ 1 Cor. 15–Rev. 20 foretold Zion, Banquet, Resurrection- Unfulfilled-- (Rev. 20)??
Joel, what is the difference?
What is the hermeneutic of distinction between these Zions, Banquets, Resurrections?   This is an un- Biblical Two Hopes!

Abraham longed for *Zion*, Matthew Chapter 8. He longed for the banquet -- or I should say Hebrews Chapter 11 and 12. And he longed for the resurrection.

Now, again, I want you to ask yourself -- and listen very carefully to see if Joel answers the question. Is the resurrection of Hebrews Chapter 11 that Abraham longed for, is it the resurrection of Zion of Isaiah 25? Well, of course it is because it's linked with Zion.

When were the Zion promises fulfilled? What did Joel say about it? I read the quote two or three times last night. All of the promises concerning Zion have been spiritualized. Well, okay, let's see.

He says Abraham's promise has to be physical -- has to be physical. No, the resurrection promise is the Zion promise and he says the Zion promise has been spiritualized, and fulfilled.

Okay. I've got to go back here, because I want to get this. I'm running out of time far, far too quickly.

I want you to notice something. Okay. We talked about *genetai* and Joel sought to escape the force of this claiming that the word does not mean fully accomplished. And I offered 1 Corinthians Chapter 15 verses 54 where Paul said that this, quote, "final resurrection," which was the hope of Israel after the flesh, to be fulfilled at the end -- the end of Israel's Old Covenant age, not the end of the Christian age, would be fully accomplished at the time of the fulfillment of Isaiah Chapter 54 (sic—Isaiah 25).

Now the question for Joel is, is that when the resurrection would be fully accomplished? Jesus said that "this generation shall not pass until all of these things are fulfilled. "Now I want you to pay very, very careful attention to 2 Timothy 2:18.

Joel on Genetai
Joel sought to escape the force of genetai claiming that the word does not mean fully accomplish.
I offered 1 Cor. 15:54– which Joel takes as the "final accomplishment" of Isaiah 25:8!
Matthew 24:36– This generation shall not pass until all these things are fulfilled (genetai)
2 Timothy 2:18- Hymenaeaus– The resurrection has already passed
If Joel's multiple resurrection theory is correct, Hymenaeus was right!
If Joel is right about all things being fulfilled at the Cross, Hymenaeus Was Right!
How could Paul condemn him???

Paul said Hymenaeus and Philetus "overthrow the faith of some saying the resurrection has passed already," *Genetai*.

Wait a minute. Joel told us last night that Isaiah 25 and the resurrection was accomplished, fulfilled, in the cross, *at the cross*. He said *genetai* doesn't mean fully accomplished. Well, listen to me really carefully.

If the resurrection promise was accomplished by Christ on the cross, then what was the problem with Hymenaeus saying the resurrection has been accomplished?

Maybe Hymenaeus was just simply saying what Joel was saying. Oh, but wait. If Hymenaeus was saying the resurrection was accomplished by Jesus on the cross, Paul said, Hymenaeus you're wrong.

Don K. Preston's First Negative

If Joel is right about the all things being fulfilled at the cross, then Hymenaeus was right after all. But Joel is going to say, oh, no, no, no, Hymenaeus was saying it was actually accomplished. It had come to be that is exactly right, because that's what *genetai* means.

Let me catch something else. Let me go to John Chapter 5. I want you to notice, ladies and gentlemen, in John Chapter 5 Jesus predicted the resurrection of the just and the unjust. He was predicting the resurrection of Daniel Chapter 12.

Now let me put it like this. The resurrection of John Chapter 5:28-29, this is a chart -- this is an argument that I made three times last night. It was completely ignored.

Restoration -In the Fullness of Time
God's *ultimate plan* was to reunite heaven and earth– Eph. 1:9-10- Edenic eschatology This is "end of the millennium" eschatology- "The restoration of all things" (Acts 3) That purpose was to be accomplished "in the stewardship of the fullness of times." <div align="center">**John the Baptizer** initiated the restoration! The fullness of time was present – Gal. 4 The goal of the ages had arrived- 1 Cor. 10 All the prophets foretold "these days" Acts 3 The time of fulfillment / restoration was present</div>

God's ultimate plan -- ultimate plan was to reunite heaven and earth; that's Genesis eschatology. This is end of the millennium resurrection eschatology, the restoration of all things, is the resurrection of John Chapter 5. Joel agrees with that. But that purpose was to be accomplished in the stewardship of the fullness of time, Ephesians Chapter 1 verse 10.

Now I want you to notice, John the Baptizer initiated the process of restoration. John was Elijah who was to come and to fulfill all things, Matthew Chapter 17:10-12, and Elijah has already come, Jesus said. But watch, the fullness of time was present, which is the time for the

Don K. Preston's First Negative

fulfillment -- restoration of all things. The reconciliation of heaven and earth, the restoration Eden.

Paul said in 1 Corinthians Chapter 10 and 11 -- boy, you got to catch this. Paul said the end of the ages has come. Now please listen to me very carefully.

Joel says the true goal in the word there is *telos* meaning goal. Paul said the goal of the ages has come upon us. Greek for *katantao* meaning the destination has arrived. In other words, all previous ages pointed to the end -- to the goal. Paul said the goal of all the previous ages has arrived.

It's interesting that Paul said that the resurrection was the hope of Israel to which they hoped to attain, *katantao*, Acts Chapter 26. But watch.

Peter, in speaking the restoration of all things, which is the resurrection of Job, which is the resurrection of Abraham, which is the restoration of Eden, Peter said all of the prophets spoke of *"these days."* Joel says no, they didn't. They spoke of your future and mine. They spoke of some time at the end of an indeterminate period of time which some Dominionists say may be as long as 30,000 to 40,000 years away. That violates what Peter said.

Paul said the fullness of time for the restoration for reconciliation of both heaven and earth, Genesis eschatology, was the fullness of time and it was there. He said the goal of all the previous ages had arrived. Peter said all the prophets who spoke of the restoration of all things, spoke of his days. Just like Joel (sic—Job) said at the last, "My redeemer shall stand upon the earth."

Peter said that Christ had been revealed in "these last days." Their salvation -- their eternal salvation -- their eternal inheritance was about to be revealed, because the coming of Christ, when he would judge the living and the dead, at his appearing in judgment, the end of all things had drawn near. The time for *the judgment*, the judgment of *the living* and *the dead* had come. I'll leave it at that.

Joel McDurmon's Second Affirmative

****

Well, thanks to Don for a very vigorous response. Yesterday the burden of proof was on him, and I had the hatchet. Today the burden of proof is on me, and he's got the hatchet. It's always good to have it feel like what you did to the other guy.

This idea that I'm trapped in Luke 20 because of the passing of the ages, I would draw your attention to the parallel versions of this; first, Matthew 22 and Mark 12. In both of these passages, the evangelist only records Jesus talking about the resurrection. There is no mention of this age and that age. Now I don't want to be guilty of this, "It's not there," so we don't want to get into that. But I will bring your focus to the fact -- your attention to the fact the focus in this narrative in the other gospels is specifically on the resurrection.

And we get to Luke, and Luke records what must have been a little bit more of the discussion. And he says the children of this age marry and are given in marriage. But they which shall be accounted worthy to obtain that age and the resurrection from the dead neither marry nor are given in marriage. Neither can they die anymore, et cetera, et cetera, et cetera.

Does this pose a problem for me seeing that I do make the distinction throughout scripture between this age, spoken in that era as being the Mosaic age and to the age to come as the Christian age, if you want to call it that? And therefore, we have to deal with this reality that there is no marrying or giving of marriage and this must therefore be what Paul is talking about in Galatians 3:24-25, "There's neither male nor female."

I think if you just pay close attention to the text, you'll realize that there's a fallacy being pulled here. Well, I shouldn't put it that strongly; I wouldn't accuse Don of making a fallacy. I just think there's an oversight.

The children of this world marry and are given in marriage. But they which shall be accounted worthy to obtain that age and the resurrection of the dead neither marry nor are given in marriage.

Joel McDurmon's Second Affirmative

Now, again, consider the context of the other evangelists. The focus here is on the resurrection, that neither marriage or giving of marriage isn't focused on the resurrection. Luke does add fuller context of this age and that age, but of course those that obtain that age were believers. The other ones weren't going to make it out anyway. I don't think the focus is on here. And in Luke, in narrative Jesus is giving two criteria. One is that you're in the new age, which must have been that they were regenerate; and the second is in pertaining to the marriage issue, the resurrection.

If not, this does force us to take seriously the issue of physical marriage. If those who will make it into the new age, if that's what he's saying, neither marrying or given in marriage, then folks, we shouldn't be marrying or giving in marriage in this age. Now I don't care what Galatians 3 says about male or female. That whole passage is talking about how is a person justified. And you know the arguments that are going on in the book of Galatians. They're dealing with Jew verses Gentile. Distinctions in which this person can be saved and that person can't because they're not circumcised. And Paul blasts that out of the water by saying it's not by works, it's by faith. And in faith in Christ there are no distinctions. It doesn't matter if you're Jew or Greek, barbarian, slave or free; even male or female doesn't exist. This is about justification, folks, not about the nature of the kingdom in general.

Jesus is talking about something that is fundamental to the age and the resurrection. Now if you believe you're living in the age after the resurrection, then you have an obligation to take that marriage passage seriously. This is not one of these arguments as Don wants to dismiss it, where if preterism is true therefore this, and this is scary, so preterism is not true. I didn't make that argument. You didn't hear me put a "therefore" like that on there. This is what I call sort of like *reductio absurdum*. Where you take an opponent's position, you drive it to its logical conclusions of what must be true, and you show that that's an absurdity. Not just scary, not just, "I don't want to do that." Absurd.

And you and I know that in this age we still struggle with sin. We still struggle with the lusts of our bodies. We still have reproduction. And to not have marriage is a big thing, folks. It's absurd. And to try to get out of it by saying, well, in Christ neither male or female is to introduce that dualism I talked about last night.

Joel McDurmon's Second Affirmative

Well, up there in heaven, we're not really married. Down here we're having the time of our life. But some of your full preterist friends have seen the fallacy of that dualism. I know people, friends of friends, who have disbanded their marriage because of full preterist and they see the logic of it and they've done it. There's no getting around this. If you believe you're in this age and post-resurrection, marriage is gone. And don't tell me that that's a ridiculous argument to be dismissed, as oh, if preterism is true, whatever.

Preston introduces this notion that this resurrection spoken of here is the Edenic Abrahamic comprehensive hope. This is one of Don's Frankensteins where he has gone all over scripture and quoted all of these things together and said they must be the same thing, and, therefore, I can talk about them in this way. And I do believe there is a comprehensive hope. But this issue about one hope just needs to be -- hold on. You can't say there's one hope in Ephesians 4. Paul's talking about there's one hope, one Lord, one faith in the baptism. Then go over to Hebrews 11 and see faith is the substance of things hoped for and things not seen, and say, oh, there's hope, so that one hope must be this one hope, and then therefore it's Abel's hope and Noah's hope and Enoch's hope and everybody else's hope. They've got the same hope; it's an Edenic Abrahamic comprehensive hope. Talk about a word that doesn't appear in scripture.

First of all, pay attention to what Hebrews actually says. Faith is the substance of things -- plural -- hoped for. It's one word. It's a plural passive participle, (*elpizomenon*), and it's plural. Well, I got accused last night of you must believe in many hopes. Here's many hopes right here. Many things hoped for.

And indeed, in that list, people were hoping after different things that they overcame. How do you know what they had in mind? That ultimately they were all looking down the line at Jesus Christ and the resurrection of A.D. 70 especially?

By faith Noah went through the flood. I think he probably had his mind on the flood and not much else.

Joel McDurmon's Second Affirmative

By faith others did other things. I think they were hoping for many things. It's not the emphasis on hope on that passage. It's certainly not an emphasis on one single hope through that passage. The emphasis is on their faith and the person they put it in.

Let me just address one more part about the Luke 20 issue. This issue about prior to the fall of Adam and Eve, they married and gave in marriage, and therefore this is pre-fall and Joel believes in Eden restored as an object of the full restoration, and therefore why can't there be marriage in that part? You know, I may have used the phrase paradise restored or something like that, Eden restored somewhere. That certainly doesn't mean I believe there's marriage at that time, especially when Jesus said it's not going to be. I think that's ridiculous to impute to me, a straw man, that I have never said publicly or written anywhere. Now, I should back up. Possibly I have written that somewhere, but I can't imagine that I ever did it. If Don finds it, I'll be glad to revise it as necessary.

The Pharisees believed in physical resurrection. And he said that I used this argument last night, physical resurrection. But were they right? I never said they were right. I'm the one that criticized Don for going to the Jewish exegetes. I didn't say that. That's just another straw man. And then he tried to bring it in and say, well, they believed in a physical kingdom too, and they were wrong about that, therefore they must be wrong about the physical resurrection. I don't think they were wrong about the physical kingdom. I think they were wrong about the nature of the physical kingdom and the timing of the physical kingdom. But who cares what they said. I'm not basing my arguments on Jewish exegetes.

The Abrahamic land promises. Dan -- or Don, I'm sorry -- you called me Job. I can call you Dan. It feels like Job being up here sometimes, I've got to say. But I'm not ripping my skin off yet.

Don quoted a few verses apparently to controvert the idea that Abraham received the land promise. Folks, not a single one of those verses addressed Abraham himself. The only one that got close was Nehemiah Chapter 9 verses 6-7. I'll flip to it and read it. Starting at verse 7 and 8: "Thou art the Lord thy God who didst choose Abram and brought him forth out of Ur of Chaldees and gave him the name Abraham and found his heart faithful before thee and made a covenant with him to give the land of the

Joel McDurmon's Second Affirmative

Canaanites, the Hittites, and the Amorites, and the Perizzites, and the Jebusites, and the Gergashites, to give it *to his seed*. And you have performed those words, for You are righteous."

I don't know if Don paid attention when I went through that argument, but I said, "Yeah, the seed inherited it"; Joshua 24:43-45 proves that. So, yeah, the seed inherited it in there. They inherited it again at the United Kingdom. They inherited it again in the Nehemiah 9. Not Abraham.

And quoting all these passages imputing that to Abraham through his seed will not work, folks. If that's the case, then *Stephen is a liar*. Stephen clearly said God gave him no inheritance, not even a foot -- not a single foot in the land. And Don seemed to think that I missed the fact that he sojourned there and he did dwell in the land, but he never inherited it. Folks, you've got to deal with this.

I was accused of missing part of the context, and if I remember correctly, the implications was that I deliberately left this out, so you wouldn't see it, and therefore, you know, not know the weaknesses in my argument. Well, look at Genesis 15. I'll read you the passage. You know this is said in Acts 17. Chapter 7 verses 17-18. "But when the time of the promise draw nigh which God has sworn to Abraham, the people grew and multiplied in Egypt until another king arose and knew not Joseph."

Don thought he had me really trapped here -- backed in a corner. This is clearly the promise God gave to Abraham that these people would be brought out and dwell in the land. All you got to do is flip back and realize that its -- yeah, it's the promise that he made about his *seed*. Again not to him personally inheriting the land, to his seed.

Verse 13 of Chapter 15. "And he said to Abram, know of a surety that thy seed shall be a stranger in the land that is not theirs and shall serve them, and they shall afflict them 400 years. And also that nation whom they shall serve will I judge and afterwards shall I come out with great substance. And thou" -- catch the power of this. "Shall go to thy fathers in peace. Thou shalt be buried in a good old age. But in the fourth generation, they, your seed, shall come hither again for the iniquity of the Amorites is not yet full." That is the promise Stephen is talking about later in the passage. If

Joel McDurmon's Second Affirmative

he's talking about Abraham inheriting the land, obviously he's contradicting himself, which means the Holy Ghost is contradicting himself.

He didn't contradict himself, folks. Abraham never inherited the land. The only way he can inherit it is if he's resurrected from the dead, period, on the land.

Now Don said a whole lot of things I didn't get to. I have not ignored them on purpose contrary to what some people might say or imply. And, again, if we missed them, like I said last night, bring them up at Q and A tomorrow, we'll do it. Thank you.

Don K. Preston's Second Negative

****

Let me see if I can pick up kind of where I left off as I was responding to Joel's first affirmative, and then I'll do my very best -- dead-level best to get some of the things that he brought up in this.

I find it rather remarkable that he says that he agrees with the Pharisees to a certain extent. Well, it turns out that the Pharisees thought they agreed with Paul. If you will remember Paul was standing before the Sanhedrin, and he said: "Brethren, I'm a Pharisee of the Pharisees. For the hope of resurrection my arms are out this day." And all of a sudden, the Pharisees, who believed in the resurrection, patted him on the back and said what a good fella you are." The Sadducees, of course, still hated him.

Now I want you to catch the power of this (that's my saying, Joel, by the way).

About 14 days passed. Now, Paul is on trial. And he says, "This I confess to you that after the way which they call a sect, so I worship the God of my fathers. I believe *like they do* that there's a resurrection -- about to be a resurrection of the just and of the unjust."

Now, folks, I want to ask you a question. Why -- if Paul and the Pharisees are on the same page in any way whatsoever concerning the nature of the Abrahamic hope, the resurrection hope, the kingdom hope, why do the Pharisees -- we know it's not the Sadducees. Because Paul says they agree with me:"I agree that there is about to be a resurrection," but if they agreed as to nature, why did they want to kill him?

It's exactly like it was in John Chapter 6. The Pharisees wanted to come and make Jesus their king. *He rejected them*. Why? Because their concept of the nature of the kingdom was of a physical kingdom, on earth. And Jesus would have nothing to do with it.

Now remember, the kingdom and the resurrection go hand in hand. You cannot delineate; you cannot divorce the kingdom from the resurrection. So if Jesus rejected the Jewish concept of the nature of the kingdom and the offer of being a physical king on earth, which is where Joel wants

Don K. Preston's Second Negative

Abraham to come and rule. Are we supposed to believe that the same class of people, the same theologically-oriented people, the Pharisees, really do agree with Paul theologically when they want to kill him for his doctrine of the resurrection?

The Jews wanted to kill Jesus because he rejected their concept of the kingdom. The Jews, Pharisees, wanted to kill Paul for his resurrection doctrine. What do we have in common here? Paul and Jesus rejected the Pharisaic notions of the kingdom.

Now Joel says it's a kingdom on earth for Abraham to rule over. For Abraham to live/reign here on earth and he can inherit the world. That's what the Pharisees had in mind evidently. Jesus rejected it. No, it's not a resurrection.

Now I have asked Joel a lot of questions here and Joel says that when we go to Hebrews Chapter 11 because there is a word there, that is "hopes," that I am absolutely wrong to conflate, that is join together, Hebrews Chapter 11, and Ephesians Chapter 4. No, I'm not wrong on that at all.

One Hope or Two?

Joel divorces Israel's eschaton from the Edenic eschatology– This is a false dichotomy.
Matthew 8:11- Abraham- Resurrection- Banquet!

Romans 5 – Death of Adam conjoined with Moses To Christ the solution– **at the end of Torah – Rom. 16:20 (Joel agrees on 16.20) There was "<u>one hope</u>"**

1 Cor. 15.22-55-56 – Death of Adam Subsumed Under Torah– **Conquered at the End of Torah**

Hebrews 11– Abel (Creation) To Abraham- To Moses– **<u>To Zion</u> and the New Heaven and Earth– End of Torah** (11-12)!!

This is One Story- One Hope- One Eschaton!

- **Edenic eschatology Fulfilled-- At The End of Torah**

Don K. Preston's Second Negative

I want Joel to tell us perhaps how many Zion hopes there are in Hebrews Chapter 11. How many spiritual countries are in Hebrews Chapter 11. How many better resurrections are in Hebrews Chapter 11. And, folks, listen to me -- I have made this point repeatedly and Joel has not touched it top, side, or bottom.

The end of the millennium resurrection, the resurrection 1 Corinthians 15 was nothing but the hope of Israel after the flesh. You cannot affirm a yet future resurrection of Abraham, Abraham's resurrection hope was the resurrection hope of Israel. If not, I want *proof*. I want *exegesis*.

Again how many resurrection hopes are found in Hebrews Chapter 11? And if the resurrection hope of Hebrews Chapter 11 is not the resurrection hope of Acts 24, Acts 26, 1 Corinthians 15, I want proof for it.

So, the resurrection hope of 1 Corinthians 15 is the hope of Abraham. But the hope of Abraham and the hope of 1 Corinthians 15 was the hope of Israel after the flesh. And remember Jesus said, "Not one jot, not one tittle shall pass from the law until it is all fully accomplished." Just like 1 Corinthians 15:54 said, "When the corruptible has put on incorruptibility it shall be brought to pass the saying, death is swallowed up." That's when the resurrection will take place on Zion. And let me remind you, once again, Joel says all of the Zion promises have been spiritualized and fulfilled in Christ.

Folks, if the Zion promises have been spiritualized, the resurrection promise to *Abraham* has been *spiritualized*. Just as I showed repeatedly from the Book of Colossians where Paul quotes, cites, and alludes to Genesis 1-3 and applies it spiritually as fulfilled in Christ and the church.

By the way, Joel says that the emphasis in Luke Chapter 20 is not on the ages, it's really on the marrying and getting married. And he says we've got to deal with no marrying and getting married. Well, we've got to deal with this age and the age to come.

And he says he knows preterists who have disbanded. Well, I don't know of any. And whether or not they have or not doesn't prove or disprove. That's that Red Herring argument once again. Oh, look, look, if Don's doctrine is true, look what he has led some people to do. If Don's doctrine is true, look what it might lead to. It's a Red Herring doctrine that Joel McDurmon himself says, "You can't base truth -- or determine truth based on what-ifs."

Paul was dealing with people in 1 Corinthians 7, who were taking Jesus' statement that in the age to come there is neither marrying or giving of marriage, and Paul has to address them because they asked, "If I married and I'm a Christian in the new creation, do I stay married?" And Paul said, "Yes. Do not divorce."

Now did Paul believe that the age to come had broken in? Joel believes it had. But Paul said if you as Christians who are part of the new creation -- 2 Corinthians 5:17, you a part of new creation, and if you're married, *do not get a divorce*.

Joel needs to deal with that. Because Paul is dealing with the concrete objective reality of marriage and the new creation, and he said in the new creation, that is the age to come, that was breaking into Paul's this age, did not nullify physical marriage. What Joel is completely overlooking and ignoring is what I pointed out from Luke Chapter 20, which is in Matthew 22, in the parallel in Mark. It is a contrast of the nature of the covenant worlds.

The Sadducees were assuming, wrongly. So in their argument against the Pharisees – "Well, in the age to come, Torah remains valid. Torah in the age to come, or Torah now, in Jesus' this age, says if a man is married and dies without children, his brother marries her, produce children.

And the Pharisees go, okay. Boy, whose husband will she be? And Jesus said, you do not understand the scriptures. Why? Because in the age to come, Levirate marriage doesn't apply at all. Because the kingdom is not sustained by marrying and giving in marriage. The kingdom is not expanded by producing children through conjugal relationships. The kingdom is expanded by going and telling people the wonderful news of the gospel of Jesus Christ. Under the Old Covenant, they were born into the kingdom. They were then *taught* who they were, what they were. The kingdom was maintained through marrying and giving in marriage. In the age to come, which Joel admits is the Christian age, guess what? We are *taught*, *then* we are born.

Don K. Preston's Second Negative

By the way, Joel brought up another Red Herring argument. He said if Don is true, then we shouldn't be teaching anyone anymore. No, it's exactly the opposite. Because we are not born first into the family of God. We have to be *taught*, then born. And when we are born into the family of God, then we all know him from the least of the greatest. It's not a denial of evangelism. That's a misunderstanding, *completely*, of the nature of Fulfilled eschatology.

Okay. Let me go on very quickly. He brought up John Chapter 5 and John Chapter 6..

Now I've introduced Daniel Chapter 12 repeatedly. I have said repeatedly, I have offered the argument, Daniel Chapter 12. Number 1, it is the promise of the resurrection. It is the resurrection at the end of the age. It is the resurrection to eternal life.

I want to know is that the resurrection that Abraham longed for? Is it a different resurrection hope from Daniel who is told, "Go your way, you shall rest with your fathers until the time of" the end, and you shall arise to your inheritance at the time of the end? Not the end of time. Not the end of the Christian age. The time of the end.

Now, Daniel was going to receive eternal life. Daniel would be dead in the grave at the time of the end and the resurrection. Abraham would be dead in the grave when he would receive the heavenly city and the heavenly country.

Now I want you to go to Revelation Chapter 11:15 and following.

The seventh trumpet sounded -- trumpet sounded. And by the way, Joel believes that the sounding of the seventh trumpet was in A.D. 70 when the mystery of God was completed. Daniel -- or excuse me, Revelation Chapter 10:7 at the end of Israel's Old Covenant age at the fall of Jerusalem in A.D. 70. "At the sounding of the trumpet a great voice said the kingdoms of this world had become the kingdoms of our God and of his Christ, and they shall rule forever and forever."

Don K. Preston's Second Negative

I just have to say this: Joel says, "Preston, you need to explain how saints rule on the earth." Well, in Ephesians Chapter 2, a passage that Joel brought up, Paul is writing the first century living saints, and he said, "You been raised together with him and seated in heavenly places." They were ruling with him at the right hand.

Now what kind of a rule was that? If you would have looked at it from the external sources, just like in the Book of Revelation in which Jesus used the word that *Nikao*, victory, conqueror, to him that overcomes of the one that conquerors, I will give this. But if you looked at them in their earthly state, you would have said, "They're winning?"

Revelation Chapter 11, "The time has come for the dead to be judged and the rewarding of the prophets." Well, here is Daniel, who is dead in the grave. He's a prophet, but the time for the rewarding of the prophets is in A.D. 70. Now I want you to contemplate the following, ladies and gentlemen.

If Abraham received the Zion promise, which is the promise of incorruptibility and immortality, according to 1 Corinthians 15 and Isaiah 25, the resurrection on Zion. Okay?

If Abraham received eternal life in A.D. 70, (Joel says he did), Matthew Chapter 8. If Daniel received eternal life in A.D. 70, then they got their reward long before you and I ever get ours. You know what Paul had to say about that? Hebrews Chapter 11:39-40, his generation and the Old Covenant saints were going to enter into the inheritance together.

Do you mean to tell me that the first century saints, the Old Covenant saints received their eternal inheritance, eternal life, incorruptibility, and immortality in A.D. 70 and you and I are still waiting on it? We've got a different hope than they did if that's true. Paul said, no: One hope. The hope of Israel after the flesh.

To be fulfilled Paul said, when the law, that is the strength of sin, as I have said repeatedly, which is Torah, because only one law is the strength of sin and that's the Old Covenant law. Paul said, I have not known sin except "the law," Torah, said "thou shalt not covet."

Don K. Preston's Second Negative

The resurrection, the end of the millennium resurrection, 1 Corinthians 15, the hope of Abraham, Isaac, and Jacob, the hope of Daniel, the reception of eternal life. According to Joel himself was in A.D. 70. If they got their reward, we have our reward. Thank you.

Joel McDurmon's Third (Final) Affirmative

****

I'm going to kick off with some of his earlier comments. I'll try to get through the responses he's made in the last go around too. If I don't, again, like I said multiple times now, anything that I miss, I'm not doing it on purpose. I'm not ignoring it. Bring it up tomorrow and I'll give it a shot.

Job 19. First of all, it says we don't know where it was written. It has to be inserted however somewhere between Abel and Moses. I think most scholars agree with that.

He attributed to me that I said that it had nothing to do with Torah. I did say that about Abraham and I'll talk about that in a minute. I don't remember saying that about Job. But it does bring up an interesting question. The only thing we know about Job's nationality is written as an appendix to the Septuagint version, which is the Greek translation made of Job in the second century B.C. or forward, somewhere; we're not sure when it was completed.

And there is an addendum on there about Job's lineage and he was actually a son of one of the son's of Esau. So he was not through Isaac, if that's correct. Which would bring up the question whether he was ever under Torah or not as a Jew. That's an open question. I'm sure Don has some kind of answer for it. He's writing feverishly. But whether that's true or not, I didn't make that statement. I don't remember.

Is Job's resurrection hope the same as the New Testament resurrection? I have a definitive answer to that actually. It is yes and no.

As I tried, labored to explain last night, we have this mistaken concept of fulfillment as a single prediction and a single fulfillment and nothing else can happen except those two things and so when I see this fulfillment in the New Testament, it has to be done, final, over with. And I gave you multiple examples through the scriptures of where that is simply not the case. Don says it has to be defined by its context, and to a certain extent I agree. But number one, like I said last night, you would not have known that living at the time. And number two, what is our context? What we're arguing over. So you can't assume one way or another and assert. But my

Joel McDurmon's Third Affirmative

position since last night has been when the curse is finally removed from this earth, then we'll know if it's fully fulfilled. If death is reversed-- Adamic death -- and really that's what this argument is boiling down to. Does the curse involve physical death? Preston has to say no to maintain his position, and therefore say that the death and corruption that we undergo is part of God's good creation that he pronounced good and very good. And therefore the corruption that follows with the decay and corpse -- which the entire rest of scripture describes as something to be avoided, something disgusting, something vile as the very image of death itself -- was part of God's good original design. I just don't see that.

But Don went through a few passages where "all" has to be defined in context. Well, like I said, I agree with that to a large extent, but you wouldn't have known that at the time. He said none of them were talking about the passing of the law. In what time or place was the promise of the passing of the law part of the law? Why would those people have expected anything like that? Why would they have thought some day this law is going to pass away and then we're going to know the final end has come. There is nothing like that in the law. Maybe I'm wrong about that. I'd be glad to hear it and talk about it.

Then Don went to this part about when I am guilty of distinguishing between text and events by different or omitted words. I hope you notice what he was doing there and caught some of the irony of it. Essentially what he was doing was taking my very tactic by which I pulled the rug out of his arguments last night and his entire methodology for his fulfillment, and he tried to turn the tables back on me. Saying that, well, since I see a distinction over here or I see a word omitted here that I make this absolute argument on there to say therefore it can't be done. And I would agree with him to a large extent on that. You can't do it. You can't do it either way. You can't say, well, these two words are similar or even these two words are the same and therefore it must be the same event all the time. And it must be happening at the same time. You can't do that with scripture.

And I would agree, just because a word is missing here or a word is missing there doesn't necessarily mean they're different topics or times.

Joel McDurmon's Third Affirmative

I was the one trying to argue with you last night that scripture is not put together like that. And lo and behold, praise the Lord, Don Preston comes along tonight and confirms my position. He said apocalyptic language cannot be screwed down like that. Thank you. That's all I was trying to say. And I agree. It can't be screwed down in that way, either for or against.

Galatians 3:17 and forward was brought up, I forget exactly what it was -- how it was supposed to dismiss my position. It says, "And this I say that the covenant that was confirmed before of God in Christ the law which was 430 years after cannot disannul, that it should make the promise of none effect. For if the inheritance be of the law, it is of no more of promise, but God gave it to Abraham by promise. Wherefore then serves the law? It was added because of transgressions until the seed should come to whom the promise was made and it was ordained by angels in the hand of a mediator."

To me that more establishes my position, in which I said -- this is where I brought in the comment about Torah having nothing to do with it.

Torah had nothing to do with the promise -- the land promise given to Abraham. And I quoted a scripture to back that up. I didn't see Don reference this in any of his rebuttals. Maybe he is saving it for the last.

Romans 4:13. "For the promise that he should be the heir of the world" -- and there Paul is changing the promise from just land, earth, to the entire world, *cosmos*, "was not to Abraham or his seed through the law, but through the righteousness of faith." That's all Paul's affirming in Galatians 3:17, that this didn't come through the law. There was a promise there, the law, came, yeah. And we can even say the law passed away. But it's coming and going had no effect whatsoever on the land of promise made to Abraham.

The refusal to deal with *genetai*. I was accused of saying this doesn't mean fully accomplished. I didn't say that in general. I said that's not necessarily the case. I quoted you from one of the most preeminent authorities, Lexicons whose first sentence after the inquiry of *genomai* is "capable of many translations." That's all I did. And I said therefore you can't go to any given verse and necessarily impress a particular meaning on it and say, oh, well, this means fully accomplished, therefore it's over with, done, and

Joel McDurmon's Third Affirmative

final. You can't do that. Again, the language -- not just apocalyptic language but all biblical language-- is not meant to be screwed down like that.

As origin of Matthew 5:17 and forward, I agree. In a way it depends on how you understand it. Don and I understand it differently. The law was fulfilled in Christ, in the person and finished the work of Christ. In the cross and resurrection and the ascension. That was done, but I can tell you one thing that doesn't mean, and that is that it was not abolished. Because that's exactly what Christ is saying. "Do not think that I have come to destroy or abolish the law or the prophets. I did not come to destroy, but to fulfill. For verily I say unto you until heaven and earth pass, not one jot or one tittle in the law shall in no wise be destroyed, passed from the law till all be destroyed," (fulfilled). Now one thing I do know is that in these passages, there's a clear contrast being drawn between destruction or abolishing and fulfillment.

Now I said last night, I'm not sure that we have a fully good understanding of what fulfillment is. I've shown you ways where Don's absolute use of it doesn't work. But one thing I know it doesn't mean is abolish and do away with.

We are invited to look at these other passages of *genetai*, Corinthians 5:54, Matthew 24:36, 2 Timothy 2:18. I would agree with Don. The context is going to determine a lot how we apply those words in those contexts in those passages. So, yeah, it may mean fully accomplished. It may mean some other shade of meaning. I'm okay with exploring those and for what they mean.

Besides I also gave you something last night for when words are definitively used to say things are fulfilled, and then they happen again later. Over and over and over. So I'm perfectly fine with saying that a resurrection in 1 Corinthians 15, Daniel 12, any of those passages happened in A.D. 70. And I have said this on many occasions. I think I said it last night. But is the curse removed? No. Is physical death gone? No. And that is the issue we really have to deal with.

This business about the Pharisees agreeing with Paul, and then all of sudden they realized it was a a completely different understanding. Paul was on a completely different page, and therefore they sought to kill him.

Joel McDurmon's Third Affirmative

That wasn't the reason they sought to kill him. They weren't arguing over the nature of the resurrection. Show me that in the text. I hear all these appeals for exegesis. Here's my appeal for exegesis. Where did they say "wait a minute, you're interpreting the resurrection as a prologue, we didn't realize that. I think we want to kill you."

Now obviously that's too much for me to ask to have that literal of a rendition put in scripture. But you think there would be something if that was the case. No, they wanted to kill Paul because he said it was being fulfilled in Jesus. They wanted to kill Paul because he was claiming Jesus was the Messiah. Same reason Paul was killing them to begin with -- or the other Christians to begin with. And news of this doctrine spread throughout all the regions. Of course when they found out what he was talking about and saying it had already happened in Jesus, and therefore the destruction of Jerusalem was coming, which was again brought upon the Jews in another chapter of Acts. Of course they wanted to kill him. It wasn't because they had a different definition of resurrection.

The same thing with these ideas of Jesus rejecting the earthly rule. The people wanted to come and make him an earthly ruler. But Jesus rejected that. Therefore, Preston implies, if not clearly states, that Jesus rejected their definition of the kingdom. That's not the truth. Jesus knew it wasn't time yet. Which it says throughout the gospels when things like this happened. His time had not yet come.

There will be a future bodily earthly kingdom of Christ with his saints ruling on the earth just as the text says in several places. But Jesus knew it wasn't time for that yet because he had to suffer and die bodily. Suffering came first, then the resurrection and glorification.

And certainly we know that Jesus didn't reject that view. The issue there is, like I said, the timing. So Jesus had a dispute not over the nature of the earthly rule, but over the time texts.

Kingdom on earth. Pharisees had in mind an earthly kingdom, and this was wrong. Jesus rejected this. No, he didn't. He rejected it at the time. Paul certainly didn't reject it because of the verse I just read you a while ago, that Abraham was to become the heir of the world.

Joel McDurmon's Third Affirmative

How many Zions are there in Hebrews, I'm asked. I don't know how many times it's referred to, but I would say it was probably one, maybe two if he's referring to earthly versus heavenly in some contexts. And then we're asked how many spiritual countries are there in Hebrews. Well, there are zero. There is a reference to spiritual Jerusalem, which is a city. But the word country as I told you doesn't apply; it's an anachronism. So we're stretching when we talk in those terms. Now granted we can argue over those things and tickey-tack, granted. But the spiritual country there does not negate the fact that God envisioned and promised to Abraham that he would inherit the land, and through Paul, the world. So yeah, of course, there's a spiritual version of this in heaven; it's the pattern. But as I told you once and it was not controverted; in Revelation 22 that city comes down out of heaven and to the earth.

Don K. Preston's Third (Final) Negative

****

Let me again go back and catch as much as I possibly can so that I can cover as much as he has said.

He kept calling attention to Acts Chapter 7, and he said, "Well, Stephen must have lied." No, I think what is -- what is missing here because very clearly verses -- verse 17 and following says the time had come for the fulfillment of the promise. Now did Stephen lie about saying that the time of the promise? Who was the promise made to? Abraham and his descendents.

There is a concept at work here that is very, very common in scripture, and that is someone receiving something representatively through their descendants. Now that's a perfectly scriptural concept of someone doing something through their descendents.

In Hebrews Chapter 7 and verse 9, *Levi* paid tithes to Melchisedec through Abraham. Now Levi wasn't alive. But Levi paid tithes to Melchisedec. How? Because Abraham his father paid tithes.

Now, could Abraham rule the world, today? I would suggest that Abraham rules the world through the body of Christ through Christ himself. Because it is through the one single seed that that promise was to be obtained and realized, and the seed has come. And Galatians Chapter 3, by the way, makes it abundantly clear, here is the Abrahamic promise: The law was added to that. But the inheritance, the fulfillment of the promise, would come when? Well, Galatians Chapter 4 makes it very clear.

Paul said we were under tutors and guardians until the time of the inheritance. Just like a man would put his children under tutors and guardians until the appointed time, the time of the inheritance. When would the time of the inheritance be? When Old Covenant Israel was cast out. But, you see, Old Covenant Israel was added to that promise.

I hope I didn't misunderstand, but he said the Abrahamic land promise had nothing to do with Torah. Well, I can tell you this, Israel under Torah had absolutely no right to the land unless they kept the Torah. There is an inextricable link between Torah and Abraham's land promise. Genesis makes it abundantly clear. Deuteronomy makes it abundantly clear.

Now I'm only going to reference this again because I want you to realize how powerful this is. Joel is trying to escape the force of it, but Luke Chapter 20.

THE AGE TO COME HAS COME!

> Jesus' "This Age" Was the Mosaic Age- Joel
>
> "The Age To Come" Would Follow Jesus' "this age" And Be The Age
> *Introduced By The Resurrection*
>
> We are living in the "age to come" that followed Jesus' "this age" (Joel)
>
> Therefore, The Resurrection Luke 20 Has Been Fulfilled!
>
> This is the Edenic-Abrahamic- Comprehensive Hope!
>
> *If not, why not?*

Luke Chapter 20 is the end of the millennium resurrection of 1 Corinthians 15. It is the end of the millennium resurrection of Revelation Chapter 20.

Jesus was living in, quote, "this age." Joel agrees. And the state of no marrying, giving in marriage, would come in "the age to come," which Joel agrees is the Christian age. Now do you know what that means by the way? It means the end of the millennium arrived in the first century. I won't go into that. But it is a definitive proof that the end of the millennium arrived. If we are in the state in which there is no marrying and giving of marriage, according to Luke Chapter 20, which would be in the age to come, guess what? The end of millennium has come. Okay.

You just simply cannot miss this. Joel wanted to divert the power of this by saying the focus is not on the ages, but rather it is marrying and giving of marriage.

Don K. Preston's Third Negative
Well, I already pointed out that Paul dealt with those in 1 Corinthians Chapter 7, who were part of the new creation. They were part of the age to come that was breaking into this age. And they believed they did not have to literally stay married. Paul said you're dead wrong.

Now Joel didn't have time to get to that. He did have a lot of material to cover. So I'm not going to accuse him of ignoring it. I hope somebody will bring it up tomorrow. But here we have a concrete example of that very question coming up: Is literal marriage to be practiced in the age to come, in the new creation? Paul said literal marriage is to be practiced in the new creation. You are the new creation; don't you get divorced from your mate. Because Joel is ignoring the simple covenant contrast between the nature of the age -- this age and the nature of the age to come. The age to come would not be the age dominated by Torah.

Let me get to my summary if I can. I want to go back. I want to summarize the things that I have dealt with and presented to you in this debate. And if I have time to get through with this, I'm going to come back to some notes here.

SUMMARY OF THIS DEBATE

I have proven that there was ONE HOPE-- that the One (final) eschatological hope was ***nothing but the hope of Israel after the flesh.***

Joel cannot affirm a final resurrection hope apart from or different from, that ONE HOPE

He cannot affirm a "final" resurrection at the end of the Christian age, without affirming that Old Covenant Israel After the flesh remains as God's covenant people!

That ONE HOPE was From Abel-Israel- and was One Resurrection Hope— This means that Daniel 12 was that one hope and fulfilled in AD 70!!

Paul's ONE EoM resurrection HOPE was the accomplishment (genetai) of the prophecy of Isaiah 25- the Hope of Israel after the flesh!

That one Hope was to be fulfilled on Zion— Joel says "Fulfilled!"

Don K. Preston's Third Negative

I have proven beyond any shadow of a doubt -- ten minutes? Okay. I have proven beyond a shadow of a doubt that there is only one hope. Joel has repeated, says, no, no, no, there are all sorts of hopes. There was one eschatological hope. Paul only had one hope of the resurrection, 1 Corinthians Chapter 15.

Didn't you find it remarkable that Joel said he doesn't have a problem in the world acknowledging that the resurrection of 1 Corinthians 15 was sort of, kind of, fulfilled in A.D. 70, but we're still looking for the end? No, Paul said that that hope that he was looking for, the hope of the resurrection, immortality, incorruptibility would be at the time of the end. The end. That is when the death would be overcome.

Now Joel simply cannot admit that the resurrection of 1 Corinthians 15 could have been fulfilled in A.D. 70 and still have a hope beyond that.

Paul's one resurrection doctrine was nothing but the hope of Israel. I stated this repeatedly. I hope you'll catch this. Paul said when the mortal has put on immortality, when the corruptible has put on incorruptibility, then will be brought to pass the saying, "death is swallowed up in victory." That's Isaiah 25:8 as I have repeatedly, repeatedly, repeatedly pointed out. That resurrection would be fulfilled on Zion.

Joel has admitted, he's on record, he has said, "Well, yeah, the Zion promise has been fulfilled." I pointed out that he is on record of saying the Zion promises have all been fulfilled, spiritualized in Christ. But he wants to somehow say there's something beyond that. No, there's nothing beyond 1 Corinthians Chapter 15.

To admit that 1 Corinthians 15 could have been fulfilled in A.D. 70 is to admit that the definitive, objective, *final* resurrection could have been, and in fact, was. How do I know that? Because it would be when "the law," as I have said repeatedly, which was the "strength of sin," was removed. Not abolished, but overcome.

Joel said there's a huge difference between abolish and fulfilled. Well, obviously, I agree with that. Jesus did not come to negate the law as of no meaning, no consequence, and without being completely accomplished. That's Jesus' point.

Don K. Preston's Third Negative

In Hebrews Chapter 8, the writer there makes it abundantly clear, as I have repeatedly taken note, that the Old *Covenant* -- notice this. The Greek there is not unclear. That Old *Covenant*, not the administration. That Old Covenant was *ready to vanish away*. Just as Hebrews Chapter 7 verse 9-10 that I took note of, "the priesthood being changed there is of necessity a change of law."

Change of *law*, Old Law, getting ready to vanish away. That simply has not been touched topside or bottom.

Let me say again Joel cannot affirm a final resurrection -- a final resurrection hope-- apart from or different from Israel after the flesh's one resurrection hope.

Now, folks, I don't know how to overemphasize this. If you have a resurrection hope that is different from, or divorced from, the Old Covenant promises made to Old Covenant Israel after the flesh (and that is Joel's resurrection hope divorced from Old Covenant Israel after the flesh. God's Old Covenant with Israel after the flesh would remain valid and binding, and that includes, as I have said repeatedly, as I have noted repeatedly, chart after chart showing the Old Covenant Sabbath foreshadowed the end of the millennium, final resurrection), you cannot affirm a yet future resurrection divorced from Israel without affirming that Israel's promises failed or that Torah, is still binding, including the seventh day Sabbath.

Joel has gone on record with this saying, "No, no, no, the Sabbath passed away." He says the symbols of the ceremonies of the Old Covenant were removed, taken out of the way. But do you know what that means? He says that the seventh day Sabbath, and all of the festivals Sabbaths of Israel, were not completely consummated.

Joel would need to answer how many times were Israel's festival Sabbaths -- how many times was Israel's seventh day Sabbaths which foreshadowed the end of the millennium resurrection? How many times was that fulfilled? How many times was it supposed to be fulfilled? It was only supposed to be fulfilled one time at the end of the millennium, at the end of Israel's Old Covenant age. Not the end of the New Covenant age.

Don K. Preston's Third Negative

So let me say again, if the end of the millennium resurrection has not occurred, fully -- been fully accomplished, taken place-- then the seventh day Sabbath and Israel's symbols and ceremonies are still just as binding today as they were in Moses' day. And yet strangely enough what Joel has really affirmed is this, as one of my charts demonstrated. Joel is affirming the passing of *part* of Torah, *some* jots and tittles, i.e., Sabbath, festival sacrifices, feast days, without the fulfilling, without the accomplishment of what those festival Sabbaths and feast days actually foreshadowed.

Is there any way in this world that you could get that out of Jesus' words? Could you ever get out of Jesus' words, "not one jot, not one tittle shall pass from the law until it's all fulfilled", Could you ever get out of that to mean Joel's belief, Joel's doctrine? Now some jots, some tittles are going to pass away before they're ever fulfilled.

Folks, if you've got a doctrine that says some jots and some tittles passed away without it even being fulfilled, that is a direct, incontrovertible, contradiction of the words of our Lord Jesus Christ. I would suggest that's not a healthy doctrine to have.

So, to go back to a point that I made earlier, the one hope of Abraham, Isaac, and Jacob, the one hope of Noah, the one hope of Enoch, the one hope of Genesis, that one hope is labeled in -- as the better resurrection and Zion -- I won't use heavenly country, if you please. And Joel is on record of saying it was fulfilled.

I want to go on, and I want to get to a point very, very quickly. He says again, "I am fully comfortable with the resurrection of 1 Corinthians 15 and Daniel Chapter 12 being fulfilled in A.D. 70," but not -- of course not removed. That won't be until the New Jerusalem comes down in heaven.

Folks, you need to go to American Vision's website in which Joel McDurmon affirms that the New Heaven, New Earth, the New Jerusalem of Revelation 21 and 22 *came down from God out of heaven in A.D. 70!* And what is true of that new creation? What is true of that new Zion? Well, Revelation 21 verse 3, in that new Zion in which you and I now abide, in tabernacles dwelling with Him, He dwells with us. There is no more *the death*.

Don K. Preston's Third Negative

Revelation 22 verse 3-4 in that New Jerusalem in which you and now abide there is *"no more curse no more."* Joel says no other curse hasn't been removed. Yet he tells us the New Jerusalem has come down. God dwells with us, we in His presence. In the New Jerusalem of Revelation 21 and 22 -- which by the way, would be in fulfillment of God's Old Covenant promises made Old Covenant Israel. We now dwell in that city. There is no more *the death*. The curse of Adam has been removed. There is no more curse, *no more*. There is no greater eschatology than that. Thank you.

Question and Answer Session

July 21, 2012.

Mr. Bell: Good morning. Welcome to our Q and A session this morning. I'm sure you all are excited about what's about to take place.

We thank the contenders in the debate. They did an excellent job. We are looking forward to digesting that material as we go along. But today we're going to have some live interchange. It's going to be much faster. And we appreciate all of you for submitting your questions. And we just have a couple of things that we wanted to ask you to do. Number one, remember to turn off your cell phones. Put them on silent. If you have or expect an emergency and you know you're going to have to answer your cell phone, you might want to move to the back so you can step out and not disturb anyone while the Q and A session is going on.

Once again we want to thank all of you for your presence, for your participation. We hope you're well rested because this is going to be a lively exchange.

Thanks again to Joel McDurmon and Don Preston for their work, their labor, and for the information they're about to present.

The next voice you will hear will be Jack Gibbert; he's the moderator for the Q and A session. And he will give you the protocol for this morning.

Jack Gibbet: Good morning. We stayed up until after midnight last night sorting through the questions.

We had quite a few questions to go through. Rod and I stayed up until after midnight last night. And we were very impressed with the quality of the questions. Personal things were the first that were cast aside. We're not going to get into personal stuff with either of the speakers. As these questions are really straight, punchy, right to the point asking the speakers to talk about this or that subject.

We're expecting to give them two minutes and we will give them the two-minute sign. That doesn't mean they're cut off at two minutes; it means, "Come on now let's wrap it on down and hopefully get it finished within the next minute." So we will get a lot of questions answered and dealt with during the first hour. And the second hour we'll get into a little bit more of the nuanced ones. We have some that were almost a thesis -- a doctrinal thesis. And we may get to some of those. But if you wrote one of those or two -- on both sides of the card in small print, you're down at the bottom of the pile somewhere. Just let you know that.

But they were good. In fact, when we read those, I had to say, you know, the guy really put some thought into this, and I really like it, but my goodness, if the guy is going to have two minutes to deal with this, that's not really something we want to have at the front end of the discussion.

So that's pretty well the way it is. We're excited about it and I hope that you are too.

Question to Joel McDurmon: What New Testament coming passages, Joel, point, to a yet future fulfillment? And how which ones don't and can we distinguish between those that do and those that do not?

Joel McDurmon: The question was, "Which New Testament coming passages point to a future fulfillment? And which ones don't, and how do you tell the difference?"

Well, I think that's looking at those texts strongly. Someone actually asked me that this morning when I was explaining my position to them. The reason I talked so much about the fulfillment and re-fulfillment and variations on a theme and that kind of thing, until you come to full fulfillment, is because many of those passages can be seen as both applying to A.D. 70, fulfilled in A.D. 70, but then again remember when we talked about the word fulfilled. It doesn't mean stop. And yet not being fully fulfilled until A.D. 70.

So I don't parse those -- when someone calls me a partial preterist and says, well, therefore you see some of these texts fulfilled and some that aren't, that's not my version or variety. I look at it more as "both-and." There is a fulfillment here, all of these in a sense, and that's why I said last night, that, yeah, I can see a way in which 1 Corinthians 15 and these other passages were fulfilled in A.D. 70. I didn't say the resurrection in 1 Corinthians was fulfilled in A.D. 70, period, it's done. And that is now under the preterist category. Now, I see a fulfillment of it in A.D. 70, but I don't see the full fulfillment of it until the bodies come out of the grave and the curse is removed from this earth.

So how do you distinguish between it? I see them as fulfillments, but they're not fully fulfilled until that final curse is removed from the earth.

And that's just my position on that. I know Don and I disagree with that. He's going to say that death, you know, is only spiritual, speaking in separation of God, and we disagree on that.

But that's how I would see it. I don't see it as drawing lines between some that are and some that aren't. It's "both-and" in almost all cases.

Don Preston: Well, obviously, we do disagree on that. And the question to me revolves around the fact how can you say that 1 Corinthians 15 would have had a fulfillment, but be looking forward to something else? I would simply go back to what I had pointed out before and there was simply one hope. Joel says there has to be a consummative end. So I would like to ask why? Why does there have to be an end?

I'd like to share something with you here. We are told that because there were many Days of the Lord historically, many passings of heaven and earth, as Joel would express that, this demands an ultimate end. Well, I would suggest that Joel has an ultimate end, the end. He calls it "then comes the end of 1 Corinthians 15."

James Jordan has written very well pointing out that the reason that all previous -- if you wish to use the term -- ages, but kingdoms, the reason that they came to an end is because they were somehow *deficient*. They filled a measure of their sin. They were manmade. They were not God's kingdom goal.

God's eschatological promises were not being finally fulfilled. Now the question is, does that apply to the body of Christ? Again, James Jordan said, "Each time that God establishes a new heaven and new earth there comes a time when that system has run its course and is no longer operating either due to sin or due to its historical inadequacy. Then we see that the heavens and earth begin to break apart and then be reconstructed."

So my question is, what is the inadequacy of the Christian heaven and earth? What is the inadequacy of the gospel of Christ? If there must be an ultimate end, i.e., the Christian age, then by all means there's something wrong with the Christian age that necessitates that it comes to an end. I think that is a major -- major problem.

Question to Don Preston: What was the hope of Israel? If you were to ask the leaders of the common people living back at that time, what would they think of as their hope?

Don Preston: Excellent question.

What was the hope of Israel? If you were to ask a common man -- Jew on the street, so to speak- what was their hope, what would they have answered?

I think we can look at that question and the answer to that question in two ways. Number one, there was the misapprehension of the nature of the kingdom. Now I categorically disagree with Joel when he said last night that Jesus did not disagree with the Jews about the nature of the kingdom, just about the timing.

Well, it's interesting to me that in 1 Samuel Chapter 8 -- Chapter 10 and Chapter 12 when Israel desired a physical king on a physical throne God said that request for that kind of a kingdom was a rejection of his sovereignty. In 1 Samuel Chapter 10 after being accused of rejecting God, Israel confessed, "We have committed a great sin this day in desiring a king over us."

1 Samuel Chapter 12, he reiterates it. And the people confess, "We have rejected the Lord God and committed a great sin in seeking a king over us." The reason Jesus rejected a physical throne over a physical kingdom in John 6:15 is not because of a matter of timing. It is because he knew that from the very beginning a physical king on a physical throne over a physical

kingdom was an expression of the rejection of God's sovereignty. I think that is part of the answer.

Now, did the Jews expect that? Some of them obviously did. The second part of the question is, and the real question is, what was the *true* hope of Israel? Paul said, "For the hope of resurrection I stand on trial this day."

Speaking of the resurrection, he said that resurrection hope "to which our 12 tribes hoped to attain." So from Paul's inspired perspective, the proper and true hope of Israel was the resurrection, i.e., the kingdom, because as I have noted there is no dichotomy between the kingdom and the resurrection.

And I would take note of this. Romans 11 verse 7 Paul says, "Israel has not attained that which she or he sought, but the elect has obtained it." So Israel may have had a misapprehension of the kingdom, but that didn't mean there is not a kernel of Biblical truth behind it. And Paul says, you know what, the real truth, the real hope of Abraham, the real hope of Israel is now being achieved by the righteous remnant.

Joel McDurmon: I would agree with Don that what the average Jew on the street thought was the hope and what the hope actually were, were probably two different things. At least in the near side.

There is nothing in John 6:15 that says Jesus rejected taking that throne because it was the wrong way to do things. It just simply says he perceived they would come take him by force to make him a king. And he knew that he had to suffer and die first before he was exalted the glory.

So, going back to 1 Samuel 8 doesn't really solve the problem. Yeah, they rejected God in having themselves a king, not just a *king*, people, a king like other nations to lead them into battle. Okay. God's way of bringing in the kingdom is not through warfare or bloodshed. They were not to have a king *like other nations*. They were not to put their trust in men. If you read the laws for kings in Deuteronomy 17, he makes it very clear you're not to have a standing army. You're not to have a large treasury, which is always a temptation to buy a standing army and to go to war and conquer through that means. You are not to multiply wives, which means you're not -- which back in those days was a way of having foreign alliances with the daughters of other kings. In other words, don't get involved in foreign affairs and entangling alliances as Jefferson said.

So there's this whole list of things you weren't supposed to do and acting like the nations of other places. God says you have rejected me in this regard by asking for a king like other nations. And here's what's going to come upon you for it.

My whole book *God Verses Socialism* is taking 1 Samuel 8 and applying this in society, showing you that the same things that went wrong in that society go wrong in our society. This doesn't mean that they couldn't have a king -- an earthly kingdom in general, especially when God's telling them the meek shall inherit the earth, the saints shall rule on the earth, et cetera, et cetera, et cetera.

So, yeah, there was this hope of resurrection and the new heavens and new earth and all that on the heavenly side, but as Revelation 22 says that kingdom comes down out of heaven, and where do you think it comes? It has to go somewhere. If it's not heaven, where is it? I believe it's on the earth, as per all those other scriptures. And there will be an earthly kingdom of resurrected bodily saints. And that has nothing to do with 1 Samuel 8. 1 Samuel 8 has to do with acting like pagan nations.

And the king in that regard is going to be God himself. Not a king like other nations, not one from among the midst of you, it will be God himself in the flesh who is that king. And in that respect you cannot say they rejected God because it's God himself.

Question to Joel McDurmon: Okay. Since 1 Corinthians 15 says that flesh and blood cannot inherit the kingdom of God, of what use is a physical resurrection?

Joel McDurmon: Well, I don't see that as literally as talking about -- literally talking about the flesh and blood from your body, obviously. I think it's talking about the flesh and blood under the fallen system. That is the fallen flesh and blood that we're constantly told throughout scripture that has to do with fleshly lust and those types of things.

I think it also has to do with Israel after the flesh. We know that ultimately the promise was not to Israel after the flesh. It came through Israel after the flesh. It was to them in the sense that it was -- to them in the Mosaic Covenant, but ultimately the promise was through faith in Abraham.

Well, what happens when John the Baptist comes? Even with the Abrahamic promise it was to him and his seed. And both Jesus and John the Baptist are telling the people of that time period -- that the Jews of that time period, don't think to yourselves that you're children of Abraham just because you're his flesh and blood. Because God can raise up from these stones children of Abraham. Of course we find out in Galatians Chapter 3 that the real seed of Abraham is singular; it's Jesus Christ. And his posterity is all from those who believe in him through faith, not his flesh.

And so I think that's being loaded in -- and keep in mind, there was tremendous Jew and gentile controversy going on in all of Paul's Apostles including 1 Corinthians. And when he's bringing this in, he's contrasting that promise or that covenant, if you will, with the future covenant. That doesn't mean flesh and blood literally cannot inhabit the kingdom of heaven. It just has to be gloried bodies.

There is this distinction that follows right there after it between what is translated as natural bodies and spiritual bodies. But that's not actually what the text says. The Greek word is *psuchikon*. A lot of people confuse that for *phusikon* and translate it as "natural physical." *Phusikon* – where we get our words physics, and physical, physical earth stuff like that. But the word is *psuchikon*. Very similar, but different. And it refers to the psyche, the soul. All through the New Testament, it's translated as soul of life.

So now you have a little bit different contrast between the two types of bodies. Okay? The first Adam is a soul body, *psychical* body. The new Adam is a spiritual body. Well, how different is that, and is that really contrasting to the flesh versus the non-flesh? I don't think it's quite that distinct. I think there are other ideas being loaded in here, and it's easy to look on the surface and make this distinction between the two, but I think there's something deeper at work here.

Don Preston: Well, actually I agreed with an awful lot of what he had to say under the identity of flesh and blood. I don't think Paul's concern there is for us to say physical does not inherit the kingdom of God. That's not his focus.

However, it seems to me when Joel says that flesh and blood has to do with the Old Covenant body, that he overlooks the fact that that flesh and blood has to do with the natural body. Those are direct corollaries with one another. He has shifted from the natural body being *this* that has to be glorified, and then all of a sudden he goes to flesh and blood being the body of Israel, the Old Covenant.

I would also point out that as I see the text, the flesh and blood certainly is Israel as William so eloquently pointed out, and others have. Paul says have you begun in the flesh? Or having begun in the spirit are you now perfected by the flesh? Having nothing to do with the biological fleshly body or a spirit separated from the body.

Paul is talking about the flesh as Joel so eloquently expressed it being an expression of life under Torah verses spirit life in Christ. I don't see how we can shift from the natural body, all of a sudden, to flesh and blood and see natural body is somehow being related to an individual body versus a corporate body in the exact same context. I think that's misapplication.

And by the way, let me point this out. If we take flesh and blood there to be the body of flesh, the body of Moses, if you please, as is called in the book of Jude if we take a body of flesh and blood there to be Old Covenant, then it very clearly places the resurrection of 1 Corinthians 15. The final resurrection -- the end of the millennium resurrection and the context of the putting away of the flesh and blood, i.e., the old body of Israel.

So to suggest that flesh and blood -- and I agree with him a hundred percent there that flesh and blood is not a reference to the biological body; it's the Old Covenant body of Israel after the flesh. Okay.

The resurrection 1 Corinthians 15 would be putting off the body of flesh and blood.

But the putting off the body of flesh and blood is putting off the Old Covenant world of Israel.

Therefore the resurrection of 1 Corinthians 15 would be putting off the old body -- the body, flesh and blood, Old Covenant Israel.

Question to Don Preston: Don, doesn't the curse in Genesis include pain in childbirth? And if the curse is removed, how is it that the pain remains?

Don Preston: If the curse in Genesis is physical, i.e., for instance, childbirth -- am I getting all that in there -- then why is there still pain today?

Well, let me point out and get in as much on this as I possibly can. It overlooks the fact, number one, that even if we acknowledge -- and I say *even if* we acknowledge and agree, that we're talking about physical realities in Genesis, and I have emphasized this before, it completely overlooks how the New Testament writers interpret Genesis.

I think Joel will agree with me. I would certainly hope that he would. That any proper hermeneutic is that the New Testament writers are the divine interpreters of the Old Testament realities.

Now let me carry that forward just a little bit and take note of a chart that I put up the very first night. Does a physical reality, i.e., physical pain and physical childbirth -- by the way, there was obviously physical pain involved in childbirth prior to the curse. Because that pain was supposed to be, quote, "increased." They're supposed to be fruitful and multiply. There was obviously death in the world before this curse. I mean, eating itself demands some kind of a death process. There were, quote, "negative things," if you want to look at them negatively. Obviously, God didn't look as a dying process of eating and procreation involving pain. He didn't see that as any kind of a curse. But Joel has expressed the idea that a physical beginning, i.e., a physical curse of childbirth demands physical alleviation of that.

But, again, that overlooks how the New Testament writers interpret those physical realities. Israel had a literal, physical, temple literal, physical sacrifices. Israel dwelt in a literal land. Israel practiced literal physical circumcision. And it overlooks that this, "curse of Eden" became incorporated into and expressed under the Mosaic Law. And I hope I can have time to do this a little bit later on and to show how passage after passage after passage in the Law of Moses talks about the -- that Edenic curse, uses Edenic curse language and shows that Edenic curse to be solved in Christ in the first century.

But back to this very, very quickly: Joel understands that all of Israel's physical realities were fulfilled and *interpreted* by the New Testament writers, interpreted spiritually. I have demonstrated that in Colossians, Paul uses Edenic Genesis curse language, but he sees it as being overturned and fulfilled in Christ and his body in the first century.

Paul utilizes a process of what is known as *Raz Pesher.* It was a hermeneutic that was well understood in the first century, a Jewish Hermeneutic. That is, the Old Testament prophets did not fully understand what it was they were even describing and predicting, but the New Testament writers were interpreting and explaining what was being talked about and fulfilled in their day. And Peter makes it abundantly clear that it was being interpreted and fulfilled spiritually in Christ. I'll just stop right there.

Joel McDurmon: First, yeah, I would agree. And I think I made this fairly clear in speeches on both nights that in Christ *all of the curse* is borne in his body. All of the law is borne in his body. And he is resurrected as a new creation. Now what that does to the law is a different question. Maybe we'll get to that.

But what that does to the curse is, yes, in Christ there is no curse. And I believe in Revelation 21 and 22, where we're given an idealistic picture of the new heavens and new earth, which I believe is definitively carried out in the church in the heavenly realms -- but I continually go back to the earthly nature of that rule, which is promised over and over in scripture.

And I go back to Daniel 2 verse 35 and 44 where it says, The stone that is cut out without hands will smash the statute on the feet of the statute of the four kingdoms, and that statute will be shattered. And then that stone will grow -- *grow* -- this is an organic process over time -- to fill the whole earth *kal-ara.*

That section of Daniel is written in Aramaic, the Hebrew equivalent is *kal-eretz*. It means the "whole earth." Not a portion of it. Not a piece of it. Not a corner of it. Not a representation of it somewhere else. It's the whole earth.

So when I look at that aspect of the promise, I go back to the traditional Christian view of progressive sanctification, of sanctification in general. It is definitively done in Christ. There is nothing left to be fulfilled. That's why for example the scriptures -- Paul can say Christ abolished death. It was already done. You didn't have to wait until 1 Corinthians 15; you didn't have to wait until A.D. 70 or any other time. It was done. Death was abolished and gone. It was defeated.

Why then can we say later that death is going to going to be defeated again? I thought it was already defeated. Because it's a definitive reality that is meant to be worked out in history as that kingdom grows and fills the earth.

And so, yes, I do believe there is a definitive fulfillment in Christ, but it is going to going to be a reality over time. And as it does that, as we move toward that consummation, wherever it is, the curse is going to going to gradually be removed. Well, I can't say it will gradually be removed. Maybe he's going to wait until the end to do it at a more momentous time.

But to say that there was pain beforehand, before the fall, and therefore because it says it was increased, I think is a little gratuitous. When God says He's going to increase something, it doesn't necessarily mean it existed beforehand. We can make that logically in our language, but again, apocalyptic language is not always meant to be screwed down like that.

So that would be a discussion we can have, but I'm well over my time already. Thank you.

Question to Joel McDurmon: Can you point to any verses that clearly show the final end is projected into our future?

Joel McDurmon: Yes and no. The question is, can I point to any verses that clearly show the final end is projected into our future? And, you know, I feel like I've already explained this many, many times from my own perspective. There is no verse that says the end will be in the future of the 20th century. I mean, that's what you would need to answer that question in the way that he's asking it. There's also no verse that says A.D. 70 is the final fulfillment of everything and there will be nothing else.

So the discussion really is what is the nature of the curse, and what is the nature of the kingdom that is to be fulfilled? Because I've already shown you fulfillment doesn't always mean the end; in fact, it rarely means the end. I've already shown you that you can't drag Old Testament context into the New Testament passages and say this was fulfilled, and therefore all this other stuff must have been fulfilled at this time. And all those things working together completely destroy any attitude of saying everything in A.D. 70 had to be final.

So I look at the passages like 1 Corinthians 15, like Romans 8, like Revelation 20, and I do see, yes, there are near fulfillments on those things. But as long as the physical curse remains on the earth, and childbirth is as terrible as it is and pain -- if you've ever been by the side of a woman who's going through natural childbirth, you know what I'm talking about. Or if you've been a woman who went through it.

And all the other stuff, attending to the curse? What about thorns, thistles? I'm an avid gardener. I don't -- I wish I didn't have to go out there and pull weeds all the time. I think that's all part of the curse, and I think it will be reversed. I think the nature of animals literally will be changed in the future. And, yes, the stuff is appropriated in scripture to explain the Mosaic Covenant to explain aspects of resurrection and death and life and exile and coming out of exile. But why does it constantly go back to that Edenic language? Why does it constantly go back to that language? Why is that physical aspect the dominating metaphor from Genesis to Revelation? Why? Why is it not the other way around?

Now I think that the result there is that is the overarching theme of the entire symphony.

Don Preston: Joel is certainly correct to say that the curse theme and the curse language is reiterated throughout the scripture. It seems to me that it's extremely problematic to say -- as I pointed out last night, to say that you can believe that 1 Corinthians Chapter 15 had a fulfillment in A.D. 70 and yet awaits a future.

I would simply point out, you know, Joel has appealed -- not extensively, and I appreciate this -- but he has appealed nonetheless to the fact that the church historically has always believed in a final consummation. Well, the church historically has never, ever, ever, ever believed that 1 Corinthians 15 has been in multiple applications and fulfillments. That simply is not in church history. If it is, I'd like to see it.

And by the way, every Postmillennialist-- may I use the term Dominionist-- because Joel prefers that. Every Dominionist that I am currently aware of with the possible exception of James Jordan -- and he tried to say these things that Joel is saying in my public debate with him some years ago -- is that okay, yeah, we have over and over and over again -- James Jordan said, "I don't have a problem believing that 1 Corinthians 15 was fulfilled in A.D. 70." It's in the book back there on the table.

Well, let me say again, virtually every Dominionist believes that Revelation Chapter 20 is the, quote, "final resurrection." Well, how can you say, well, it may not be? There may be something beyond that. There may be another final one. I would ask the question again. Why must there be an ultimate end of human history in the first place?

Now, back to the idea that the language of curse and the language of correction is used throughout Israel's scripture. Now remember, this resurrection of the end in 1 Corinthians 15 is the hope of Israel specifically quoting Hosea. I want you to notice how Hosea uses this language.

God said, "I will make a covenant of peace for you with the animals of the field." Now this is -- this is harkening back to Genesis. This is the redemption of creation. This is back to Isaiah 24 and 25. There's the destruction of the old creation, but a new creation being brought in at the end of the millennium resurrection of Chapter 25 and verse 8.

But notice this: This recreation, this removal of the curse, when the animals of the field would be at peace once again, so to speak, is being applied *when God would remarry Israel* -- watch this -- when He made a New Covenant with her. So marriage and the New Covenant go hand in hand, because Hosea 2:19, "I will betroth you to me again in righteousness." So watch this, the curse is removed, animals would be made peaceful, if you please, the new creation, the New Covenant, and marriage go hand in hand.

When did the marriage take place? When was the New Covenant brought in? Matthew 22, the remarriage of God with Israel, A.D. 70. Revelation 19, the destruction of Babylon, the city where the Lord was slain: "Let us rejoice and be glad for the marriage of the son has come."

This is when the curse of Eden, expressed in Hosea, was removed.

Question to Don Preston: How should we understand the word "world" as it is used in Romans 4:13 and Colossians 1:6? Is this global? Is it covenantal? Just what is it? How do we know?

Don Preston: How do we understand the word "world" in Colossians 1:6? What was the other text?)

Jack Gibbert: Let's see. That was Romans 4:13.

Don Preston: Romans 4:13. Well, I think we are basically forced to understand the words in the same context. Joel will certainly agree with me. I know James Jordan did in my debate with him.

There are a variety of different words used for the word "world" in the New Testament. The word "world" used in Romans 4:13 is *kosmos*; the word "world" in Colossians Chapter 1 verse 6 is *kosmos*. And that *kosmos* as virtually all common lexicons will agree has a variety of meanings.

But the word "kosmos" can have a very limited scope. It does not have to mean the globe as we think of it. As a matter of fact, *kosmos* probably has to do with the order of creation of society and not physical dirt at all referring to a globe.

Now notice this. Paul said that the gospel had been preached into all of the *kosmos* and was bringing forth fruit. How do we limit that *kosmos* from, and make it different from the *kosmos* of Romans Chapter 4?

Now, I'd like to address very, very quickly Joel's comment that God said that Abraham would inherit the world. Has he not inherited the world through Christ? Is Christ not the seed, the representative of Abraham? Well, Christ has all power, or literally more authority, in heaven and in earth.

We have to understand the representative nature of ruling and reigning. When Christ was on earth, he was doing the work of the Father. When the Holy Spirit was here during the interim period of time, he was doing the work of Christ. These are representative works.

Abraham has inherited the world through Christ who has all power and all dominion. Now specifically to this, the word *kosmos* is determined by the context. And so in Colossians Chapter 1, how far had the gospel been preached? It had been preached to the very extent that Jesus said it had to be preached. The gospel will be preached into all of the world. Paul said it had been done. Those aren't not two different worlds. We cannot begin redefining the word *kosmos* because of our own preconceived theological concepts.

Joel McDurmon: The reason Don and I keep going back to sit down is because we're both humble and sharing people who don't want the spotlight. We want to give it to the other guy. So I just want to clarify that. [Audience laughter]

Well, the comments on Romans 4:13 and the interpretation of that, of course, not withstanding, I had something to say that may shock everyone in the room. And that is, I agree with Don entirely. [Laughter]

Yeah, the word "world" of course is capable of many translations. And many of the synonyms that are translated that way throughout the Bible overlap. For example, what we hear in Colossians 1:6 where it says the gospel which is coming to you as it is in all the world, *kosmou* -- or *tou kosmou* -- or *kosmoi*, That is the same as Jesus predicted back in Matthew 24, but I believe the word back there is only *oikoumene*, which means the inhabited house made literally, rather than world. So obviously it's a different word with the same concept.

That doesn't mean everywhere in scripture the word "world" for example therefore must be this limited view. And I know where the background of this question is coming from, the Beyond Creation Science guys, who not only want to use the redefined words the way we understand them now in the preterist world for the destruction of Jerusalem in Matthew 24 in those regards but then import those limited meanings of the word "world" back into other things in the Old Testament, for example creation itself, and for example, 2 Peter 3:6, which is talking about the flood of Noah, which says, "Whereby the world that then was being overflowed with water." Oh, that means it must have been a limited world. That means it was a limited flood. It wasn't a global flood after all. Well, now maybe the *Darwinists* are correct. Maybe the modern scientists are correct. So now we're relieved of that issue. And I think Don will probably agree with me on that issue; that it was a global flood.

Is that the case?

Don Preston: [No response. Audience laughter.]

Joel McDurmon: And probably agree with me on a literal six-day creation and not that the creation narrative is a framework in which we understand other things, and that it's not meant to be taken literally in all that other kind of stuff.

So there are consequences into how we interpret these. And of course you also need some framework or hermeneutic by which you determine when and where you take it one way or the other. And I think the context usually determines that. But that's longer than I have time for now.

Question to Joel McDurmon: Jesus' followers were to be raised on the last day. If that day is in our future, how is it that the last hour of John 2:18 was at hand? How do you reconcile those two "lasts"?

Joel McDurmon: Okay. I haven't looked at the Greek of John to know if the definite article's there.

The question is -- and it's probably one of the best questions I've seen. If "the last day of John," which is exclusive to his language, is to be an hour of our own future, and yet in the apostle of John -- 1 John Chapter 2, I believe

-- 2:18, is talking about the coming of anti-christ and he says, "Now dear children this is the last hour," and the implications is if there's a last day, then the last hour obviously is a subset of that last day and it's even shortened even more and he was expecting it in his time period. In fact, he said these anti-christs are coming and now are. So he was clearly talking about his time. That on the surface does present a conundrum. But if you go back to the overarching framework that I'm working with, that you can have a near fulfillment of these things and so you can apply a language on the near side, and yet what is the controlling narrative? It is the curse removed from the earth? And if it's not, then you can take both of those and move them into the future.

Now I realize that drags up other things like future anti-christs, future Armageddons. We can deal with that if you want to. But that's basically how I would view that. On the surface, it looks like a conundrum, but it's not insurmountable.

Don Preston: I would clearly disagree with the fact that it's not insurmountable. John is very consistent in his eschatological concepts. Notice back in John Chapter 5:28 -- or 24-- and following. He talks about the hour that now is when the dead shall hear the voice of the Son of Man and they shall live. He says, then "the hour is coming."

Now here's what -- an interesting thing that takes place in Joel's paradigm. He suggested to us the other night, whichever night it happened to have been, that because it's an hour coming, that it cannot be the same kind of resurrection related to the resurrection of verse 24 and 25; that it must therefore involve a period of thousands of years so far.

I would suggest to you that this -- this fails to understand that obviously a -- the initiation of the resurrection had begun. He would agree with that. And I don't know if I can find this or not. There are not two resurrections in John 5. There is a resurrection that had begun, was beginning, a resurrection to be consummated.

Notice he doesn't shift from the nature at all: those who are dead, those who are in the grave. So what's the difference? Notice that he talks about those who hear the voice of the Son of Man shall live. Well, don't marvel at this for the hour is coming in which *all* shall hear.

This is not a shift or a change in the *nature* of the resurrection. Once again, it is the initiation, awaiting consummation.

Joel will admit that the new creation was initiated in A.D. 70, but that we still await the consummation. Well, Christ was the second Adam, the new creation begun. And Colossians 1:15 as I pointed out, he was the first born of the new creation. Well, watch this. (Chart)

> The restoration (*apokatastasis*) of all things would be consummated at the End of the Millennium *parousia*—Acts 3 (McDurmon).
> John began the restoration (Mt. 17:10f– Elijah must come and restore (apokathestesai) all things; "Elijah has come" —> Acts 1– Will you *restore the kingdom (apokathestemi)– and that was <u>imminent !</u>*
> John, as Elijah, preached the kingdom and the parousia
> Peter said all the prophets who spoke of the restoration "spoke of these days."
> John, who preached the restoration, preached the imminent Day of the Lord.
> John did not preach two Great and Terrible Days of the Lord.
> So, John proclaimed the restoration of all things and began the work of restoration.
> Since the work of the restoration of all things would be consummated at the parousia, and since John began that work and proclaimed the Day of the Lord (the consummation of the restoration) to be near, <u>then it must be true</u> that the parousia of Acts 3 (Acts 1, etc) was imminent in the first century.
> The Day that John preached– as the time of restoration of all things-- was the fulfillment of Malachi 3-4—The application of Mosaic Covenant Sanctions!

I pointed this (chart above) out a couple of different times. Elijah began the restoration of all things. He began that work of restoration. The body of Christ was the continuance of that restoration. And what did Peter say? All of the Old Testament prophets, who spoke of the restoration of all things, *apokatastasis* is the Greek word.

All of those who spoke of it spoke of "these days." Now they were aware that the process, the initiation of the resurrection, had begun. They were fully aware that John had begun the work of restoration of all things. He didn't say they were waiting for it to be initiated. They were waiting for the consummation, which would be the *parousia*, and he said all of those prophets spoke of these days. They didn't speak of days far off; they spoke of Peter's "these days."

Question to Don Preston: Revelation 21:4, whose tears will be wiped away?

Don Preston: Okay. The question is Revelation 21 verse 4, whose tears will be taken away?

Well, I think if we keep this in context, number one, it is talking about the fulfillment of God's Old Covenant promises made to Old Covenant Israel.

I would also point out that in the Old Testament, there are many, many, many passages that talk about the time in which there would be no tears. Isaiah 25, the end of the millennium resurrection -- watch, Isaiah 25. "On this mountain He will establish a great feast. On this mountain He shall destroy death. On this mountain He shall wipe away all tears."

Now in this context -- now remember, this is the end of the millennium resurrection that He is predicting. Paul makes that clear in 1 Corinthians 15. This is Revelation Chapter 20. In the context, this curse that has passed upon all the nations came about as a result of Israel's violation of Torah. They have broken the everlasting covenant. Isaiah 24 and verse 5. "And the curse has passed upon all men."

Now here is the continuance of the Edenic curse that is now being incorporated as I have shown repeatedly throughout this debate. Here we have creation, Enoch, Noah, Abraham, et cetera, Zion, and Israel. But in this context, that curse that came in through Genesis is now being exacerbated just like Romans Chapter 5 says, "the law was added that sin might abound." Well, the death of Eden is now the death exacerbated under Torah, the tears, if you please, of Genesis, are now exacerbated under Torah. But when would they be taken away? "On this mountain He shall destroy death. On this mountain He shall remove all tears." On this mountain is Zion.

I call your attention once again to the fact that Joel says all of those Zion promises have been spiritualized and fulfilled in Christ. We can't take what has been -- catch this now - we cannot take what has once again been spiritualized by the New Testament writers, spiritualized in fulfillment, turn it around and make it literal and physical of a yet physical coming Zion and kingdom. I think that has very serious hermeneutical problems.

Joel McDurmon: Throughout this debate, Don's made a lot of that comment I made. I forget what article that was in where I talk about Zion's promise being spiritualized and fulfilled. Now obviously I'm referring specifically to Hebrews 12:22, and that's not a full expression of my doctrine. That promise was literally and physically fulfilled in the person and work of Jesus Christ. Definitively.

Now I have said this many times. And I believe the traditional view that things are definitively fulfilled in Christ and they're worked out progressively throughout history, and they will be consummated finally at some future point.

So, yes, there is a spiritual reality fulfillment of it and it, corresponding to that, will be an earthly fulfillment reality just as that spiritual city comes down out of heaven and goes -- I don't know where -- to Mars? Somewhere. Certainly not Oklahoma. [Laughter]

No, we know where it goes. And the definitive realities that are defined in that Revelation 21 passage that are coming *down, ek tou ouranou* out of the heaven are going to be manifested in this earth, and those tears are going to be wiped away. And the question was whose tears will be wiped away. And the text literally says men, in general, but we know of course, it's the men that are in the New Covenant, the believers, the elect, those who endure.

So, yeah, it is a spiritual fulfillment, and it will have a corresponding earthly fulfillment. It will be done gradually and it will be consummated at some point in the future.

Question to Joel McDurmon: Lay a little groundwork on this one. There is more than one curse stated in scripture. There are two curses in Genesis 3 verse 14. Given the serpent verse 17 given to the ground. Genesis 5:29 predicts the birth of Noah will ease the curse given in the garden. Genesis 8:21 says that this curse is now over.

So the question is, how do you explain the position that the curse of the ground has not been lifted when Genesis 8:21 says it has been?

Joel McDurmon: Sure. Genesis 8:21. Yeah, 5:29 I'm less worried about. The question is that there are, number one -- actually two-faceted questions: The first part was that there are multiple curses mentioned in Genesis 3, one to the serpent and one to the woman and one to the man. Then I thought the question got confused when it said, but this curse, singular, in Genesis 5:29, which says, "When He called his name Noah saying the same shall comfort us concerning our work and the toil of our hands because of the ground which the Lord has cursed."

So there would become some comfort in regard to that curse through Noah. And then in 8:21 it says -- according to the question, it says this curse has been removed. But that's not what the verse says. "And the Lord smelled a sweet savor and the Lord said in his heart I will not again curse the ground anymore for man's sake, for the imagination of man's heart is evil from his youth. Neither will I again smite any more everything living as I have done."

I don't see that as saying the curse is over; As saying God is saying I'm not going to curse it again. I'm not going to add any more to it. And in reality, if you think about it, the flood was an added curse. It was an added judgment. And that's why there's comfort in Noah because He saved the seed -- the lineage of the seed that was going to come from Genesis 3:15.

But because of the evil imaginations of men's hearts, in relation to that curse, of course, and Adam's fall, God curses the ground that's, quote/unquote, "again" through the flood. But there's comfort in Noah because he saves them out of that. Well, when the flood recedes, God, of course, He says, "I hang my bow in the clouds," and we always think of that as a rainbow, but it's poetic language. I'm hanging my bow, my bow and arrow of judgment, up in the clouds. Judgment is over with. I will not curse the ground again for man's sake. But He didn't say He removed the pain in childbirth. Didn't say He ended death. Didn't say the serpent's head was finally crushed for once and for all. He didn't say any of that. So I don't see that as a removal of the curse in that sense.

Don Preston: Well, there are two expressions of the curse. It can all be brought under the curse of Satan because of the ultimate end, the final end to use the terminology, Satan would be crushed, Genesis Chapter 3:16, which is what's classically known as the *protoevangelium*, the first expression of the gospel of Jesus Christ. It says he, that is Satan, will bruise his heel, but he, that is the seed of woman shall crush Satan's head.

Now I want you to look at Romans Chapter 16 and verse 20, in which Paul the apostle said, "And now the God of peace shall crush Satan under your feet shortly." Greek term meaning *en tachei*, however you wish to pronounce that. And it's only used seven times in the New Testament. Has nothing to do with rapidity of action as opposed to imminence of occurrence.

Therefore Paul was unequivocally expressing that the imminent overcoming, the imminent fulfillment of the *protoevangelium*. It's interesting to me that Kenneth Gentry says that Romans 16 verse 20 harkens back to the *protoevangelium*, and Paul was anticipating that. I would point out that Jesus and John, Chapters 12 and following, said two or three different times, "Now is the judgment of this world now. Now, the god of this world shall be cast out."

Now certainly I agree with Joel at least partially in some of the things that he says. He says all things were fulfilled in Christ and the person of Christ. Well, there's no question about that.

My, shall we say-- caveat on that is this: Christ in the cross is the foundation of *every single thing.* There is nothing beyond the cross if Christ didn't come out of the grave. Period. So because he came out of the grave, all promises would then be accomplished. They were not accomplished; they were *guaranteed to be accomplished.*

And that's not just a word play. That's not just semantics, but it is because the foundation was laid so securely and properly on the death, burial, and resurrection of Christ, it insured, guaranteed that all the promises in him are "yea and yea." And they would come to their full accomplishment. They were not fully accomplished. They were *guaranteed* through Christ and the cross.

So when the New Testament tells us that this crushing of the head of Satan was to occur in just a little while, and just like Revelation tells us that the overcoming of *the curse* and the death was coming in a very little while, these things must shortly come to pass, there is no temporal dichotomy between Chapter 20 and Chapter 21 and 22.

And let me remind you that Joel himself says in an article that I asked him to write, the new heavens, new earth, the new Zion arrived in A.D. 70. That means that God came down. He lives among us. He lives with us. He rules and he reigns now.

Joel McDurmon: Do you want to do a back and forth on this? Do you want to go back and forth on that?

Don Preston: It's fine if you wish.

Jack Gibbert: Absolutely.

Joel McDurmon: I only ask this as an exception to this point because the crushing of the serpent's head -- I've been waiting for this whole debate for this to come out. I knew somewhere sometime Romans 15 was going to come out. Is it verse 15 or 16? 16, right?

Don Preston: 16:20.

Joel McDurmon: 16:20. And this was going to happen shortly. And sure -- well, there you go. Genesis 3:15 is going to be accomplished. And the time indicator there does not imply rapidity in any way, shape, or form. Well, but the Bible does. The serpent's head is crushed a half a dozen times throughout scripture.

Now it doesn't say a half a dozen times that the serpent's head is going to be crushed shortly. It shows it in various ways. And this is part of the symphony I've been talking about. This is one of the most beautiful parts of the symphony in all of scripture. And the repetition of theme through several movements, okay? When Sisera invades Israel, how is he killed? Jael. (Which by the way is a wonderful name. It's the feminine version of my name. If you have a daughter, name her Jael. It's a wonderful name.)

She lures Sisera into her tent, gives him the milk, he becomes sleepy, he falls asleep, and what does she do? She, lady-like, drives a tent spike through his head. The serpent's head is crushed, folks. Why do you think the scripture records that one particular incident?

What happens to Goliath? If you read, the account is described like this big, long serpent dressed in scaly armor. And David slings the stone and crushes his head. By the way, he got that stone from the brook, which was a stone cut out without hands. Put all these things together, folks, the symphony is playing, the music is going on here.

This is repeated. Abimelech, I believe, has his head crushed from a millstone that is dropped from the tower. The enemy of Christ is crushed.

David's son Absalom has raped the daughter, he's fleeing from David. He gets his head caught in a tree and he's hung there and that's how he dies. And ultimately, folks, where does Christ die? They lead him up to a hill called Golgotha, which is being interpreted, the place of the skull. And as his physical heel was being bruised, he was crushing the serpent's head, *definitively*.

So, anything that comes after that is merely an application of the definitive reality of what Christ has done on the cross. And it's no big deal if the enemies of Christ that are defeated at a later point are referred to as the serpent having his head crushed. But that doesn't mean it's the final crushing. It doesn't mean it's a definitive crushing. You have to prove that from scripture in other ways, if you can. I say the definitive one was on Golgotha and everything has reference to that.

Don Preston: Well, shock and disbelief, I actually appreciate a lot of what he said. I see a lot of that -- I see a lot of that recapitulation. Those are all typological -- I think he would agree they're typological of the ultimate. Well, let's take take a look that. Let's see if we can dichotomize between Roman 16:20 in which the crushing of the head of Satan was to be accomplished shortly.

Paul in 1 Corinthians Chapter 15 says the *last enemy*. Now Joel says he can see that that can have a fulfillment in A.D. 70. How can you have the destruction of the last enemy in A.D. 70 and then have a repeat of that at any point of time? This has got to be the definitive thing.

Now let me go back to some comments that I made earlier. Joel says he agrees that the term flesh and blood does not refer to a biological human fleshly body. Again, I fully concur with that. It refers to the Old Covenant body of Israel. The flesh and blood of Old Covenant Israel. It's the natural body of 1 Corinthians Chapter 15.

Well, let me reiterate the argument that I made a while ago.

The resurrection of 1 Corinthians 15 is when the last enemy, death, would be destroyed, which means it would also be when Satan's head would be crushed definitively, finally, because this is the last enemy to be destroyed. Right? This is the last definitive resurrection. This is not one of many. This is the definitive one. The last enemy to be destroyed.

Okay. The resurrection of 1 Corinthians 15 is when the last enemy would be destroyed when Satan's head would be definitively, finally crushed.

The resurrection of 1 Corinthians 15 would be the putting off of the body of flesh and blood.

The body of flesh and blood in 1 Corinthians 15 is the Old Covenant body of Israel and Torah.

Therefore, the definitive, the last, the final resurrection, the crushing of Satan's head, finally was when the Old Covenant body of Israel, the Old

Covenant body of flesh and blood, was put aside at the end of the Old Covenant age of Israel.

That agrees perfectly with what Paul says when the mortal puts on immortality; it will be when the law, that is the strength of the sin, is overcome. The only law that was the strength of sin was Torah. That agrees perfectly with the putting off of the body of flesh and blood, i.e., Old Covenant Israel.

Question to Don Preston: All right. Who are the dead referred to in Mark 12:25? The dead.

Don Preston: In Mark 12:25. Well, let me get my glasses. I don't have my glasses.

Who are the dead Mark 12:25. This is in the same context -- thank you.

"Jesus answered and said to them, 'Are you not therefore mistaken because you do not know the scriptures nor the power of God? For when they rise from the dead, they neither marry nor or are given in marriage, but are like angels in heaven.'"

I believe this is a multi-varied question because he -- he then immediately asserts as Luke Chapter 20 and the parallel and Matthew Chapter 22 does. He immediately asserts that Abraham, Isaac, and Jacob are involved in this resurrection that he -- that he is talking about. But there is also the concept of those who are under Torah, who are going to come into the New Covenant of the age to come. I have said very often, and I apologize for any misunderstanding that may have been on the part of some and there is lot of a misunderstanding. But resurrection is multi-varied -- I should say multi-faceted type of thing. The resurrection for Daniel certainly included after his death, the resurrection certainly included for Abraham after his death, the reception of eternal life. Daniel Chapter 12 is very clear on that. It would be a resurrection to eternal life.

Now the great question is, did he have to be raised up by a biological body out of the dirt of the ground in order to receive eternal life? I would just simply pose this. I believe -- Joel can correct me if I'm wrong. Joel believes that when Christians die today and as a result of the fulfillment of coming to Zion -- he's said it, and the article is on the American Vision website by the way, in which he says the promises of Zion have been spiritualized. Abraham has received the Zion promises that have been spiritualized. Matthew Chapter 8 -- and that's in your book, by the way, Joel. Your comments on Matthew 8 and the Messianic Banquet that Abraham, Isaac, and Jacob had set down at the kingdom -- they set down at the kingdom in Matthew Chapter 8. Well, wait a minute.

The Messianic Banquet is the time of the end of the millennium resurrection. So here are the dead that are receiving eternal life. But wait a minute. If Abraham received that promise of eternal life, I'm pretty sure Abraham hasn't been raised up out of the dirt of the ground in order to receive eternal life. And yet Joel says he has been raised to sit at the Messianic Banquet and he sits with him. So there is one aspect of the identity of the dead. Jesus himself in Mark Chapter 2 says, but as to the dead whether they live, whether they have life, et cetera, I'm the God of Abraham, Isaac, and Jacob. There you have one facet of it. And as I said, there are multi-facets of resurrection and resurrection language. But I'm pretty much out of time.

Joel McDurmon: I very much appreciate Don appropriating my language about multi-variegated and multi-faceted. Perhaps he is about to join the symphony. And I agree, resurrection is a multi-faceted thing. It can have many interpretations. It happens on many levels. And do we have to have this understanding that therefore when the New Testament talks about the resurrection it's always talking about the exact same thing at the exact same time, once and never to be fulfilled again?

This is why I went through all those hermeneutical exercises the very first night to show that that is not necessarily the case. And burden of proof is on anyone who says it is.

So, again, the marriage passage. That's why I didn't necessarily hear it, I don't mean this to be a criticism, but I wasn't clear on who his answer to the dead in that passage were.

And honestly, I don't know if it is necessarily talking about the spiritual dead -- well, no, I would say definitely it's talking about the end resurrection. They rise from the dead. Then they neither marry nor are given in marriage. If that's talking about the A.D. 70 resurrection as full preterists believe, and you believe you are living in that resurrection now, then it's logical that you neither marry nor give in marriage. If you believe you've obtained that resurrection, then that has to logically follow.

Now last night, Don went to 1 Corinthians 7 and said here is a clear case where issue came up in the Corinthian church, and Paul responded to them by saying since you're in the new creation, new heavens, new earth now, these rules apply, and don't get divorced.

But I invite you to go for yourselves and read the entire chapter of 1 Corinthian 7. There is no mention anywhere about being in the new heavens and new earth. There is no mention anywhere that the ethical principles he's laying down are to be considered as post-resurrection principles, which of course if the resurrection was to be in A.D. 70, it hasn't happened yet.

So why would these people be concerned about these issues? I particularly look at the verses about virgins and should I get my daughter married and considering the fact that they were expecting some great upheaval of society attending the resurrection of the dead -- what I mean is A.D. 70. That was a slip of the tongue, by the way. Should I bother having my daughters marry? If we're about to live through this great conflagration, we may lose our lives. Should we bother going through this long process? No. That's what I see going on there. And of course my time's up here.

Final Question of the First Hour: to Joel McDurmon: Joel, what is your exegesis of 1 Corinthians 15:28, "that God may be all in all"? When does or did this occur? Give a picture of how you perceive being "all in all." Repeat the question.

Joel McDurmon: What is my exegesis of 1 Corinthians 15:28. I'll read the whole verse. They only reference part of it, but I'll read the whole verse. "And when all things shall be subdued unto him, then shall the son also be subject unto him that put all things under Him, that God may be all in all."

And the question was what is my vision of what all -- number one, when will God be all in all? And what does that look like, that God will be all in all? And I've got to say, in the big picture, I have no idea. And that is my very highly studied theological, almost Ph.D. opinion on that.

You know, when we start talking about these kind of speculative ideas, well, what's that going to look like or what was God doing before creation -- you remember the story about Saint Augustine. One of his pupils asked him what was God doing before He created the world. And Augustine responded by saying He was creating hell for curious students.

So I think we are rushing into places where angels dare to tread. When did this happen? Again, I can see a definitive fulfillment in Christ himself. But then, I can also see aspects and applications of it in A.D. 70. But as Christ therefore turned over the kingdom of the Father, if he has, then he's no longer interceding for anyone. And if he's no longer interceding for anyone, then how does anyone come to the father? Therefore why evangelize? Therefore all those other practical issues that come out -- and these are not just full preterism's true, then this must be scary. These are real practical concerns. I mean, if all that is true up in heavenly realm -- this is done, it's over with, God is all in all now -- then there Moreno more enemies of God, how can sin exists anywhere in the universe? What about Ephesians 4? All of the offices are gone because the place is perfected. We don't need to be teaching each other.

Don, I believe, turns that backwards on its head and says, oh, no, they have to be taught before they're in. But, no, at this point, it's all in all. And it says they shall no more be taught. They shall no more teach one another. So, how do you get -- they have to teach one another, out of "they shall no more teach one another." I don't understand that. So I look at this and I say, no, there's obviously some definitive fulfillment of this or some final fulfillment of this in the future.

And, again, I look at my overall scheme definitive in Christ, progressive in history, final at some point in the future. And that's why I was saying, what's that going to look like in the future? I have got no idea.

Don Preston: I'd like to point out that in 1 Corinthians 15, Paul is not only drawing from Isaiah and Hosea and Daniel, but he is also drawing very, very heavily from the Book of Zechariah.

I'd like to point out that in Zechariah Chapter 14, it begins with the prediction of the coming of the Lord, just as Paul is discussing the prediction of the coming of the Lord.

It is a time of the coming of salvation. It is a time, notice if you will, verse 8 and following. "It shall be *in that day* that living waters shall flow from Jerusalem. Half of them towards the Eastern sea, half of them towards the western sea. In both summer and winter it shall occur."

Now this is very clearly a picture of the River of Life. This is a resurrection motif. Ezekiel Chapter 47 speaks of the River of Life flowing out from under the throne. Well, here you have the River of Life flowing out from Jerusalem, which is where the throne was.

And by the way, let me go back to a comment that Joel made the other night. That if you espouse full preterism, it may, as some have lamentably espoused, lead to universalism. I don't think that's a logical trip at all for Ezekiel Chapter 47. Although it talks about everywhere the river flows, that it brings life, verse 11 specifically and emphatically says the marshes in the subsidiaries thereof "do not come to life."

They don't get life. Just like Revelation Chapter 21 depicts a situation outside the city where there are dogs and liars. Well, that is another issue. But the point of fact is here we have the River of Life, which is Revelation 22.

I would remind you once again that Joel has said that this Zion, this new creation, came down from God out of heaven in A.D. 70. Okay. Here we have the River of Life. Back to 1 Corinthians Chapter 15 verse 28. God being all in all, verse 9. "And the Lord shall be king over all the earth. *In that day* it shall be the Lord is *one* and his *name one*."

Here is a direct prophecy of 1 Corinthians 15:28. Zechariah emphatically places it within the context of the judgment of Old Covenant Israel: the coming of the Lord with all of his saints. Revelation puts this at the end of the millennium. Same prophecy, 1 Corinthians 15 was to be fulfilled in putting off the body of flesh of Old Covenant Israel. Just like Zechariah coming of the Lord in judgment of Israel.

Q & A – Second Hour

Jack Gibbert: Okay. We're ready to begin the second hour of the question discussion section. This is a question that came from an American Vision reader, fan, follower, and supporter, and it's directed to Joel. It's a little bit complicated; that's why I'm up here, so you won't have to repeat it. Okay?

Question to Joel McDurmon: Sam Frost has just authored a new book entitled *Why I Left Full Preterism*, which you have handed out free copies of it at this debate. This person has read this book, during this conference has read it from cover to cover. And he notes that on Page 69 of this book, Frost writes: "I have many friends among full preterists, though I cannot in good faith call them brothers and sisters in the Lord." It goes on and says, "I do not wish to state that a full Preterist is automatically damned to hell either. It's a tough call."

What the questioner asks is, "Will you comment on Frost's quote? And does belief in full preterism damn one to hell?"

Joel McDurmon: Response to the first question, will I comment on Sam Frost's comments? No. I'll let Sam speak for himself.

But the second question is basically the same question. What are my thoughts on the same subject? So, I agree with Sam. Oh? That wasn't enough? Okay.

No, I do agree with Sam. From the perspective of the historic church, it's a heresy. But what is a heresy? Historically people have used the word heresy -- at one point, it meant *damnable* heresy. At other points, it was meant simply a sect that we recognize as these kind of odd brothers over there and we don't want them teaching in the main line church. But we recognize that, yeah, they have faith in Christ, even if they have other aspects misguided. And then of course when you get to the Reformation, particularly the English Reformation, and the views of Richard Hooker, I believe late 1600's, I could be wrong about that. Late 1500's? And he says the terms of communion are the terms of salvation. And the terms of salvation are faith in Christ. And he says, folks, we're -- he even went and took the Reformation doctrine himself. We are not saved *sola fide*, by faith alone. We are not saved by believing in the doctrine of *sola fide.*

So he even brought in Roman Catholics and other people who, as long as they had genuine faith in Christ, may have had some of their doctrines messed up in their mind, he accepted them as brothers. So I say by his standards he would accept most full preterists.

That's also a problematic aspect of the question. There is a whole range of people who call themselves full preterists. What about the Tim Kings and these guys who are Universalists? What about the guys who do reject any standard for morality? What about the libertines and all these other people who are full preterists, but they carry all these other heretical doctrines? Well, you can say, well, there are damnable heretics for those reasons and not their full preterism.

But I think there's a range of things in which you have to discuss this. And in some aspects, yes, it is damnable, but other aspects, nah, I think there's grace to be shown here. So, that's how I agree with Sam.

Don Preston: The entire issue calling one another heretics as Joel has expressed, the word heretic has a wide range of meaning. It seems to me that throughout the history of the church, we have sought ways to call one another heretics instead of finding ways to come together. And that is a really sad testimony.

In the fellowship in which I was raised as a fifth generation member of the churches of Christ, you can be called a heretic for a woman not cutting her hair, or if you got two cups on the communion, or if you got a Bible class room for kids instead of meeting in the auditorium, and about 14,000 other different things that you could be called a heretic for.

To me that is the ultimate expression of legalism. I appreciate Joel's struggle if I may use that term.

Joel McDurmon: No, it's not a struggle. I'm at peace.

Don Preston: Okay. Ambivalence perhaps of whether or not to call us damnable heretics.

I remember some years ago, James Jordan had written that we are damnable heretics. In my debate with him, he then recanted that position and said while he now believes that we are simply serious -- or while we are guilty of serious error, he no longer believes we are damnable heretics.

It seems to me, once again, that we are far, far too quick to call one another damnable heretics. Every preterist that I am personally aware of affirms the inerrancy of scripture, the Deity of Jesus Christ, the reality of Jesus' death, burial, and resurrection, the glorification of the body of Christ, and we affirm the completion of his work. Now how in the world we could be labeled as heretics for standing fast upon some of these foundational tenets of Christianity itself is, quite frankly is beyond me.

Now I have applauded and I do applaud Joel for having the courage to come here and to discuss issues. I think it is way past time for even more dialogue, even more discussion, more debate, if you please. I think it has been manifested abundantly clearly that the " partial preterist", or may I just use the generic term, futurist view, is pretty seriously flawed. There are a lot of questions about it. It is not, quote, cut and dried. And it certainly should never be settled on the issue of the creeds and what the creeds say. It should never be settled upon the testimony of church history.

If, in fact, we are going to make the appeal as the Reformers did, it is surely *sola scriptura*. Let's get about discussing *sola scriptura*.

Question to Don Preston: Do you think that the sole purpose of the Sabbath law was to serve as a shadow? Did it contain no other purpose? And if so, have they also been fulfilled?

Don Preston: Was the sole purpose of the Sabbath to foreshadow the resurrection? And it has been -- or were there other issues?

Question to Don Preston: Was its purpose to serve as a foreshadow and did it have no other purposes? And if so, were those also fulfilled?

Don Preston: Okay. Was its purpose solely as a foreshadow, and were those other purposes fulfilled?

Well, I think sort of like resurrection, the Sabbath was kind of a multi-varied type thing. It was obviously to give man relief from physical labor: "Six days you shall work and the seventh day you shall do no work at all."

I think there's a fundamental primary release from physical labors, but certainly was not exhaustion of the meaning. Because it pointed to how God rested from his labors, which in turn pointed to the ultimate rest.

So I think it would be misguided to say that there is only one meaning. It certainly would be wrong to stop at the primary meaning of, hey, "I get a day off," because that's clearly not.

Look also at Exodus Chapter 31:16-17 in which the Sabbath was specifically said to be a sign -- a covenant sign between God, indicative of creation. Well, Deuteronomy Chapter 5 likewise says, "I delivered you from the land of bondage. *Therefore* I gave you the Sabbath." If we want to see two things at work there, then the Sabbath was indicative of the creation of Genesis. It was likewise indicative of the deliverance from Israel -- from Egyptian bondage.

Let's keep this in mind. Whatever variegated meanings or definitions we might put to it, Paul said that Israel's new moon feast days and Sabbaths were, when he wrote, it's present tense there, shadows of good things that are about to come. That's obviously in future tense.

The typological significance of Sabbath had not yet reached its fulfillment. Now so far as typology of Sabbath, I don't see a multitude of typological applications. The typological application was designated as the Sabbath's cessation from labor. The writer of Hebrews says there remains therefore a rest for the children of God. That rest was to be found in Zion and the resurrection. They had arrived at Zion.

The writer says we have here no abiding city, but we seek one that is about to come. There is the ultimate rest, and that city that was about to come came down in A.D. 70. I hope that answers your question.

Joel McDurmon: If they had already arrived at Zion and the rest was supposed to be in Zion, then they already had the rest. Then how in Hebrews can he say there's yet another rest to enter into? Obviously there are variations on the theme being played here. And I agree with Don: the Sabbath can be interpreted in many ways and it is used throughout scripture in many ways, in the ways he mentioned.

I did think it was curious that he makes this long list of all these places throughout the Pentateuch, not just in the law of the Mosaic Covenant itself, but in Genesis and Exodus and other places and in other contexts. The return from exile and all this kind of stuff.

And then he says, but I don't see a whole lot of typological application of the Sabbath. What do you think all that is? You just gave three or four or five examples of how it's typologically applied. How that part of the symphony is played over and over and over again.

And Hebrews has it going on twice itself. You have arrived at Zion, and yet there is yet another rest to enter into. And you can say, well, that is the post-A.D. 70 rest when the temple is destroyed and all those rites and sacrifices and Sabbath days and everything were done with.

And I would agree that as for as the Mosaic administration and those things, that is true. But, as far as that curse is still here, there is yet another rest to enter into.

Question to Joel McDurmon: Is physical death the enemy of the child of God?

Joel McDurmon: Is physical death the enemy of the child of God?

Yes. Is it the only? Is it the fullness of the enemy? Is it the whole thing? No. But it is obviously part of the curse. It's obviously part of the curse. And when the Bible talks about death, I believe it's talking about the curse of death; it's talking about the whole picture. As Paul says in 1 Thessalonians 5, I believe 23, that I want you to be sanctified in your whole body, soul, and spirit. The vision of redemption is for the body, the soul, and the spirit, includes the body. And to me, if you go back, like I said, and read Genesis 3, clearly the curse includes bodily death.

So, yeah, that is the enemy of God. And so in 1 Corinthians 15, when it says the last enemy that shall be destroyed is death, that can't have been finally fulfilled in A.D. 70: even if there is some kind of typological application that happened in A.D. 70.

Then you say, well, why then is that that is about to come upon them in their generation. But again, there's still a future fulfillment. And the New Testament itself shows multiple fulfillments of this as I have stressed over and over and over. That death was abolished in Christ's death and resurrection. Why then does it have to be killed again? Death is defeated in Christ's resurrection. Didn't say a process of killing death was started. Didn't say anything like that. It says death is abolished. It's gone. Definitively in Christ.

Ephesians 4 says "When he ascended on high, he led captivity captive and gave gifts to men." That's definitive in his ascension. Didn't have to wait until A.D. 70. And yet we're told that this is going to happen again. And yet we get to Revelation 20 and we see death and Hades being thrown into the lake of fire. Why? Because there are variations on a theme being played here. The definitive one being Christ and his body and his resurrection. And the finality of that being worked out over history until there is a consummation point which includes our bodily death.

Don Preston: Okay. I find it very troubling to suggest that physical death is the enemy of the child of God.

Let's look at it like this: Sin brings death. The wages of sin is death. That's supposedly biological death. So the great question therefore is what happens when I as a child of God, am forgiven, cleansed, redeemed by the blood of Christ? Has not that sin which brings my biological death been removed? Yes or no? Now if that sin, which brings my biological death, has been removed, I should no longer be under the penalty and the sting or the penalty itself of biological deaths. So it raises the question. If I am redeemed, cleansed, and purified by the blood of Christ, his righteousness is now my righteousness, why do I as a child of God die biologically? Does not therefore my physical death demonstrate I am not forgiven? After all, I'm still under the penalty of sin, i.e., physical death.

Now seems to me we also have quite a -- quite a conundrum here. Again, Joel can correct me if I'm wrong. But I believe that Joel believes that when the faithful child of God dies today, they go to heaven.

You mean to tell me that biological death, that ushers us into the presence of God is our enemy? How so is that? But you see the real question here comes back to the very nature of the substitutionary of death of Christ and the work of the atonement.

To refer to it in church history if I may, the historical view of the church is that Christ died *in my place*. He is the Passover that died in the place of, as a substitute, instead of.

Okay. If Christ's physical death was a substitutionary death so that I do not have to suffer the consequences of the curse of Adam, of the penalty of my sin, then why do I have to die? I am paying the atonement for my own sin. Physical sin results in physical death. I die; I paid the penalty for my sin.

What happened to the substitutionary death of Christ? Did I not believe enough? These are very serious issues. Physical death is not the enemy of the child of God, forgiven of their sin or else there is no forgiveness.

Question to Don Preston: If the resurrection is spiritual in nature only, can you explain the change in 1 Corinthians 15:51 those alive, meaning Christ in the spiritual realm, that is in the air, in 1 Thessalonians 4:17?

Don Preston: Okay. If resurrection is spiritual only, then please explain the death in 1 Corinthians 15.

Moderator Clarification: Explain the change in 1 Corinthians 15:51.

Don Preston: Okay.

Moderator Clarification: And then the meeting in the air -- in the meeting of Christ in the spiritual realm in the air, 1 Thessalonians 4.

Don Preston: Okay. Explain the change of 1 Corinthians 15:51, and then the meeting the air in 1 Thessalonians Chapter 4. Well, there's only about three month's worth of talking.

Well, let's look at 1 Corinthians 15. In the context of flesh and blood, once again, what is the change? The change that Paul has in mind in 1

Corinthians 15 is the change from the natural man to the spiritual. It is the change from flesh and blood to the spirit. So if that change in 1 Corinthians 15 -- let me rephrase that. If flesh and blood in 1 Corinthians 15 is the body of flesh of Old Covenant Israel, then the change in 1 Corinthians 15 from the natural man and the flesh and blood body of Israel is the new change to the New Covenant body of Christ, life, and immortality in Christ Jesus. Not talking about individualistic. It's the body of flesh and blood, which Joel has already told us is indeed the body of Israel.

Now, I have already pointed out, and Joel agrees, resurrection is a multi-varied thing. For those who are biologically dead -- and I've appealed to this repeatedly. All of those listed in Hebrews Chapter 11 -- Abel, you know, Enoch, Noah, et cetera, et cetera -- they were longing for resurrection. They were longing for eternal life. Daniel Chapter 12 says that the end of the age when the power of the holy people would be completely shattered, they themselves would receive their eternal life.

Now, I have to remind you one more time, Joel says they received that promise. They have received that promise. Now Joel says it has to be with biological bodies coming out of the ground. Well, then they haven't received their eternal life. They haven't received their mortality. They haven't received incorruptibility because they haven't come out of the ground.

But, again, Revelation Chapter 11 emphatically shows us that at the time of the fall of Jerusalem in A.D. 70 the resurrection and the rewarding of the prophets, i.e., Daniel and Abraham and Noah and all of those, was to take place, their rewarding, eternal life, was to take place at that time.

So here is a change for those who are biologically dead. There is a covenantal transformation from the administration of death to the ministration of life. That is not a biological transformation of any kind. Here is a living, breathing human being under one covenant, but he is dead under Torah. Now he comes into Christ, now he is alive. So to try to limit resurrection, and Joel and I do agree on the multi-varied aspect of it; we cannot limit it to a single thing. We have to take all facets of this beautiful diamond called resurrection into consideration. And the Bible invariably places the consummate, end of the age final resurrection in A.D. 70.

Joel McDurmon: Still looking for that word *final*. The question was about 1 Corinthians 15:51 and forward: "Behold I show you a mystery. We shall not all sleep, but we shall all be changed. In a moment in the twinkling of an eye of the last trumpet for the trumpet shall sound and the dead shall be raised incorruptible, and "we..." plural, "...shall be changed. For this corruptible must put on incorruption, and this mortal must put on immortality."

This is not talking about a single body. It doesn't say that the Old Testament Covenant, the covenant, anything like that will be changed. That the body of the believers as a corporate unit will be changed. He says this is talking about individuals. Clearly it is because it uses the plural references. There are places in the scripture where the body is talked about in the singular, and full preterists always latch on to that: "See, there's where we're talking about one corporate body." Well, here it's not. It's talking about "we." "We shall all," inclusive, "be changed."

There's even a division made between those who are living, "You shall be changed"; and those who are dead, "You shall be changed."

And what is that change? This corruptible must put on incorruption. This mortal must put on immortality. Okay. That's not simply talking about a change of covenants. It's talking about *them*. It's talking about their *bodies*. Just as it's talking about in Romans 8, which full preterists also incorporate, and they have to spiritualize in language and say this is talking about a spiritual reality.

But Paul is very clearly using Genesis language -- physical language for the creation was made subject to vanity; that is the curse. Not willingly, but by reason of him who subjected the same of hope because the creature itself also shall be delivered from the bondage of corruption. Greek word is *phthoras*, which is used all through the Psalms to talk about corruption of a body lying in a grave. Not an Old Covenant.

Delivered from that into the glorious liberty of the children of God for we know that the whole creation groans and travails and pain together until now. And not only they but we ourselves of which have the first fruits of the spirit. Even we ourselves groan within ourselves waiting for the adoption; to wit: The redemption of our body." And in that way, Paul -- I assume still talking the about the same event -- says we shall all be changed. Jesus says when this change happens, we'll neither marry nor give in marriage.

So, again, I ask you to put all these things together and say, was all this fulfilled in A.D. 70 in a spiritual way, when it's specifically talking about things we do in our bodies? And things we do with our spouses and our bodies. All these things go together. And even if we grant that there is some kind of a fulfillment in A.D. 70, it doesn't get to the heart of it. It doesn't get to the fullness -- the full fullness of it. So it's a fallacy to simply add that this must be final.

Question to Joel McDurmon: Luke 20:35 speaks of the age to come, which you have agreed is the age in which we now live. What is the resurrection of this age and what does the Bible say with regard to when this age will end?

Well, like I said last night, I see a distinction that Jesus is talking about two distinctive events here: they that are accounted worthy to obtain that world, which is the age we're living in, *and* the resurrection. Okay.

I don't think he was talking about the spiritual resurrection; however you want to define it of A.D. 70. And if he was, then you have the marriage and non-marriage problem. So I think he is talking about a resurrection that is in that age, which is this age we're talking about now, which has to have happened after A.D. 70.

And, of course, I bring in the rest of my world view and theology with the curse and everything else, and I say this must have to happen at some point in the future. That's fairly easy.

Don Preston: Pardon me. Well, once again I think Joel is overlooking what he is really honestly on record as saying. He acknowledges that we are in the age to come. Well, according to the Bible the age to come has no end.

Isaiah spoke of the coming of the kingdom of Christ and the establishment of what we call the church age, and he says that "the increase of his government, that's Messiah, and a peace there will be, no end." I don't know how much clearer a Bible text could be when it says there shall be end.

Back to Mark and Luke and what have you. I would like to return in order to answer this question just a little bit. He says it's not a spiritual resurrection, but the question was posed to me, who are the dead.

Well, the answer to that and even addressing this specific question is found in the contrast of this age verses that age. Jesus' "this age" was the age of death characterized by the ministration of death.

2 Corinthians Chapter 3, they lived under the ministration of death, written and graven in stones. Well, is that physical death or is that spiritual death?

Now did it include, as we have already pointed out, Daniel, Abraham, and all those who are biologically dead because they lived prior to the work of Christ? Certainly it did. But Jesus' this age was the age that was characterized by death. *They died.* Paul says I was alive once without the law, the commandment came, sin revived, and I *died*. And as he struggled with life under Torah, he said, "Oh, wretched man that I am, who shall deliver me from the body of *this death*?"

He wasn't wanting to be out of the biological body. Paul didn't consider the biological body subject to human death as the enemy. The body of death that he was talking about was the body of the death under Torah condemned because of violation of Torah.

But what did he anticipate? Look at what Jesus said, "In the age to come they will never die." Now this places a real conundrum, does it not? If death, under Torah, Adam, into Torah, is physical death, then here we have Jesus proclaiming unequivocally that in the age to come, the age in which we live, there will be no physical death.

Well I'm in the age to come. Joel admits that he's in the age to come. Why are we still dying biologically? Jesus said in the age to come they do not die.

Question to both debaters: It seems that an agreement concerning the truth of scripture may never be realized by the varying Christian denominations. Since our beliefs vary so much, I'm wondering if it really matters what we believe. Realistically, no one will ever get it all right. Knowing we will always embrace some sort of error, why keep attempting to figure it out? Does salvation depend on adhering to correct doctrine? If God is sovereign, He has given each of us the knowledge we have of Him, He grants salvation by his will, what difference does it really make if we have it all figured out or not?

Don Preston: Well, first of all, truth does matter. But I would say in the final analysis, we are not saved by what we know; we are saved by who we know. Our faith is in Jesus Christ. My faith is not in the perfection of my knowledge or the perfection of what I do. *Praise God for his grace.* Praise God for -- *faith*.

[Applause.]

Now with that said, Paul makes it abundantly clear that the scriptures are for edification, for learning, for doctrine. And does it not matter anything whatsoever about what we believe?

Well, Paul makes it abundantly clear in 1 Corinthians Chapter 15 that if we reject the resurrection of Jesus Christ, we are yet in our sins. *That truth matters.* But you know the reason for that is because the resurrection of Jesus Christ is the foundation of our belief in *who* or in *him*, not in what, but in *him*.

Now eschatology is very clearly, an important doctrine. I have struggled with this issue insofar as fellowship, and what have you, for many years. It's very clearly true that Peter said in 2 Peter Chapter 3 that some twisted scriptures to their own destruction. That's pretty serious stuff, isn't it? That's pretty serious stuff.

Paul said that Hymenaeus and Philetus had overthrown the faith of some. Saying the resurrection has passed already. Now unfortunately too many people look at that passage in what I would consider a way, way, way too simplistic matter. They don't do any exegesis of the text. They impose an anachronistic view of the resurrection on the text and lo and behold preterists are declared as heretics. I've already demonstrated to you last night that if Joel's view of everything being fully accomplished in Christ at the cross, then Hymenaeus wasn't wrong. Hymenaeus could have been saying exactly like Joel is saying everything is fulfilled in Christ at the cross. Well, then how can Paul accuse him of being guilty of heresy in saying the resurrection has passed, because it was fulfilled? It was passed in Christ. Paul said, no, that's not right. That's not the meaning of *genetai* at all.

So, it does matter on some level, on many levels what we believe. But our faith has to ultimately be in Jesus Christ and his death, burial, and resurrection.

I don't know if that gets us all the way back to some of the views of Anselm and some of the other philosophers and theologians of the past. I don't know if it even gets us back to the view of Alexander Campbell, the Restoration Movement. Those who believe in Jesus Christ are my brothers. That's as far as he took it basically.

So it is somewhat of a perplexing issue. We cannot simply discount doctrine. We are called to know doctrine, to teach doctrine, to know truth, to love truth. So we can't discount it. But we must never lose sight of the fact that it's not theology that saves us. It is the person of Jesus Christ.

Joel McDurmon: The question is obviously coming from someone who is beginning to understand the implications of full preterism. Does it matter what we teach? Well, if Hebrews 8 is correct, we don't have to teach anything. If Ephesians 4 is fulfilled, we don't need pastors and teachers or we don't need apostles or evangelists. They were all for the pre A.D. 70 era, and therefore at this point in time, it doesn't really matter what you say you believe. It matters -- I don't know. But we don't need teachers, we know that much.

So, I would say that that question is really beginning to verge on that reality. Now I think Don responded more to the spirit of the person who was saying it. And I'm coming at the side that was unwitting.

And I think I agree with Don a lot on some of that as I expressed a while ago, Richard Hooker's view of salvation. You can have some doctrines wrong in your mind and still have a genuine thread of faith hanging on Christ and through that be saved by the skin of your teeth, to use a phrase from Job.

But then again, there are some doctrines that if you deny explicitly, are you not denying the very reality on which you must be saved? And if you deny that, then you're really verging on territory where, yes, it does matter what you believe.

This is talking about salvation. Now Don also brought up the issue of does it matter in life. And I would say, of course it matters in life. Your view of the continuing incarnation of Jesus Christ matters greatly for how you view human society.

And I would invite every one of you to get a book by R. J. Rushdoony entitled *The Foundations of Social Order* where he goes through the historic creeds of the church and shows how these doctrines have consequences, the trinity, incarnation, et cetera.

If you believe in an eschatology that says this earth will never be redeemed and my reward is only in heaven, why get involved? Why get involved in politics or economics or anything like that. And indeed many Christians use that rationale to say, I'm not doing that stuff. My reward is in heaven. But if you realize that this earth is going to be progressively redeemed throughout history toward a consummate end, you might have a different view of things. You might realize that you need to apply the Bible to every area of life, to your own life, to your business, to economics, to politics, things like that the way this nation was founded. So, yes, it does matter *greatly*.

Question to Joel McDurmon: Genesis 2, God told Adam the day that he ate thereof he would die. What death did he die and what is the day as mentioned in the text?

Joel McDurmon: The question was, the Bible says that in the day that Adam would eat of the fruit then that day he would die. And if I recall correctly it is what was the nature of that death, how did he die that day?

Question Clarification: The death and the day.

Joel McDurmon: The death, and what was that day?

Well the nature of that day, I assume, was the day they literally ate the fruit. I don't think it was 40 years later or anything like that. And the death that they suffered was the full consequence death, separation from God in body, soul, and spirit.

Now you say, well, wait a minute. Why did they not die bodily that day? And it's because that day God came down and showed them grace, instituted the covenant of grace that lasts all through history. Promised them a coming Messiah. Indeed in the very curse itself upon the serpent promises a coming Messiah and in faith in that Messiah they didn't experience bodily death yet.

Although in a way they did, in two ways. God curses the ground, which is the *adamah* from which Adam was taken, which implies a curse on his body. And of course the curse does come through his body with increased toil, labor, sweat, et cetera, increased pain in child birth. These things are all intricately linked.

And secondly a physical death did occur that day. God sacrificed an animal. He provided a substitutionary atonement so that they could continue their existence on earth and continue working toward that which they had been commanded to do, which was to fill the earth, multiply, and subdue itself. But God did provide a substitute. He brought animal skins for Adam and Eve and replaced their fig leaves with animal skins. Where do you think he got the animal skins?

God performed the first ritual sacrifice. And in doing that, he taught them how to worship him in that way which he later institutes in the Law of Moses with all the animal sacrifice. Why do you think Abel's sacrifice was preferred and Cain's was not? Because Abel offered from the beast of the field a sacrifice, a blood atonement sacrifice, whereas Cain offered from the vegetables that he had grown. That doesn't cut it. The fig leaves don't cut it, Cain. You got to have the blood.

Now the blood of the animals themselves didn't save, but it was pointing to the Savior that was promised. But a physical death did occur that day.

Don Preston: It is interesting to me that in order to maintain a theology we have to deny the threat that God made to Adam and Eve. "In the day that you eat thereof *you* will surely die." Not an animal, *you*.

Now he admits that it was Adam and Eve who died spiritually by being cast out of the Garden that day. Well, if God created that animal sacrifice to keep them from dying physically, why didn't that animal sacrifice do the same job for spiritual?

Well, Joel would immediately respond, well, the blood of bulls and goats cannot take away sin. Well, it kept them from dying physically ostensibly.

The point of fact is God didn't say a death will occur. He said *you* will surely die. It seems to me disingenuous at the very least to say that, yes, Adam and Eve did in reality objectively die spiritually that day, and then turn around and say that the real focus of this death is biological death, but they didn't really die that day after all.

Wasn't the sacrifice as equally efficacious for spiritual as well as biological? Why would an animal sacrifice be efficacious physically but not spiritually? See, we get into all sorts of problems here. The bottom line gets back down, he didn't say a death will occur. *"You will die."*

And we have to deal with that reality and not change it to a death, some death, an animal will die. *You* will die that day.

Now Jesus, it says in 1 Corinthians 15, was the first born from the dead. Acts Chapter 26:21 and following says he was the first to be raised from the dead. He wasn't the first person to be biologically raised, but he was the very first person to be raised from the death of Adam. But now he's telling us that Adam and Eve didn't even die that day, biologically. So he has created a dichotomy between Jesus being the first born of the death of Adam, when Adam didn't even die that day. I think that's troublesome.

Question to Don Preston: If Torah was covenantally fulfilled, can it, should it, still be used for showing God's law principles in society on earth?

Don Preston: Okay. If Torah was abolished, then should it be used for showing God's law of principles of God's attitude toward man on earth, society, et cetera, et cetera? I think that's correct.

Well, Paul was convinced that "whatsoever things were written before time were written for our learning that we through patience might have comfort" through the scriptures. Paul's not referring to the New Covenant there. Paul was living during the transitional period of time in which he was certainly appealing to Torah and what have you.

I think, however, it is absolutely vitally critical that we understand that the New Covenant is not the old. Jeremiah promised -- a God through Jeremiah, I will make a New Covenant with the house of Israel and Jacob not according, not like the old. And somebody says, well, wait a minute, God says it's still -- thou shall not steal, that's Torah. No, it's not. These commands spring, not from codified law, but from the very heart of God himself.

We cannot look for law and look for Torah in the New Testament commandments. The Decalogue itself was a distinctly covenantal reality. How do I know that? Because the Sabbath is imbedded squarely in the Decalogue. And the Sabbath was a covenant sign between God and Israel. Thou shall not kill, thou shall not lie, thou shall not steal, are not simply arbitrary laws that God made up. They spring from the heart, the mind, and the characteristics of God's heart and mind.

Therefore, can we see how God operated through Torah? Now, Gary North says if Deuteronomy Chapter 8 is not still judicially binding in the New Testament, then there is no basis or any ground for Theonomy in our world. Well, that's re-imposing the Law of Moses. The Law of Moses died in A.D. 70. Not one jot, not one tittle shall pass until it's all fulfilled. But if Deuteronomy Chapter 8 is applicable, judicially binding on us today, then Sabbath is judicially binding on us today.

I posed the question last night. I repose the question. Would anyone get from reading Matthew Chapter 5:17-18, which says "not one jot, not one tittle shall pass from the law until it is all fulfilled" -- would anybody get -- part of the law will pass even though that part of the law is not fulfilled. If you can't get that from the text, it's not in the text.

Joel McDurmon: Would you please repeat the question?

Question Repeated: If Torah is covenantally fulfilled, can it, should it still be used for showing God's law principles in society on earth?

Joel McDurmon: If Torah is completely fulfilled --

Question Clarification: Covenantally.

Joel McDurmon: Covenantally fulfilled, should it still be used for -- looked to for providing principles on earth? And I would say absolutely. Not because I don't think the Mosaic Covenant was not fulfilled in Christ. But remember the one thing we said last night, the one thing that we know it doesn't mean is that it was abolished, as in it disappeared.

Notice what Jeremiah's version of the making of a New Covenant actually says: "For this is the covenant that I will make with the house of Israel after those days saith the Lord." Actually back up a verse.

"Behold…" this is Hebrews 8:8. "…the days to come saith the Lord when I will make a New Covenant with the house of Israel and with the house of Judah, not according to the covenant that I made with their fathers in the day when I took them by the hand to lead them out of the land of Egypt. Because they continued not in my covenant, and I regarded them not, saith the Lord."

So indeed he is making a covenant that is not like the Old Covenant but is that in regards to the *law* of that covenant.

Read on. "For this is my covenant." Obviously he's talking in regard to their disobedience and their inability to keep it as what he just said. "For this is the covenant that I will make with the house of Israel after those, saith the Lord. I will *put my laws* into their mind and write them in their hearts and I will be to them a God and they shall be to me a people. And they shall not teach every man and his neighbor and every man his brother saying know the Lord for all shall know me from the least to the greatest."

Now, did the law completely change when Torah was gone? No. Is that the distinction he's making when he says, I'll make them a New Covenant not like the old one? No. He's talking about the mode of administration of that covenant is no longer through thou shalt do this without the Spirit. But instead God says, "I will write my laws in their hearts and in their minds," and through that means it will bring about obedience.

So, while I say, yes, there are some things that are -- that are fulfilled, and this is -- this is what distinction -- fulfilled does not mean abolished. Christ fulfilled that law. He fulfilled every single ceremony, Sabbath day, right, and everything else. He fulfilled all of the moral code that Don says is apart from the Law of Moses out there. And he fulfilled all of the judicial law. He fulfilled everything. But when he was resurrected and that new priesthood, new law comes along, does the content of that law completely change? No. In fact, I would argue it's for the most part identical. But we don't observe those covenants and rights and ceremonies because they're fulfilled in the body of Christ to which those things typologically pointed. But as far as the civil laws go, the judicial aspects, and the judgments, the case laws, and the moral law, he fulfills that, but we're also told to mimic him

So where do we go to find out what it means to love your neighbor? Where do we go? You can say thou shalt not steal is written in God's character. Well, yeah, and I would say thou shalt not muzzle the mouth of the ox that treads out the corn is also written in his character. And that's what Paul quotes in the New Testament in order to justify the payment of ministers. That's Old Testament case law.

So this is a much more complex issue than just harping on not one jot, not one tittle shall pass until all is fulfilled. What is the nature of that fulfillment and what does it look like on the other side? And you've got to deal with the content of that law and where you can find it.

Question to Joel McDurmon: Romans Chapter 8 verses 1-4, if the law of the spirit and life made us free from the law of sin and death, what has occurred to put the church back under the law of sin and death?

Joel McDurmon: I understand what the question says. I don't really understand where they're going. I don't understand how they're saying that I'm putting them back under the law of sin and death.

Question Clarification: The law of the spirit of life made us free from the law of sin and death. So what has occurred that puts the church back under the law of sin and death?

Joel McDurmon: I would say we are not under the law of sin and death. It's that simple. Because the old covenant administration was a covenant of death. We just read and I just explained that there is a New Covenant. But in that covenant, God writes the law, his laws, in our hearts and minds. That is a new way of doing things. It doesn't mean the content of what we obey and do and how we should live in society is different. It's a new way of doing things. So when we're freed from the curse of the law and we're free from law in that regard, that doesn't mean that we can go live as libertines, but it also doesn't mean that we go and find the source of our ethical codes by which we live and by which we interpret how to live somewhere besides God's word. I mean, that's the only place in the world where God has ever revealed ethical laws, civil laws. No civil law code in human history can claim that except the Mosaic Code.

And we're not following that on our own, by our own works on pains and death anymore. God has written that in our hearts and minds, and we are to aspire to that in society. That is not placing us under the law; that is the Spirit of life freeing us to obey the law.

Don Preston: It's interesting that Joel says that we are free from the law of sin and death and yet he still says that we die biologically because of sin.

Well, it seems to me if I still die biologically because of sin, I am subject to the law of sin and death.

Let me point out that the law of sin and death was prior to Torah. That was the Garden. The law of sin and death was incorporated into and exacerbated by Torah. Romans Chapter 5, "the law entered that sin might abound." So Torah exacerbated, compounded, magnified if you please, the law of sin and death and provided no solution for it.

Now Joel says I'm not subject -- we are not subject to the law of sin and death. But to reiterate, he says we still are subject to physical death which is the result of sin. I'm sorry. That is a very, very serious logical contradiction.

Now let me make a comment on something that Joel has kind of harped on because it has directly to do with the New Covenant and law, resurrection, et cetera. He said if what Preston is true -- says is true, then we shouldn't even be teaching anyone. We shouldn't have evangelism. Now wait just a minute.

Joel just stated and has stated repeatedly, we are in the age to come. The age to come is the covenant of -- the age of the New Covenant. What did -- what did Jeremiah say would characterize the age of the new covenant? "I'll put my law in their hearts and minds and their sins and their iniquities will I remember no more, and they shall not teach every man, his neighbor, and every man, his brother, saying know the Lord, for they shall all know me."

Okay. Now watch this, folks. Joel says we're under the New Covenant promise by Jeremiah. Jeremiah said under the New Covenant they won't teach their neighbor, teach their brother. Now remember Joel says we're under that New Covenant. And yet Joel says we ought to be teaching one another. Another self-contradiction. Well, this gets back to the nature of resurrection and death and the entire panoramic story, to use his term, the symphony.

We are in that age to come that was promised. That does not *negate* evangelism as Revelation Chapter 21 and 22 says. Joel himself has admitted we're in the age to come. He admits that we are supposed to be teaching, therefore he has nullified everything he has said about if what Preston says is true we shouldn't be evangelizing. Because he says we're under the New Covenant promised by Jeremiah.

And I'm way out of time. Sorry.

Question to Don Preston: If Eve's pain was increased in the curse, wouldn't that mean that her pain already existed before the fall?

Don Preston: Yes. I'm sorry. No, I'm not really trying to be facetious.

If Eve's pain was supposed to be multiplied in childbirth, does that not prove that pain existed? Yes.

It certainly proves that. Joel says, no, it doesn't necessarily prove that. Well, you know, if I've got a dollar and I increase it by two, does that mean I didn't have a dollar? I mean, we can't ignore this language, ladies and gentlemen. Pain shall be increased. That means there was pain present.

Now, if animals were eating plants, wasn't that death? If man was eating plants, wasn't that death? You -- you simply cannot deny the reality that some form of death was present in the Garden before sin. I don't have time to draw up. I've got about ten charts giving ten reasons why this death cannot be biological. That's not the focus. But I've already demonstrated over and over that the focus is not on Adam and Eve's biological body.

So, again, does the -- her pain shall be increased mean that there was already pain? Yes.

Joel McDurmon: So of the increase of Christ's government there shall be no end means that he had a government before that. But you know it didn't. He didn't receive a government until he set it on high. According to Daniel 7. I know you put that in A.D. 70; we disagree on that.

So, obviously, this language is not meant to be absolutized in that manner as I have warned you about a couple of nights ago. Now, would I absolutely positively deny that there was any of the slightest discomfort on Eve's part? I won't go into all the details of a ten-pound baby again.

But, you know, the problem is, number one, this language is not always used that way. It can't be absolutized, and number two, I have no idea. I wasn't in the Garden. Preston has no idea. He wasn't in the Garden. Were you?

I'm not going to imply that you were the third animal that was there. But, we don't know. We don't really know what it was like. So when God uses a phrase like that, I will greatly multiply your pain in child birth, even if there was some level of discomfort before that, we know that the curse greatly multiplied it. And I think we can imply from our experience today that

that's pretty much still in place. Now, granted, when you see it in the movies, it's way over dramatized. But it's not a cake walk, folks.

So to dismiss this in that regard I think is a little cheap. That should be enough for now.

Question to Joel McDurmon: This is a question that Rod and I, as we sorted through them, we said that's a really good question. And I don't know if we ought to ask it. And we thought, well, we'll hold it towards the end and see if we can get it in. So, everybody, bear with us on this. This is a question before the fall. I want to know what you think of it. It's before the fall.

Did Adam sweat? Did Adam's sweat smell? Did his feces stink? And then what about the non-fallen Jesus? Same question.

Joel McDurmon: I have no idea. I wasn't in the Garden. I don't know. I don't know if there were different odors. I don't know if we received odors the same way we do today.

The only person who has even tried to imagine this, and again this is rushing in where eagles -- angels -- eagles too probably, fear to tread, is -- what's the guy's name down in Texas that has the creation science?

Don Preston: Karl Baugh.

Joel McDurmon: Karl Baugh. He tried to recreate what -- creation all these misapplications of scripture here and scripture there -- and he created this world in which he was -- but he did have some really weird results. By creating certain conditions, he grew fish in fish tanks that were two and a half, three, four times the size they were supposed to be in the wild. Where normally fish grow larger in the wild than they do in captivity.

And then they noticed something else. The feces of the fish began to have positive effects. And I'm not trying to say that that answers your question by any means. But it's not unimaginable that things were different then. But as far as did his sweat smell and that kind of stuff, I have no idea. Did he sweat? I don't know. I wasn't there.

And what was the last -- oh, about the sinless Jesus. I have no idea. That's a difficult question. We're never told anything in scripture about Jesus' feces.

And so -- for lack of scientific data, I'll suspend judgment.

Don Preston: I appreciate Joel's candor. There are some things that we do not know. However, if we know that they ate, there's certainly a process of death that must occur unless we want to postulate some great unknown mystery about those processes.

If we want to say that Adam and Eve didn't sweat perhaps, then we're going to have to postulate some different biological and physiological processes in the human body.

And it seems to me that if we are going to be candid enough to say I don't know about any of this, it is therefore a little bit illogical and disingenuous to say now I am going to build my case on the curse saying that the curse is radically different from that. Well, if you don't know if it's radically different than that, you can't build your theological case on that.

I'd like to go back to the point that I have made repeatedly. When we come to the prophetic books of the Old Testament, when we come to the New Testament, the Genesis curse is incorporated into Israel, the predictions of the overcoming of that curse, *using Edenic language,* are without fail, *without fail,* posited at the end of the Old Covenant law of Israel in A.D. 70.

I have pointed out repeatedly how Paul in Colossians cites, quotes, and alludes, to Genesis 1-3. He talks about the reconciliation of heaven and earth. Well, what happened because of the curse of Adam? Heaven and earth were divided. I would remind you that Paul said in Ephesians Chapter 1:9-10 that it was God's eternal purpose -- purposed before time to reconcile all things both in heaven and on earth, all things in him, in one body, in Christ, in the dispensation of the fullness of time.

When was the dispensation of fullness of time? The Old Covenant age, the last days of Israel. Joel agrees with that. Now, he didn't say beyond and again and again and again I'm going to restore heaven and earth. He said the reconciliation of all things would occur in the dispensation of the fullness of time. Paul said that time was present in the first century.

Moderator: Would you want a rejoinder on that?

Joel McDurmon: Do you want to go back and forth on that?

Don Preston: Whatever.

Moderator: Because what this is dealing with is, of course, death being present in the Garden before the fall. That's why I think that we've always viewed questions. So if you would like to --

Don Preston: Sure.

Joel McDurmon: Let's back and forth. Let's do it two minutes.

Joel McDurmon: Two things, first of all, about the sweat. Two things on that. It's one thing to say I have no data on this and therefore I can't make a conclusion, but I do have absolutely clear data on the other part that says this is part of the curse. So while I have to suspend judgment on the one part, I don't on the other part. And so to say therefore it is wrong to build a doctrine on that is just absolutely fallacious. What else do you build doctrine on except God's own explicit words.

Now, last night, I believe it was, maybe the night before, I mentioned, have you ever done a Biblical study on the word sweat? It appears three times in scripture. Now I jokingly said it would change your life. Perhaps it won't go that far, but it may, you know, make you go back and reconcile with an old friend or something.

Sweat appears three times in scripture. Once in the Garden after the curse. Okay? This is part of the curse. And the second time it is in -- its either Ezekiel or Jeremiah, I don't have it off the top of my head. And it's a reference to the clothing of the priest. In this idealized view of the new heavens, new earth, for lack of a better term at the moment, they shall be coated in linen, which actually was the undergarments of the priest. That says they will wear nothing but linen. And it explicitly says so that nothing -- they will wear nothing that makes them sweat. Now what is that image? Removal of physical curse.

Now we'll get to this in just a second. The third place sweat is mentioned is in another garden. The Garden of Gethsemane when Jesus kneels down with the thorns of that curse on his head. (Well, about to wear those) He kneels down in the Garden of Gethsemane and prays until, as it were, he sweats blood.

And what does blood symbolize? This is not just a dramatic statement. It is symbolizing the blood he is about to shed to overcome that curse. And then he wears the thorns of that curse on his head.

Now, granted the Edenic language is incorporated into the Mosaic Covenant. And then that language is used explicitly to say that this is being reversed, they're coming out of the exile, out of the Mosaic Covenant, out of this and that. But is it being equated? Is it being totalized in the Mosaic Covenant? See, Preston's position, as far as I understand it, requires that you do that. That at the moment that the Mosaic Covenant appropriates the Edenic language, therefore all the clear physical language of Eden is no longer applicable; only the Mosaic Covenant is. When in reality the Mosaic Covenant itself was really just a set of types to lead us to the Messiah that was going to come from Genesis 3:15.

So I see it as a typological reality. Just because it's appropriating the language by no means means that the original curse, and original promise, won't be fulfilled literally, and it certainly doesn't mean that what happened in A.D. 70 was final. To say that is too add way to much to the text and the documents.

Don Preston: Well, it's interesting that an agreement is made, in fact, that these things are typological. Adam himself was specifically said to be typological of Christ who was about to come when Paul wrote. So that means that these events, these physical events that happened in the Garden are explicitly being said to be typological.

Types go from the physical to the spiritual. Joel has admitted that these promises have been fulfilled spiritually in Christ, but then he turns around and says they must yet be fulfilled physically.

Now I want you to notice what this means. Physical then spiritual then back to physical. I'd like to have some real good scriptural proof for that. The spiritual is always the ultimate goal. The physical has never been the physical goal.

For Joel to submit or to agree that Israel's language incorporates the language of Eden, and yet it's not the same thing, it seems to me, denies the reality of what Hebrews Chapter 11 has been saying. And that is there is one hope, there is one resurrection hope. They are not many resurrections. And so if that hope from creation all the way to Zion has been fulfilled -- to agree that Israel's language incorporates the Edenic curse language, and to say it's been fulfilled spiritually is to say in essence that it's been fulfilled finally because the spiritual is the ultimate goal. Physical has *never* been God's ultimate goal.

So we will leave it at that.

Joel McDurmon – Afterthoughts

****

Throughout this debate run a few themes that help to summarize it. I'll look at a couple of these in this appendix, and tie up a few loose ends as well. Toward this effort of summarizing and clarifying what I have argued in this debate, the interested reader will want to see the fuller summaries available in my recent book *We Shall All Be Changed: A Critique of Full Preterism and a Defense of a Future Bodily Resurrection*.

Themes

Perhaps the most important theme upon which Don's position and mine diverge is that of the nature of the curse and death of Adam. Is it "spiritual" only, or does it include physical death? As we cover this issue, the reader will see just why it is so crucial, and just why Don attempted to halt discussion of it at the very outset.

The crucial centrality of this issue is obvious: if Adamic death includes physical death, then any "resurrection" we speak of as having occurred in AD 70 must have included *physical* resurrection *or it was not final*. If, however, Adamic death does not pertain to physical death *at all*, then Preston may—I stress, *may*, for even in this case it is not conclusive—have a case as to the *finality* of resurrection in AD 70. The reader can see easily why this is perhaps the most important theme running through this debate.

The only chance Don had at maintaining his claim to finality in AD 70 was to keep physical death and physical earth *completely* out of the discussion. One budge on this issue and he has not only failed to establish his position beyond a reasonable doubt (which was true anyway), but utterly falsified any possibility that his resolution is true.

Thus the reader can understand why virtually the first thing Don said in his opening statement was an attempt to marginalize and dismiss this specific issue, and thereby head off any discussion of it:

No matter what our concept of protology—that is, creation in Genesis, no matter what our concept of the protology may be. No matter what our concept of the curse of Adam and the death of Adam may be . . . no matter what our concept of the body, or our concept of the resurrection may be, scripture posits . . . the end of the millennium resurrection to overcome the Adamic curse and the Adamic death at the end of the old covenant age of Israel and fulfillment of God's promises to Abraham and Israel after the flesh (p. 5).

As I noted at least twice in the debate, I can sure understand why Don wants to say our concepts of these topics *don't matter*. If the Bible even in a single instance suggests that *it's* (not "our") concept of Adamic curse and Adamic death includes physical death, then whatever happened in AD 70 must not have been final, as already noted. So, *of course*, this matters! It is of central and utmost importance. And Don's attempt to sweep it under the rug at the outset was nothing short of an admission of a crippling weakness in his eschatology.

What ensued was a feat of hermeneutical reductionism—that is, an attempt to reduce nearly everything in Scripture, including Genesis 1–3, to spiritual-only realities and fulfillment.

I had expected this logical result in advance of the debate, and based on that expectation I specifically requested a format that allowed me freedom to introduce my own negative material up front. Don agreed, and then subsequently neglected what he agreed to, and then pretended I did not address the vast majority of his salient arguments. I am glad he apologized when I called him out on this during the debate, but then he continued doing so on other occasions.

In anticipation of this logical corner into which he would be forced, I presented multiple exegetical examples of when Scripture speaks of fulfillments of prophecy in terms of finality, "the end," "fulfilled," totality (such as "all"), and yet it was impossible that any of these instances was the *final* end of God's redemptive history. This impossibility resulted in the very least because the curse upon the ground and upon Adam and Eve was not yet removed in those instances. Physical curse was the only obvious criteria by which anyone could have determined.

Don never engaged these multiple exegetical instances in that debate. In the one passing reference he gave to the problem in general, he stated, "How would we *know* if the Biblical writers were intending to point to the consummative end? Wouldn't they say something like 'the end of all things has drawn near'?" (Cp. p. 44). This obviously missed the point of the argument which had already rendered this very question impotent. It almost a good thing Don did not realize it; he would likely have been embarrassed. Preston was left making an impotent argument as a bare assertion without proof, and then concluding his position was proven. This is a classic example of the fallacy of begging the question, but worse, it was begging a question with an assumption *that had already been refuted*.

Don's neglect to address my examples was such a gaping deficiency in his performance that he actually broke debate protocol and used a large portion of his time the *following* night to double back and offer responses to some of those instances. When he should have been addressing *my* positive arguments, or offering negative material to undermine them, he instead tried to keep administering life-support to his own positive arguments from the night before. This indicated to me that he thought he had been stung, and wanted more time to support his tottering position.

But even after sleeping on it, and then cheating a little for his own affirmative, the best he could offer in response was that: 1) the instances of totality and finality I referenced are limited by their contexts, and, 2) none of them included the passing away of Torah (the Sinaitic Covenant). Since, he argued, the "end" and "all things" spoken of in the New Testament *did* include the passing away of the Mosaic Covenant (Matt. 5; Heb. 8), it therefore *must* be the complete finality of God's redemptive history.

These responses still left Preston's position deficient. While scriptures must of course be interpreted within context, to impose limits upon some pronouncements and not others that are very similar is arbitrary. And thus to draw conclusions based upon such distinctions is to beg the question again. The question at hand involves, among other things, *when exactly is the finality?* Is it AD 70, or later? How do we know? My examples proved that you cannot simply point to a word like "fulfilled" as proof of finality. With that option removed, one must point to *other* biblical indications. In hindsight, *all pronouncements of fulfillment can be said to have limited contexts*. Thus, any such descriptor we have from Scripture, even allegedly for AD 70, cannot in itself be the deciding factor on this issue apart from assuming without evidence that *this* time is categorically different from all the previous incidences in scope and nature.

Preston thought he was countering the conundrum I placed him in by arguing the previous contexts were limited. But besides begging the question, all he actually did was prove my point: all does not necessarily mean all, end does not necessarily mean end, fulfill does not necessarily mean over and done, once for all. It was encouraging to see him progress somewhat toward my position during the debate.

To his credit, Preston attempted to overcome his question-begging by giving a reason why AD 70 was different than all those times before. The distinction, he argued, was the passing away of the Mosaic Covenant. But it is here that his argument added incoherence to its arbitrariness. This argument amounts to a tremendous assumption that because of this passing away, the "resurrection" of the covenant body in AD 70 *must* be the final and exclusive end of all things.

The incoherence here lies in the fact that this argument is a *non sequitur*—the conclusion simply *does not follow* from the premises. This is why I mentioned during the debate that the Mosaic Covenant was like a covenant within a covenant. As we discussed, it was *added* for the sole purpose of keeping Israel after the flesh under strict discipline until Christ arrived (Gal. 3:16–24). At that point, the purpose of that Old administration was finished. But if the covenant that was *added* passed away, does that mean that the larger covenant to which it was added *also* passed away? Does it mean that the even larger overarching deliverance from Adamic corruption and death was finalized? Don *assumed* so, but was unable to give any reasons why this *must be* the case.

While the relationship of all these covenants and redemptive history needs fuller explanation than I can give here, the basic point should be clear: the Mosaic administration *itself* was *added* for a limited purpose, and thus was itself a *limited context* within the Abrahamic covenant! Thus, to speak of the passing of the Mosaic covenant is to speak of the passing of a *limited context* within God's overall redemptive history—not the totality of it. Thus, Don's arbitrary separation of AD 70 "finality" as somehow different from all of those other instances was further falsified.

In this view, then, we must look to other factors in determining the finality of God's plan. I argued consistently that these factors involved the nature of the curse, the earth, and the nature of God's kingdom promises as including the earth. The transition from Old to New Covenant administrations brought us the advent of the Messiah, His death, burial, and resurrection, His ascension and session at God's right hand, and the beginning of the rule of His saints with Him, and the destruction of that Old Covenant administration in AD 70. But it could hardly be said that the inauguration of the New Creation was also the fullness of it in history. In light of the facts I brought up over and over, including the inheritance and rule in the earth by the saints (Matt. 5:5; Rev. 5, et al), the growth of Christ's kingdom until it destroys all other kingdoms and fills the whole earth (Daniel 2), not to mention the issues of the curse already discussed, there is simply no way we can honestly say that the complete finality of God's redemptive history has arrived.

I say one cannot maintain such a position, that is, *unless* he radically redefines everything stated to be earthly as somehow spiritual-only. But to do this and overcome all that has been argued so far, one must be very strident and stubborn in the effort, while overlooking a good deal to the contrary.

This is what I observed from Don: an effort to maintain ultimate finality based upon Torah-finality in AD 70 by means of a radical hermeneutic. That is, limiting the application of the fullness of the kingdom promises to the poetical adaptations of Edenic language used later in Scripture. Since AD 70 was a limited context within redemptive history, we should therefore expect its references to the covenant worldview that is larger than itself to be limited in a similar way. But the larger realities from which it draws still remain full realities. Within the smaller, added covenant, that language becomes limited to its poetic potential in most cases—a tool for conveying certain truths about *that smaller covenant* and *its* purposes in the meantime. But these poetic applications hardly alter the substance and reality of what already existed in the first place. In other words, the Mosaic Covenant does not subsume and thereby redefine Eden, it only alludes to it in a certain way. Likewise when Paul references Genesis 1 and applies it to Christ (Col. 1), he is not redefining and annulling the rest of the full truth of Genesis 1–3 with new "spiritual-only" definitions, he is merely appropriating that language for one particular purpose in one particular context. The larger realities still remain. What Don did in these regards, however, was to take the limited contextual meaning in Paul and impose that upon the whole reality of Genesis. He argued that Paul's "spiritualized" teaching was *all it ever meant to begin with*. Once again, this shows why Don attempted to stifle any discussion of the nature of Genesis from the outset. It puts him in a really difficult position.

One Hope

Another theme was endlessly repeated by Don throughout the debate: the refrain of "one hope" (a search of the document retrieves 90 instances of this phrase!). This phrase was alleged as the basis of Hebrews 11. Yet, as I said in the debate, "one hope" is nowhere to be found in Hebrews 11. It does not exist there. In his zeal to create an argument of proof-texts from various books and contexts, Don never even bothered to read Hebrews 11 to the audience, and he certainly never bothered to exegete it. Had he done so, he would have found the exact opposite of what he was arguing: "Now faith is the assurance of *things hoped for*" (Heb. 11:1). The Greek word is *elpidzomenon*. It is a present passive participle that is *plural* not singular. It should literally be translated, "things being hoped for." Don never rose to the level of reading the basic grammar of the text. Instead, he kept repeating his own refrain over and over despite it, and trying to force the text to mean what he said.

"Things hoped for" remains *plural* here despite Don's best efforts to convince us otherwise. The chapter outlines the feats and endurances of several of God's faithful people who had various short-term hopes toward which they acted in faith. It is faith, of course, that is the theme of the chapter, not "one hope."

Yet Don repeatedly stated this error boldly, even going so far as to post a chart that posited "The One Hope of Abel-Noah-Abraham-Moses→ Zion! (Heb.11:11-35)" (p. 15, 26-27, 45, et al), and openly to state later, "Hebrews 11–12 inseparably joins the one hope of Abel, Noah, Abraham, and Moses" (p. 45). This is just simply false, and is easily proven so by simply reading the chapter: *it says no such thing*.

The mystery then is why Don harped on it so much, *even after I exposed this fact to the audience* very early on. As N.T. Wright once said of one of his theological opponents, this is not so much trying to shut the barn door after the horse got out, it's trying to ride across open country on a hobby-horse.

Someone should tell Don that stating the same falsehood over and over does not make it true, it just makes you a repeat offender.

Loose Ends

Misquoting and attributing non-existent ideas is not an isolated incident with Don. At least twice in this debate he attempted to prove from quotations of my own that I actually supported his positions. Unfortunately, on both occasions, he twisted or pulled from context what I said and meant. In one case (which he repeated more than once), he attributed a direct quotation to me I never even said or wrote. Allegedly, Joel McDurmon said, "Zion has been spiritualized and fulfilled" (chart, p. 15). In other places, I allegedly said "all" of the Zion promises have been so (p. 90, 99, 111, 124).

During the debate, I responded by saying Don's treatment was "not a full expression of my doctrine" (p. 148). Indeed, it was *hardly* a full expression of my doctrine! Let's have a little context: this comes from an article I wrote which was later published as an appendix to my book *Jesus v. Jerusalem*. It was specifically refuting the idea of rebuilding of a literal *temple* in the future upon Mt. Zion. In that context, I wrote:

"I say let the Dome-of-the-Rock stand. In fact, I will go so far as to say that it would be non-Christian and unbiblical to call for its replacement by a Jewish Temple. Rather, in due time, Christ reigning from his current throne will spread the Gospel and subdue all His enemies—even the Muslim and Jewish enemies. He will bring them into the Church—His body—the only True Temple and Dwelling Place of God. *Even Zion has been "spiritualized," if you will—revealed to be fulfilled in the person of the Ascended Christ . . . What is Zion but the Spirit-Indwelt people of God?* What is the Temple except these same Indwelt people of God? To trade this truth for any stack of concrete blocks on any hill is to trample the Son of God underfoot and slap God in the face" (*Jesus v. Jerusalem*, p. 178).

For starters, let's note that I *never* said "Zion has been spiritualized and fulfilled." When Don attributes this to me as a direct quotation, it is simply sloppy scholarship and is thus irresponsible and bearing on false witness.

But even against his paraphrased versions, perhaps you can see that my application is totally different and certainly more nuanced that Don presented it. By "spiritualized," it is clear that I *did not* mean "no earthly manifestation," because I clearly went on to say Christ would subdue all His enemies, and that Spirit-indwelt Church (obviously on earth, at least in part) was itself "Zion." I also made abundantly clear, first, that by "spiritualized" I was choosing a term that could be misunderstood, and thus I said, "if you will," which is classically a request for clemency in interpreting the phrase at hand. Don refused such clemency and imposed his own narrow definition upon my meaning. More importantly, second, I noted that this "spiritualized" promise was fulfilled in the *ascension* of Christ—*not in His AD 70 judgment!* Don not only totally ignored this part, he misled the audience in suggesting it could be applied to AD 70.

Don went through so much trouble to prepare charts based on alleged quotations of me, it would have been more helpful (not to mention more honest) if he had told the whole truth, and not suppressed most of it.

As I stated in the debate itself, Hebrews 12:22 attests to something that was true already *before AD 70*. Don never addressed this point, obviously because it throws a monkey wrench into his hermeneutic. If Christ has already fulfilled "all things," including the Zion promises, *before AD 70*, then obviously AD 70 must be of some secondary importance. Don cannot stomach that idea, as biblical as it may be.

In another instance, Don quoted me in a chart as affirming that the Law of Moses "died in AD 70." I pointed out immediately that this neutered quotation was bereft of its context. The context is a discussion of the Old Covenant age giving way to the New:

I believe these two periods, being hinged upon the coming and work of Christ, pertain obviously to the Old and New Covenant **administrations**. Indeed, this is what the author of Hebrews himself relates. He says the New Covenant makes the Old obsolete: "And what *is becoming obsolete* and growing old *is ready to vanish away*" (Heb. 8:13). Notice, the New had in fact made the Old obsolete definitively. But as he wrote, in his time, the Old was *becoming* obsolete and was *ready* to vanish away. It had not yet been completely wiped out, but it was certainly in its dying moments.

"**It died in ad 70,** when the symbol and ceremonies of that Old **system—the Temple and sacrifices**—were completely destroyed by the Roman armies (*Jesus v. Jerusalem*, p. 47–48; bold emphasis added)."

Now you decide, reader: did I mean that the law itself "died in AD 70," as Preston claimed, or was I writing about particular aspects of the *administration* of the law? The question of God's law itself must be taken up independently of the point I was obviously making.

Yet even after being corrected on this quotation and its meaning by me—the author of the quotation and its meaning—Don continued to defend his own erroneous misquotation. When he broke debate protocol on that second day, he even went so far as to display a *new* chart that, as he apparently thought, justified his misrepresentation:

"Joel says it was not the law that died in AD 70, but "the administration of the law."

This is false!

Hebrews 8 does not mention "administration"" (chart, p. 98).

Let me help Don understand his error by simply quoting the actual text in question:

"Behold, the days are coming, declares the Lord, when I will establish a new covenant with the house of Israel and with the house of Judah, not like the covenant that I made with their fathers. . . . For they did not continue in my covenant. . . . For this is the covenant that I will make with the house of Israel after those days, declares the Lord: *I will put my laws into their minds, and write them on their hearts,* and I will be their God, and they shall be my people (Heb. 8:8–10).

God says that in the New Covenant, He would write *His laws* in our hearts and minds. This means His law must *continue* into the New Covenant. I acknowledge this openly and teach it. So, Don Preston is misleading in trying to attribute to me that God's *law itself* **died** in AD 70. All Don needed to do (again) is simply read the text, and he would have realized that the issue is not God's law itself, but the covenantal administration of that law. Don's failure to pay attention to basic facts—either in Scripture or my arguments—seemed to be another recurring theme throughout this debate.

Conclusion

And what more shall I say, for space here fails me to discuss at length several other loose ends outstanding:

The alleged fulfillment of all of Isaiah 24–27 and Hosea 11–13 in 1 Corinthians 15 (which claims were the *very reason* I presented those exegetical examples up front!)

Don's misattribution of Abraham's children's inheritance of the land to Abraham himself (Don applies the principle of Abraham and Levi in Hebrews 7 *backwards*!)

Don's complete fabrication claiming "Abraham got it" in Nehemiah 9 (it's not there, read the text!)

Don's attempt to poison the well by suggesting that anyone who believes in bodily resurrection and earthly reign is "dispensational" (when in fact all those ideas predate dispensationalism by centuries)

Don's fruitless attempt to align me with Hymenaeus (which claim unwittingly entraps Paul himself as well—just read Ephesians 2:5–6, which makes clear that in one sense believers were already resurrected)

Don's inaccurate claim that the Pharisees wanted to kill Paul over his doctrine of resurrection (Acts 23:9 says the Pharisees *agreed* with Paul: "we find nothing wrong in this man")

Don's claim that Paul's marriage teaching pertained to the reality of the new heavens and new earth (when in reality, new heavens and new earth appears nowhere in that context, and if Don's claim were true, it would mean that the new heavens and new earth had already arrived *prior* to AD 70).

These problems and many more (I have not even included many issues brought up in Q&A) made this debate almost an endless series of headaches (though perhaps because of me pulling out my own hair). Through them all, however, the simple truth concerning the nature of Adamic curse and the promises of an earthly renewal and reign still defy any claims to finality in AD 70. The AD 70 event was obviously an important watershed. But while many important lessons are yet to be learned in light of acknowledging its *finality* is not one of them.

Don K. Preston – Afterthoughts

****

One Hope– The Hope of Israel

Throughout the debate I emphasized the one eschatological hope proclaimed by all NT writers.

1.) Paul said, "There is One Hope" (Eph. 4:4). The "one hope" was "nothing but the hope of Israel," found in Moses and the Prophets. (Page 9-10).

2.) This one eschatological hope extended from Abel to Moses to Zion (Hebrews 11).

3.) The Old Testament texts that serve as the source of the NT prophecies of the final resurrection invariably posit that resurrection at the time of the destruction of Old Covenant Israel (Isaiah 24-27; Daniel 12). This is indisputable. Joel did not touch it.

4.) Paul said the resurrection from the death of Adam would be fulfilled when "the law" that was the strength of sin would be overcome. *The only law* described as the strength of sin was Torah. Thus, the "final" resurrection would be at the end of Torah. This is *critical*, yet, Joel *never offered one word of response.* This argument alone falsified his eschatology.

5.) The One Resurrection Hope, from Genesis onward, climaxes in *Zion* (Isaiah 25:8; Hebrews 11; chart, page 15). Genesis eschatology is not different from Israel's eschatology.

Joel continually divorced Genesis from the climax of Israel's covenant history. This creates two eschatologies: one for Israel, fulfilled in AD 70, and another, at the end of the Christian age. *Let this soak in.* Joel's Dominionism is an overt denial of Paul's inspired word.

Matthew 5:17-18[1]

Jesus said not one jot or one tittle of the Law would pass until it was all fulfilled. Jesus' emphatic words pose a severe problem for Dominionism..

For instance, the ceremonial Sabbath- an integral part of "the law" - foreshadowed the "final salvation." (Page 13f) Thus, until fulfillment of the resurrection, Torah could not pass. Joel said the Sabbath law, and attendant cultic practices, have passed away, yet, final salvation has not come!

The contrast between Joel and Jesus is stark: Jesus said NONE would pass until it was ALL fulfilled. Joel says *some passed, without being fulfilled!* I challenged Joel to show how anyone could get from Jesus' words, "not one jot or one tittle shall pass from the law, until it is all fulfilled" that Jesus meant: "Some of the law will pass without being fulfilled."No response.

Joel attempted to negate the comprehensive definition of "all" in Matthew 5:17-18 by offering some passages where "all" is restricted. This is not disputed. But, for Joel to go to texts *unrelated to Matthew 5–* and find a limited "all"-- and impose that limited definition on Matthew 5 is an "illegitimate transfer of context."

If we adopt Joel's hermeneutic then "all" can *never* be defined as comprehensive. If "all" in Joshua limits "all" in Matthew 5, then by Joel's "logic," it likewise limits the "all" in John 3:16!

I produced a chart– (page 59) from Greg Bahnsen, McDurmon's former mentor. Bahnsen demonstrated that when "all" is used in an "unparticularized" manner, *as in Matthew 5*, it is wrong to impose a limitation on it as Joel did. *There is delimitation of "all" in Matthew 5!* This is fatal to Joel's view. McDurmon offered not a word of response.

Jesus said not one iota of Torah would pass until it was all fulfilled. The word "fulfill" is from *genetai*, and means "fully accomplish." Joel argued

---

[1] See my book *From Torah To Telos: The Passing of the Law of Moses*, for an in-depth study of Matthew 5:17-18. The book is available from my websites, www.eschatology.org, or, www.bibleprophecy.com; http://www.donkpreston.com, Amazon, Kindle and other retailers.

that *genetai* can have many definitions. But, this does not negate the fact it does mean "fully accomplish" as Bahnsen insists.

Joel's desperation to escape the force of *genetai* came into full view when he claimed all things were fulfilled in Christ on the cross. I responded by noting Hymenaeus said the resurrection was past (*genetai*, 2 Timothy 2:18). So, if Hymenaeus took Joel's position, i.e. the resurrection was "fulfilled" at the cross, *he was right! Paul was patently wrong to condemn Hymenaeus!* After all, Hymenaeus was simply teaching what Joel does! Joel uttered not a word in response.

The Curse of Genesis[1]

Joel's theology rests on the *assumption* that biological death is the curse of Genesis 2:15-17: "in the day you eat you will surely die." His argument was, a physical death demands a physical resurrection. I refuted this in a variety of ways.

I asked if Adam and Eve died *the very day they ate the fruit*. Joel said they died *spiritually*, but not physically, except symbolically, when God killed the animals to provide skins for their nakedness. Joel insisted the death of the animals provided an "atonement" so Adam did not have to die biologically. This raises serious problems.

If the death of the animals was efficacious enough to prevent biological death, why did it not prevent spiritual death? I also posed a challenge directly from the text: "In the day that you eat thereof *you* will surely die." Not an *animal*, *"you."* Also, (page 31) Paul said Christ was "the first to be raised from the dead" (Acts 26:21f) *i.e. from the death of Adam. This is critical. Christ was patently not the first to be raised from biological death.* So, Joel says Adam did not die that day, but, Christ was the first to be raised from that non-occurring death!

---

[1] See my *We Shall Meet Him In The Air, The Wedding of the King of kings*. This book offers devastating evidence that refutes McDurmon's emphasis on physical death as the Curse of Adam. The book is available from my websites, Amazon, Kindle and other retailers.

Joel says a physical Adamic death demands a physical resurrection, else there is no "restoration of all things." I produced a chart, "Does physical demand physical?"(Page 115) that reveals a glaring inconsistency in Joel's hermeneutic. Joel ignored this chart.

Dispensationalists say Israel's physical city, temple, sacrifices demand a physical restoration of those things. Joel *ostensibly* rejects this. Yet, in our debate he argued that physical realities demand physical restoration!

I argued repeatedly that *it does not matter what our concept of the death of Adam was,*[2] because there are two indisputable facts.

The language of Genesis and the Curse is incorporated into God's OT promises to Israel.

That Curse language is posited as overcome at the end of Israel's aeon.

In Hosea 2:18f, the Genesis Curse is reversed- at the time *God would remarry Israel and make the New Covenant with her*. The NT posits the New Covenant and the remarriage at AD 70 (Matthew 22). Thus, no matter our concept of the nature of the Curse in Genesis, YHVH promised to reverse that Curse *when He made the New Covenant with Israel and remarried her.* Joel agreed that Hosea uses Genesis Curse language and Hosea posited fulfillment under the New Covenant. Yet, he denied the fulfillment of Genesis at that time.

Joel simply resorted to his "belief system" that Israel's promises were fulfilled, but, we are waiting for "the final fulfillment." No, there is not another New Covenant promised, and God will not remarry Israel again.[3] Hosea undeniably posited removal of the Genesis Curse with the making of

---

[2] Joel changed my argument from, "It does not matter what *our concept of the nature* of the death of Adam was" to, "It does not matter the nature of the death of Adam." This is not what I said. Joel approached Genesis pre-suppositionally, rejecting the NT spiritual interpretation of Genesis.

[3] See my book *AD 70: A Shadow of the (Real) End?* for an unprecedented, extensive and revealing examination of the Wedding issue as it relates to Joel's argument that AD 70 was a type of the real end of the age. There is *no evidence* that AD 70 foreshadowed another eschaton.

the New (Marriage) Covenant. This falsifies Joel's concept of the nature of the Adamic Curse.

In Colossians (see page 20f) Paul utilized the language of Genesis 1-3. Paul interpreted that language *spiritually*, and affirmed its first century fulfillment. You *must* catch the disingenuous nature of Joel's response. He admitted Paul interpreted Genesis spiritually in Colossians. Nonetheless, we are still waiting for the physical fulfillment! Yet, *Paul says not one word* to suggest that what was being spiritually fulfilled pointed to a future physical fulfillment.

My challenge was if Paul and the NT writers interpreted Genesis spiritually, we have no right to interpret it otherwise. Joel admits the NT writers interpret the OT prophecies *spiritually*. Joel's pre-suppositional "belief system" over rides the NT spiritual interpretation of Genesis, and this is wrong. So, once again, no matter what our preconceived idea of the nature of the death of Adam might be, the NT interprets Genesis spiritually, and that is authoritative.

I asked, in response to Joel's emphasis on physical death: "Is physical death the enemy of the child of God today?" Joel said "Yes." This is remarkable.

I offered several arguments in response.

1.) Sin brings (physical) death per Joel. But, the Christian is forgiven, all sin is removed. So, I asked Joel: If the child of God is forgiven, having no sin, why does the child of God still die physically? Joel offered no answer.

2.) Joel believes when a Christian dies physically they go to heaven. But how so? If the Christian is still under the Adamic curse, *which separates man from God* they should not go to heaven when they die! *How can physical death be the Christian's enemy when it ushers them into heaven?* No answer from Joel.

3.) Joel agrees Jesus died a *substitutionary death*. (Pages 172). But, if Christ's physical death was *substitutionary*, those in Christ should not die!

He took our place, did he not? Why do Christians, in the power of Jesus' *"substitutionary death"* still die physically? No answer from Joel.[4]

If physical death is the enemy of the child of God, there is no forgiveness today. If we are truly forgiven, death cannot be our enemy. Joel offered not a word of response.

Incredibly, Joel admitted the language of 1 Corinthians 15 demanded an imminent, AD 70 fulfillment (p. 238). So, since 1 Corinthians 15 predicted the destruction of "the last enemy" how can it be argued, with logical consistency, that 1 Corinthians 15 was fulfilled, but not fulfilled? Not one word in Corinthians suggests we look beyond the admitted imminence- and fulfillment! - of the text.

Abraham and the Land

Joel insisted, based on Acts 6:7, that Abraham must receive the land promise after a physical resurrection (Romans 4:13). This was a major element of Joel's resurrection doctrine. I offered the following:.

1.) Genesis 15 gave the *time* for the fulfillment of the promise to *Abraham*. In Acts 7:17 Stephen cited the land promise and said, "when the time of the promise drew nigh, which God had sworn to *Abraham*." Now if *the time had come* to fulfill the promise *"to Abraham"* then if the promise was not fulfilled *"to Abraham" at the time promised*, either the promise failed, or, the promise was fulfilled to Abraham *through his seed*. This is what I affirmed, but Joel ignored it.

2.) Nehemiah 9:6f specifically cites the Abrahamic land promises and says, "You have fulfilled your promise." Joel insisted this referred to Abraham's *seed* receiving the land, but not *Abraham*. This ignores the textual emphasis on the land promise being to *Abraham and his seed*.

3.) Scripture clearly posits the fulfillment of the Abrahamic promises in "the Seed." Abraham representatively rules the world through his Seed, Christ (Matthew 28:18-20). Jesus, the Seed of Abraham, has all authority. Joel never responded to this.

---

[4] See my, *We Shall Meet Him In The Air, The Wedding of the King of kings*, for an extensive discussion of the substitutionary and atoning sacrifice of Jesus. This material falsifies the idea of Adamic death as physical death.

4.) Hebrews 11 definitively refutes Joel's view of Abraham and the land promises. Hebrews shows that dirt was never Abraham's ultimate hope. He looked for a heavenly city, not an earthly one. This heavenly city was "Zion." "Zion" was a critical issue in the debate.

5.) When writing against the millennial view of a restored, literal Zion Joel says the promises of Zion have been "spiritualized" and "fulfilled in the body of Christ." So, per Joel, the Dispensationalist is wrong to preach a restored, physical city of Zion. Those promises are spiritually fulfilled in Christ. But this demands the fulfillment of the final resurrection!

The Messianic Zion promises are inextricably tied to the consummative resurrection (Isaiah 25:6-8). You *must* catch the power of this!

Scripture posits the final, end of the millennium, resurrection in Zion.

Abraham's "land promise" and "better resurrection" promise was centered in Zion, the heavenly city.

The Zion promises have been "spiritualized" and "fulfilled" in Christ (McDurmon).

Therefore, the final, end of the millennium, resurrection (the Abrahamic land promise and the "better resurrection" promise) was spiritualized and fulfilled.

In obvious desperation, Joel claimed that although the Zion promises have been spiritualized and fulfilled, Abraham is still looking for a physical city, on earth.

Zion, Resurrection and the Messianic Banquet (cf. p. 27f).

Isaiah 25:6-8 foretold the Messianic Banquet would be established on "Zion" in the day YHVH destroyed death. This is the "final" resurrection of 1 Corinthians 15. This is incredibly important, and once again demonstrated how Joel's assumptions about the nature of the death of Adam are nullified by the *spiritual interpretation* offered by Jesus and the NT– and *by Joel's own admissions*. Here is part of my argument:

The Messianic Banquet would be established "in the day" of the end of the millennium resurrection, on Zion (Isaiah 25:6-8).

Abraham, Isaac and Jacob sat down in the kingdom at the Messianic Banquet in AD 70 (McDurmon).

Therefore, the end of the millennium resurrection was fulfilled in AD 70.

This was ignored by Joel– with the exception of his claim that since the words "final resurrection" are not in Isaiah we can't say if Isaiah foretold the end of the millennium resurrection. However, Paul's "end of the millennium resurrection" doctrine of 1 Corinthians 15 was based on Isaiah. Thus, Isaiah clearly did predict the end of the millennium resurrection.

Job and the Resurrection

Another pillar of Joel's affirmatives was Job 19:25. Joel sought to prove that Job anticipated a resurrection of his physical body. His arguments, however, are specious.

1.) The translational issues in Job 19 are *incredibly* difficult. Joel admitted *some* difficulties but claimed the Hebrew of Job 19 is actually "a piece of cake." This is nonsense. The translational issues surrounding Job 19 are so daunting that many of history's greatest Hebrew scholars say Job 19 does not predict a future resurrection, much less a resurrection in the flesh!

2.) I noted that even if Job predicted a future (to him) resurrection, scripture posits the one resurrection hope at the end of Torah, on Zion, as taught in Isaiah 25-27, Daniel 12, 1 Corinthians 15, etc..[1] Joel never attempted any exegetical response to my examination of Isaiah 25-27, Daniel 12 or other texts I discussed. None.

3.) I repeatedly offered an argument in response to Job 19 from 1 Peter 4:5, 7, 17. Joel never mentioned it. (Page 71).

---

[1] See my book *Seventy Weeks Are Determined...For the Resurrection,* for a detailed discussion.

Peter said Christ was "ready (Greek, *hetoimos*, meaning not only morally prepared, but *temporally ready)* to judge "the living and the dead" (1 Peter 4:5). He said, "the end of all things has drawn near" (v. 7). He said, "*the* time has come for *the* judgment to begin" (v. 17).

In verse 17 Peter used the *anaphoric article*, the preponderant use of the article in the Greek. What this means is a writer introduces a subject. In his later discussion of that subject, he uses the definite article to refer back to that subject. This means verse 17 refers back to v. 5. Thus, in verse 17, Peter said, "the time has come for the judgment of the living and the dead" i.e. the judgment of v. 5, the resurrection at "the end of all things"!

Peter affirmed the end of "all things." Thus, Joel's demand that the word "final" or equivalents must appear in a text to identify it as the final resurrection was satisfied, and the imminence of that final end is undeniable..

Peter's declaration that the (appointed) time had come for the judgment of the living and the dead undeniably refers to the resurrection of the dead. This judgment of the living and the dead is the resurrection of Revelation 11:15f. What was clearly devastating is, *Joel applies Revelation 11 and that judgment and resurrection to AD 70!*

The application to Job 19 is clear. Both Peter and Revelation foretold the end of all things resurrection, the "final" resurrection of Job, and posited it at the destruction of Jerusalem. This was *not a type or shadow of something else*. It is little wonder Joel totally ignored my arguments on 1 Peter and Revelation 11.

No Marrying or Giving In Marriage

Joel considered his appeal to Luke 20, where Jesus said in the age to come "there is no marrying or giving in marriage," to be a "slam dunk" argument. His argument missed the entire backboard!

I offered several facts.

1.) Joel violated his own hermeneutic. Remember, Joel said since the word "final" is not found in the resurrection texts I appealed to, they cannot refer to the "final resurrection." This was Joel's *only* argument on several texts.

So, when Joel appealed to Luke 20 as a definitive refutation of Covenant Eschatology, I noted the words "final resurrection" or corollaries *are not in the text*. By Joel's own "logic" there is no way for him to prove Luke 20 refers to the final resurrection. Joel ignored this.

2.) I produced a chart giving a quote from Joel (page 155f) stating that Jesus' "this age," the age in which Jesus was living, was *the Mosaic age*. He said "the age to come" from Jesus' perspective, was the Christian age. This is a true "slam dunk" refutation of Joel's argument.

Here, in simplified form, is what I argued:

In "the age to come" there is no marrying or giving in marriage– Jesus.

The age to come, from Jesus' perspective, was the Christian age– McDurmon.

Therefore, in the Christian age, there is no marrying or giving in marriage.

Joel insisted that if preterists believe we are in the age to come, we should disband our marriages. Yet, the onus falls squarely on McDurmon. *He says we are in the "age to come" anticipated in Luke 20.* Thus, Joel should disband his marriage.

3.) Joel was clearly shaken by the exposure of his own doctrine concerning "this age" and "the age to come." So, once again his desperation was manifested when he claimed the two ages were not Jesus' real focus. This is nonsense. Jesus was undeniably contrasting "this age" and "the age come."

4.) In another desperate move, Joel espoused what may well be a historically unprecedented argument. He argued "the age to come" is to be delineated from the resurrection. I could hardly believe my ears!

5.) Joel's argument destroys his own theology. I showed that *prior to the curse*, Adam and Eve were *married* with the mandate to *procreate*. Thus, marriage, conjugal relations and children existed *in the pre-sin Eden*. Here is a concise presentation of my argument:

In the resurrection, the pre-sin state is restored (McDurmon).

In the pre-sin state, Adam and Eve were married, engaged in conjugal relations, being mandated to bear children.

Joel believes that in the restored pre-sin state, there is no marrying, conjugal relations or child bearing, per Luke 20.

Therefore, the pre-sin state, where there was marriage, conjugal relations and child bearing, cannot be restored per Joel's interpretation of Luke 20.

All Joel said in "response" was to repeat his claim that preterists must disband their marriage. But of course, this totally ignored his a *fatal* self-contradiction.

Acts 3– The Restoration of All Things[1]

I presented the following:

Paul: There is One Hope (Eph. 4:4).

That One Ultimate Hope was the reuniting of "heaven and earth"- *purposed before time* (Eph. 1:9-10).

That One Hope was to be fulfilled "in the stewardship of the Fullness of Time" (1:10).

But, the fullness of time was the last days of the Old Covenant World of Israel (Gal. 4:4).

Therefore, the fulfillment of the ONE HOPE was to be fully accomplished in the last days of Old Covenant Israel– which Joel admits was finalized in AD 70!

---

[1] See my book *Like Father Like Son, On Clouds of Glory*, for an extensive discussion of the restoration of all things. Simply stated, the restoration was to be consummated at the end of the Old Covenant age of Israel.

This argument proves that the time for the "final" realization of *God's ultimate goal* was the first century. Joel's response? *Not one word!*

No More Teaching?!?

Joel claimed if preterism is true it destroys evangelism and all teaching of the Word, because Hebrews 8 promised, "they shall teach no more his neighbor..." under the New Covenant. He claimed the establishment of the New Covenant will end all teaching functions, i.e. evangelists / evangelism. This is clearly untenable.

Joel's construct ignores the difference in the *nature* of the two covenants. Under the Old, a person was born, then taught. Under the New, a person is taught then born.

I noted if Joel's application is correct, all evangelism must stop, *now! The New Covenant has been established*! Hebrews 8 says nothing about the New Covenant being established, *as it had been*, and then, two thousand years + later, the conditions of that New Covenant finally coming into being. The state of "they shall no longer teach" is *inherent* to the very *nature of the Covenant*. Joel never touched this.

Joel's "Last" Hermeneutic

As noted, Joel argued repeatedly that if the word "final" or "last" is not in a given prophecy, it cannot be proven it refers to the "final resurrection."[2] I demonstrated the fallacy of this hermeneutic. Incredibly, Joel *said* he agreed with my chart and my claim that you cannot "screw down apocalyptic language" so tightly that the absence of given words, the use of different words, demands different topics or times are in view. But, notice what happened then.

When I pressed my points on Isaiah 24-27, the Banquet and the resurrection, Joel repeated his claim that the absence of the word "final," or "last" means Isaiah does not necessarily predict the "final" resurrection!

---

[2] See my websites for several follow up articles on points raised in this debate.

In 1 Corinthians 7, Paul dealt with those who were evidently pondering whether, since the New Creation had broken into the Old, they should still be married. Paul told them to stay married. This is a powerful refutation of McDurmon's argument on "no marrying" in the New Creation. Joel's response? Well, the words "New Creation" are not found in 1 Corinthians 7, so my argument fails!

Joel re-adopted his "last hermeneutic", the very hermeneutic he said was false!

So, Joel ostensibly agreed that just because "final" or "last" is not in given texts, it did not negate my argument. Nonetheless, when entrapped, he appealed *again* to "missing words" as fatal to my view! This is a blatant self-contradiction.

Finally, let it soak in that Joel affirmed the AD 70 fulfillment of Revelation 21-22. This means there is no more death, NOW (Revelation 21:3-4). There is "no more curse no more" (Revelation 22:3-4), NOW.

I challenged Joel to show us what could be better than this and why we need anything better. Not a word. There is not a word in Revelation 21-22 that looks beyond the, "these things must shortly come to pass" vista.

Joel's theology invents an eschatology different from Revelation *and scripture*.

His system is therefore un-Biblical and wrong.

www.ingramcontent.com/pod-product-compliance
Lightning Source LLC
Chambersburg PA
CBHW061259110426
42742CB00012BA/1987